. . The Search for . . . .
. . . . Philip K. Dick . .

THE SEARCH FOR
PHILIP K. DICK

ANNE R. DICK

TACHYON

:::::::::::::::::::::::::::::::::::::::

The Search for Philip K. Dick
Copyright © 1995, 2009, 2010 by Anne R. Dick

Cover art and design by Josh Beatman
Interior design by John Coulthart
Photos by Anne R. Dick

Passages from the writings of Philip K. Dick
used by permission of the Philip K. Dick
Testamentary Trust

Tachyon Publications
1459 18th Street #139
San Francisco, CA 94107
415.285.5615
WWW.TACHYONPUBLICATIONS.COM

Series Editor: Jacob Weisman
Editor: Jill Roberts

ISBN 13: 978-1-61696-000-1
ISBN 10: 1-61696-000-1

Printed in the United States by Worzalla
First Tachyon Edition
9 8 7 6 5 4 3 2 1

In Memoriam
Philip K. Dick

CONTENTS

Acknowledgments —————————————— 6

Introduction by David Gill —————————— 11

Prologue ——————————————————— 15

PART I 1958-64 ——————————————— 21

One   I Meet Phil Dick ————————————— 23

Two   Honeymoon for Four ——————————— 51

Three   Family Life in the Country ————————— 65

Four   Disaster in Point Reyes Station ——————— 83

A Postscript to Part I ———————————— 106

PART II 1964-82 —————————————— 109

Five   Bachelor in Oakland ——————————— 111

Six   Nancy ————————————————— 129

Seven   The *Scanner Darkly* Years ————————— 141

Eight   The Vancouver Science Fiction Convention ——— 155

Nine   More Dark-Haired Girls: Linda, Tessa ————— 163

Ten   Doris and Joan ————————————— 181

Eleven   Death of a Science Fiction Writer ————— 193

PART III 1928-58 —————————————— 211

Twelve   Early Years ——————————————— 213

Thirteen   Boyhood in Berkeley ——————————— 227

Fourteen   A Young Man ————————————— 241

Afterword 2009 —————————————— 263

Three 1982 Dreams ————————————— 265

A Legacy —————————————————— 267

Index ——————————————————— 270

About the Author ————————————— 280

ACKNOWLEDGMENTS

I would like to thank the Philip K. Dick Estate for making the Philip K. Dick papers available to me and for permission to quote letters, documents, and some small bits of text.

The material in this book was collected in 1982 and 1983, and the text was written in 1984. This paperback edition of 2009 is a revision, with new material added.

Much of the original information was from interviews, tape-recorded shortly after Phil's death. The original tapes are in the Philip K. Dick archives. My own personal memories did not include exact quotes. The dialogue is constructed but close to the spirit of the past.

My sources for Part I of this book, a personal memoir, were my three older daughters, Hatte, Jayne, and Tandy; Phil's Point Reyes novels; and old friends who still lived in the area: Sue Baty, Avis Hall, Inez Storer, and (interviewed briefly at the Palace Market) Pete Stephens. Thanks to them, Joan Stevens in Arizona, and June Kresy in southern California.

I would like to thank my oldest daughter Hatte for remembering, criticizing, and endlessly listening. Thank you, second daughter Jayne who, living next door, had to listen even more than endlessly. Thanks to third daughter Tandy for your good memories of Phil and for encouraging this project.

Paul Williams functioned as literary executor for the PKD estate for ten years after Phil's death. I frequently visited the archives at Glen Ellen, one hour's drive north of Point Reyes Station. In 1982 and 1983, Paul gave me copies of a handful of letters, childhood report cards, and newspaper clippings from the Philip K. Dick archives, which were located in Paul's garage. I donated new information that I had discovered, mostly interviews. I also made my manuscript available to other biographers: Paul himself, Larry Sutin, and Emmanuel Carrère.

Dr. Willis McNelly, professor emeritus, California State University at Fullerton, encouraged me and showed me how to most effectively study the Philip K. Dick papers at Fullerton.

Dr. Patricia Warrick, from the English Department of the University of Wisconsin at Appleton, was also the 1985 president of the Science Fiction Research Associates. An early and enthusiastic scholar of Philip K. Dick's writing, she gave me feedback on early drafts of this book over many long phone calls. At her invitation, I gave a talk about Phil, which was recorded, at the annual Science Fiction Research Association meeting at Kent State in 1985. Afterward, Jack Williamson, an old-time science fiction writer, came up to the podium and hugged me and told me I had made Phil Dick "come alive" for him.

In 1986, at the invitation of Professor George Slusser, curator of the Eaton Collection at the University of California at Riverside, and Professor Jacques Goimard of the University of Paris-Sorbonne, I gave a talk about Phil at a five-day conference at a restored château in Etampes, France, sixty miles south of Paris. The château had a grand foyer with two curving staircases going to the second floor. In the middle of the foyer, a section of the floor had been removed to show an ancient mosaic surviving from a villa that had been located there in Roman times. I was overwhelmed when I was given the Countess's enormous suite, which had two sets of huge French doors leading out to two balconies that overlooked a park of fifteen acres. It had a bathroom the size of a small living room. It was hard to get a good night's sleep; the bells of the ruined monastery next door rang all night long. Its remains had been made into a church, where I went to Mass on Sunday. I gave my talk about Phil on the last day of the conference. Kim Stanley Robinson liked it and gave me a manuscript copy of one of his short stories, which I later gave to Sam Umland.

Thanks, Professor Gregg Rickman of San Francisco State University; you were encouraging and helpful to me over the years.

Thanks, Ray Nelson and Kirsten Nelson for information and for sending kind and helpful vibrations from Albany.

Thanks, Betty Jo Rivers. It was a pleasure to meet you and talk with you.

Thanks, Nancy Hackett. You were very helpful via several interviews. It was nice to get to know you and Isa and Tina.

Thanks, Kleo Mini for your generous help. I loved talking with you at lunch in that excellent restaurant in St. Helena.

Thanks, Joan Simpson for information, encouragement, and copyediting.

Thanks, Michael Walsh, David Berner, and Michael and Susan Walsh in Vancouver.

Thanks, Joel Stein in Las Vegas and to young sci-fi writer Daniel Gilbert.

Thanks, Tim and Serena Powers. Thanks for many quotes from your journal, Tim. Thanks K. W. Jeter.

Thank you to Professor Gerald M. Ackerman at Pomona College for sharing your unpublished manuscript; to Dr. George Koehler for coming all the way from Los Angeles to Point Reyes with your carefully thought-out information about Phil's boyhood; to Dick Daniels for your warm and detailed memories of Phil in high school; to Leon Rimov and Pat Flannery for your memories of Phil in junior high and high school; to Maury (Iskander) Guy for your extensive memories of Phil, and Dorothy and Joe Hudner. Thanks many times over to Lynne Hudner Cecil, now Lynne Aalan, Phil's stepsister, for family information and documents.

Thanks to Vince and Virginia Lusby, Janet Feinstein Doyle, Alan Rich, Alan Ayle, Mrs. Anthony Boucher, Lois Mini, Pat Hollis, Grania Davis, Linda Levy, Doris Sauter, Mary Wilson, Nita Busby, and Jim Blaylock.

Thanks to the Scanner Darkly Kids, for trusting me and for sharing your past.

Thanks to old enemies for taking a risk, laying down old animosities, and helping me clear up the debris of my past. Thanks to Dr. Sam Anderson and William Wolfson.

A special thanks to Karen Pierce, who came to type my tape-recorded, dictated manuscript on the computer and, when I was close to despair, taught me that my early awkwardness and incoherence were all "part of the process." Karen helped without intruding, became my copyeditor and editorial consultant, and in the process acquired new motivation for her own writing.

Thanks to Heather Wilcox, Allan Kausch, Elizabeth Story and James DeMaiolo for the copyediting, proofreading, and vetting of the current Tachyon edition.

Thanks to Professor Samuel Umland of the University of Nebraska at Kearney for his interest in Phil and in this book. He went through it with me chapter by chapter and helped me revise it for Mellen Press for the hardcover 1993 library edition.

I could not have finished the 1993 revision without the help of my jewelry business manager, Craig Bailey, who processed the manuscript several times, struggled with an obsolete software program, fixed small errors, added italics, etc. (He's still here, correcting the 2009 revision.)

Thanks, Father Tim West, for opening a door for me when I felt perhaps I "should not" write about many of these events.

I would also like to thank all the other people mentioned in this book but not mentioned specifically in these acknowledgments.

Thanks in memoriam to Vince Lusby, Bill Christensen, Edgar Dick, John Gildersleeve, Bill Trieste, Margaret Wolfson, Jerry Kresy, Pat Jambor, Dorothy and Joe Hudner, Alys Graveson, Ben and Anita Gross, Neil Hudner, Avram Davidson, Henrietta Russell, Avis Hall, Willis McNally, and Jack Newcomb.

INTRODUCTION
by David Gill

Philip K. Dick still haunts us. A quarter century after his death, as our ever-more wired and dystopian times look more and more like a Philip K. Dick novel, the story of Phil Dick's life fascinates critics, fans, and followers almost as much as what he wrote. Perhaps this is because his long, strange trip is as enthralling as any of his novels. But this distinction, between Phil's life and his fiction, has always been blurred. Avid fans see Phil Dick in each of his world-weary protagonists, grappling with the pain and uncertainty of the universe — very much the way Phil appears in this memoir.

During Phil's recent literary ascension, which coincided with his inclusion in the prestigious Library of America series, critics took to publications like *The New Yorker* and *Newsweek* to dispassionately list the litany of bummers in his life: poverty, multiple failed marriages, drug abuse, battles with panic attacks, and agoraphobia. As a result of our media's obsession with the alleged connection between artistic genius and madness, Phil Dick was introduced to mainstream America as a caricature: a disheveled prophet, a hack churning out boilerplate genre fiction, a speed-freak. None of these impressions of Phil, taken without awareness of the sensationalism that generated them, advances our understanding of his life and work. Today the myth of Philip K. Dick threatens to drown out what evidence remains of his turbulent life.

We can never fully understand Phil Dick. He, like Walt Whitman, contained multitudes. Instead, we have to content ourselves with studying Phil through a series of lenses. Like his novels that shift from character to character between the chapters, we must examine Phil's life from the vantage point of the people who knew him. We may never be able to assemble a complete image, but the impressions that he left on the people that he loved, and that loved him, help in getting a sense of the man.

The extensive research Anne did for this book is impressive. The interviews she conducted have become an important source for all of Phil's biographers, but perhaps more importantly, the small details from his daily life provide a more intimate picture than any of Phil's other biographies. The fact that Phil chose the old, battered shoe as his avatar whenever the family played Monopoly gives us a sense of him. Even though I never met Phil, after reading Anne's memoir, he feels familiar to me. Of course, this picture is incomplete, but Anne's memoir captures, in vivid recollections, Phil at the top of his game as a writer. But her memoir also depicts a man whose creative drive and need to make a living is burning him out.

While Phil certainly had other prolific periods in his life, he produced some of his best work in rapid-fire brilliance during his years with Anne. Between 1959 and 1964 he wrote a dozen novels, including *Confessions of a Crap Artist*, *The Man in the High Castle*, *Martian Time-Slip*, *Now Wait for Last Year*, and *The Three Stigmata of Palmer Eldritch*.

When Phil moved to Point Reyes Station in 1958 and met Anne, he was finishing up his novel *Time Out of Joint*, a book that can be read as either science fiction or psychological fiction, depending on whether you believe the protagonist is sane. In this way the book combines Phil's disparate ambitions: to be a mainstream writer—spoken of in the same sentence as Faulkner and Hemingway—and to provide a stable income for his family by churning out science fiction.

In 1959 Lippincott published *Time Out of Joint* as a hardcover, Phil's first, and billed it as a "novel of menace," marketing it without any of the usual science fiction trappings. This small literary success prompted Phil to try his hand again at mainstream fiction and this resulted in *Confessions of a Crap Artist* and *The Man Whose Teeth Were All Exactly Alike*. While these novels were not successful in his lifetime, Dick's reaction when his mainstream fiction remained unpublished for many years—including *Confessions of a Crap Artist*, which has since been recognized as one of his finer works—became a pivotal moment in his career.

Feeling like he was back at square one as a writer, Phil momentarily gave up on writing and helped Anne with her fledgling jewelry business, selling her pieces to stores in the Bay Area. When he inevitably returned to writing, he decided to again combine his two ambitions by incorporating highbrow literary elements into his science fiction. The resulting success, the Hugo Award winning *The Man in the High Castle*, set the stage for an unrivaled burst of creativity that lasted until he left Anne in 1964.

Phil's writing became much more autobiographical during this period. Phil wrote in the introduction to his short story collection *The Golden Man*, that he wanted to "write about people I love, and put them into a fictional world spun out of my own mind." And so Phil wove Anne into his fiction. Anne, a talented and forward-thinking artisan, became the model for some of Phil's most heroic characters, the careful craftsman, the skilled artist, such as the jewelry maker in *The Man in the High Castle* and the ceramicist in *The Three Stigmata of Palmer Eldrich*, capable of producing an object that is not subject to the decay of the world; these objects serve as an antidote, in some ways, to the entropy so Ubikuitous in his writing. Artisans pop up again and again in Phil's writing, but not until after he meets Anne in 1958.

Anne's memoir makes it clear that Phil's characters did not suffer alone; their plight was a reflection of their creator's pain. I often find myself, upon finishing one of Phil's books, wanting to hug him and thank him for dredging up so much, for giving so much of himself. Anne is to be commended for her willingness to take an unflinching and thoughtful look at her own life and her relationship with Phil, and for sharing her search for answers.

David Gill, a scholar who has studied the life and work of Philip K. Dick for over a decade, writes the Dick-centered Total Dick-Head blog (TOTALDICKHEAD.BLOGSPOT. COM) and teaches literature and composition at San Francisco State University.

PROLOGUE

Our small Episcopal church was half-filled for the memorial service that I'd arranged at the suggestion of Paul Williams. Nancy, Phil's fourth wife, came, and Joan Simpson, who could have been his sixth wife, and Tessa's sister (Tessa was his fifth wife). Kleo, Phil's second wife, said she wouldn't come, then tried to get a ride at the last minute but didn't make it after all.

At the end of the service when Fr. Schofield said, "Into thy hands we commend thy servant, Philip K. Dick," I felt my heart twist. "No, no," I thought, "I can't let Phil go." I began asking questions I had put aside years ago. Why did Phil leave? Why didn't he come back? If I'd been different, would he have left? What were his relationships with other women like? Had any of them had the same kind of experience I'd had? Had he loved me, or had he been a colossal fake? After eighteen years, I began again pulling off the petals of that infinite daisy: He loves me...he loves me not....

I didn't have any false pride to preserve anymore. I didn't have to tiptoe around Phil's touchiness, so I decided to find out. I started phoning, writing, and visiting all the people who had known Phil. I compiled so much information that I began to think of writing a book. I'd call it *The Five Wives of Philip K. Dick*. I gave up that idea when I couldn't locate Phil's first wife, Jeannette Marlin (Phil's father, Edgar Dick, believed she was dead), and Tessa Busby Dick, his fifth wife, declined to be interviewed.

I spent the next two years interviewing wives, an extensive list of serious girlfriends, male friends, family members, psychiatrists, and lawyers. (Phil was always terrified that his ex-wives would get together and compare notes.) Other women friends of Phil's—Joan Simpson, Kirsten Nelson, Kleo Mini, Nancy Hackett, Linda Levy, Mary Wilson, Betty Jo Rivers, "Sheila," and "Cindy"—shared memories with me.

I had a lot of help from Phil. I researched when his works were written rather than when they were published and compiled a chronology. Then I read through the thirty-six science fiction novels and the 120 short stories in the sequence they were written. It was so fascinating to read Phil's science fiction as a whole, an oeuvre (or "irve," as my friend David Gill calls it) that I read through it twice, sometimes laughing out loud as Phil's novels took me back to the events of our life in the early sixties. Those books were unbelievably revealing. In effect, Phil had made notes about our life together for me. His complete oeuvre was a surrealist autobiography. Reality and imagination flicker back and forth in his fiction as it did in his everyday life, Phil playing all the roles and predicting his own future.

Search for Philip K. Dick was the first biography of him to be completed. The manuscript revealed a side of Phil that some of his friends and followers couldn't accept. Besides loving Phil, some of them had also been well primed by Phil to believe a version of his life in which I had no credibility (to put it mildly), even though at the same time he was telling them he was being watched by the KGB, the FBI, and the CIA. (Some of them believed that, too.) One of them, a dear young man, fiercely loyal to his late friend, threatened to sue me after he read my manuscript. A group of his young male followers supported his other biographers, all male, heartily. It's interesting to me that the women who read my manuscript understood it immediately, but some men took a little longer.

I discovered many new aspects of Phil's writing that I hadn't perceived when, as his first reader during his Point Reyes period, I proofread his novels. My goodness, the anti-heroines of the Point Reyes novels, more or less based on me, were always murderesses, adulteresses, and sometimes schizophrenic. In the books written at the end of our marriage, they also became drug addicts. I don't even take aspirin. Then there were the books with a theme of divorce and reconciliation, written while we were separating. I hadn't read these until after Phil's death. If I had read them in 1965, would our lives have turned out differently? We had to have bought the white Jaguar before Phil wrote *We Can Build You*, because that car was in the book. The ad in the *Baywood Press* that inspired us to buy a spinet piano was in that book also. *We Can Build You* told about our family's trip to Disneyland and Phil's fascination with the Lincoln robot there.

My children, now grown, were a great help in dating events: "That happened the year I was in third grade." "That was the month I fell and chipped my tooth." "That happened right after my birthday party, the one where the cake had yellow icing and seven white candles."

When I learned about the later part of Phil's life, I felt sad. I worried about chronicling it, even though Phil left similar information for biographers in his letters and other documents. At times, I felt that something must be terribly wrong with me that I had loved a person who was (to my way of thinking) involved in such a terrible life at one period. But he had also been my best friend as well as a good husband—he played the role beautifully for a while—and a good father to my children. He was lots of fun, too. And he was a writer. I was a lifelong reader. I love writers.

Besides his books, there was the immense amount of material that had been written about him. His life and writing existed on so many levels that I couldn't possibly cover what one critic called "the vast reality of Philip K. Dick." I have made no attempt to consider literary, political, sociological, or theological ideas. Phil's voluminous letters are a huge research project in themselves. Besides thirty-six science fiction novels and 120 short stories, Phil left nine unpublished literary manuscripts and a one-million-word theological rumination, *The Exegesis*. When I was writing this book in 1984, at least seven other books were being written about Phil. He's been compared to Kafka, Dickens, Borges, and Blake. Blake? I was astonished. I hadn't followed Phil's career after our divorce (in fact I had ignored it) and was unaware of his great success.

Writing this book was like living with Phil again. I never met anyone else like this kind, charming, brilliant, modest, responsive man, a life enhancer, a joy to be around—but there was something else, something dark. There was a real Phil, but which one was it? When I think I know, that's just when I lose the image. Did Phil change identities the way some people change their clothes?

He was isolated by his genius. No one, except years later Gregg Rickman (Phil's chosen biographer, who was literally—and literarily—persecuted for his theory) saw how hard Phil had tried and how much he had to struggle with. It is amazing that Phil was able to produce so much excellent, innovative writing with his inner problems, whatever they were. He used those problems to write his novels!

If Phil were alive he would have loved my project and encouraged me. He would have invented all sorts of theories to support my picture of his life. Then he would have invented other theories just as plausible. Bending a few facts here and there, he would have rewoven the past to present a reality that would make him look better and better and me worse and worse, but the pyrotechnics of his mind would have been so remarkable that I couldn't have helped but admire them. My advice to anyone married to a person like Phil (but there couldn't be another!) is if there is no other solution, write a book.

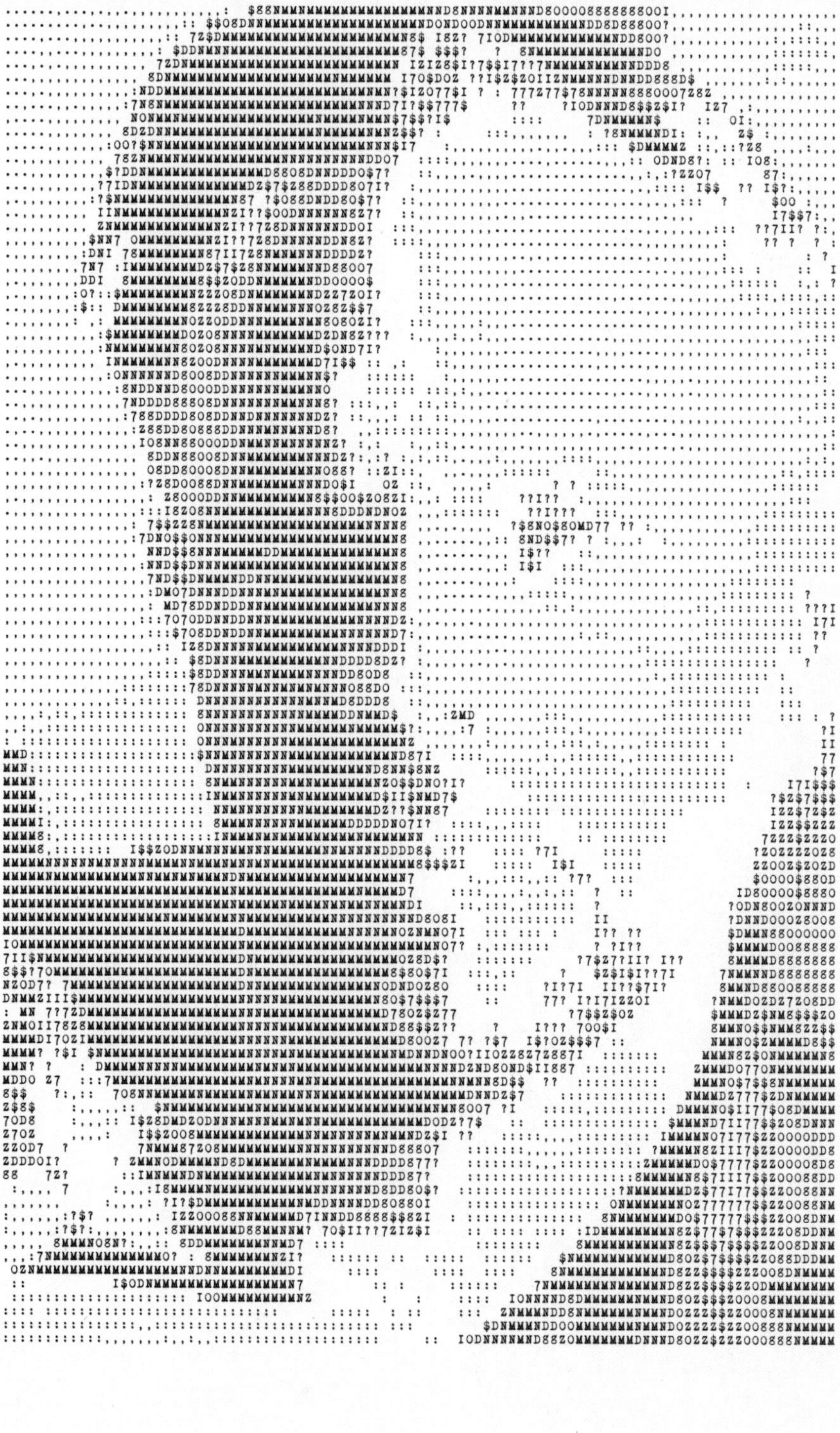

PART I: 1958–64

As I wrote this book, I became so immersed in the past that when I took a walk in the field, I was in the eternal now of 1958, the black-faced sheep just over the rise by the eucalyptus trees, and Phil and our four small girls back in the house making fudge. As I worked, I dreamed vivid dreams, more real than everyday life. My memories carried me to that timeless place where feelings never change.

One
I MEET PHIL DICK

Then she appeared, gliding at him with her springing, padding walk, meanwhile drying her hands on a dishtowel.... [S]he wore tight pants and sandals, and her hair was uncombed. God, how pretty she looks, he thought. That marvelous alert walk of hers...ready to whip around in the opposite direction. Always conscious of the ground under her.

—Philip K. Dick, *Confessions of a Crap Artist*

THE DAY I met Philip K. Dick in late October 1958, my third daughter Tandy, not old enough for school yet, and I went downtown after lunch to shop at the Palace Market in Point Reyes Station. (Its motto: "Shop at the Palace, live like a king." "And pay like an emperor," Phil added later.) We ran into my friend Avis Hall while buying brownies at the Bluebird's cake sale. She wanted to give me her condolences, but I didn't want any more sympathy and changed the subject. We got to talking about this and that, and she told me that a writer and his wife had just moved into the white frame bungalow on the corner of Manana and Lorraine.

"What kind of a writer?" I asked, thinking that it was probably someone who wrote technical manuals. She didn't know, but she said that the new couple had come from Berkeley.

When we got back home, I put Tandy down for a nap and worked in the vegetable garden while worrying about the future. Then I started worrying about the past and about Richard's tragic death. No. I didn't want to think about that. I began to feel depressed. I wrenched my thoughts around toward the new couple. "Maybe they'll turn out to be interesting," I thought and decided to call on them in the late afternoon. My oldest daughter Hatte could babysit with her sisters Jayne and Tandy.

At five o'clock, the cocktail hour, I called the children. "Hurry, girls, get your Mickey Mouse hats," and switched on the TV. The Mouseketeers were already singing "M...I...C...K...." I put our blue merle collie, Drift, out on the patio and ran into the bedroom to slip on a three-quarter-length red dirndl skirt with white fringe around the bottom, handmade leather sandals, and handmade spiral brass earrings. I walked past the Monterey cypress trees in our driveway, jumped in my middle-aged Ford Country Squire station wagon, and drove down the hill, turning up Lorraine Street just before Forester's Hall. As I parked near the new writer's house at 73 Lorraine, the late-afternoon fog was blowing through the eucalyptus trees, and a blue heron flew over on the way to its inland nest. I tried to open the gate of the white picket fence but the latch was too stiff, so I hiked up my skirt and climbed over. Passing a bed of bearded iris and old-fashioned floribunda roses in the front yard, I ran up the porch steps and knocked on the front door.

At that time I was a thirty-year-old widow. My husband, poet Richard Rubenstein, had died suddenly only three weeks before. Three years earlier we had bought a somewhat California Bauhaus house in Point Reyes Station, California—unusual architecture for the rural area of West Marin. It was in a five-acre field, and a small flock of Suffolk sheep had come with the house. Old-timers told us that the house was sitting on an arm of the San Andreas fault, the longest and most dangerous earthquake fault in the world.

Point Reyes Station is a small agricultural town on the California coast, one hour's drive north of the Golden Gate Bridge. It has one main street that in those days had only a few stores on it. A couple dozen houses were clustered around this "downtown" area, and on a nearby hill there were another few dozen houses. Beyond were very large ranches.

A half-mile west below a bluff is long, narrow Tomales Bay. To the east are large rolling hills, golden in late summer and fall, green in winter and spring, and always dotted with black and white cows. On a clear day I could see toward the west Inverness Ridge, covered with a forest of fir, oak, and bay trees. Its far side sloped down to the Pacific Ocean and miles of beaches. Point Reyes, twenty miles north, juts out into the Pacific Ocean and is the windiest and most western spot of the continental United States. It was named after *los tres reyes* by Spanish explorers when it was been first sighted on January 6, 1606, the day of epiphany.

Many of the people who lived then in West Marin, which includes Point Reyes Station, Inverness, Olema, Marshall, and Tomales, worked on dairy ranches. Another group worked for RCA ship-to-shore communications.

The Search for Philip K. Dick

College professors and old Bay Area families owned rustic summer cottages in Inverness.

My driver's license read: "Blonde hair, blue eyes, 5'4", 120 pounds, must wear glasses." I dressed in a colorful and avant-garde way in those days. I had three beautiful daughters: two blue-eyed blondes, Hatte, eight, and Tandy, three; and Jayne, six, with bronze hair and hazel eyes. Jayne was in first grade, Hatte third, and Tandy was still at home. I was glad I had her company while I went through the motions of cooking, cleaning house, and gardening, wondering all the time what to do with our lives after the loss of their father and my husband, Richard Rubenstein.

At 73 Lorraine Street, a young woman with short, curly black hair and wearing jeans answered the door. "Hi," I said, "I heard a writer and his wife moved here. Welcome to Point Reyes. My name is Anne Rubenstein. I live up the road. My late husband, Richard Rubenstein, was a writer too, a poet."

Kleo Dick was pleased that I had come by to welcome her and her husband to our town. She introduced herself and invited me to "Come in and meet Phil." As she led me through the house to the kitchen I noticed that there was hardly any furniture and what there was must have come from a sale at a Salvation Army store.

I still have in my mind a vivid picture of Phil standing with his hands in his back jean pockets, rocking on his heels, frowning slightly and staring at the floor. He was twenty-nine years old, just under six feet tall, and on the slender side. He had dark hair above a high forehead and intense gray-green eyes. An almost-handsome man, he wore an old brown leather jacket with knitted cuffs and knitted waist, a cheap plaid flannel shirt, stiff jeans, and clunky, brown Army boots. Nevertheless, he managed to look graceful and attractive—like someone wearing a disguise.

Kleo introduced him: "Meet Philip K. Dick." He looked up at me as we came in, and I looked up into his eyes, and, as I was beginning to say, "How nice to meet you," I had an odd experience unlike anything that had ever happened to me before. A voice from the depths of my mind said, "I already know this person. I've known him for eons." But my practical conscious mind, astonished, answered itself, "Ridiculous, how can that be? You just met him."

"What does the 'K' stand for?" I asked him.

"Kindred," he answered.

"Aha!" said that voice.

I considered myself to be a logical person not given to silly mysticism and brushed this whole experience out of my mind. The three of us sat down at the kitchen table and immediately plunged into an animated conversation. Phil had a most pleasant manner and a beautiful voice. He almost fell backward in his tilted chair when he heard that my late husband and I had been connected with the little magazine *Neurotica*, and that we knew William Inge, James Jones, and other poets and writers whose names I dropped with great abandon. I told him that I had edited, published, and distributed four issues of two little poetry magazines, *Inferno* and *Gryphon*, and a small chapbook of Richard's poems, *Beer and Angels*.

I told Kleo and Phil about Richard's sudden death on Yom Kippur three weeks earlier at the Yale Psychiatric Institute. He had dropped dead while getting a drink of water from the water fountain. After a long investigation, it was discovered that he had been fatally allergic to the heavy tranquilizers given to him, drugs that were still so new that their side effects were not yet known. Also, some doctors don't seem to know this, but many sensitive, creative, high-strung people react differently to pharmaceutical medicines. Maybe we've already killed many of them off.

But I didn't want to go over that tragedy again. I changed the subject and asked Phil about his writing. He said he was a science fiction writer. Interesting. I had never met this type of writer before. As we talked, I realized that I had actually read one of his stories in *The Magazine of Fantasy & Science Fiction*. He was quite pleased, although he seemed more interested in telling me about his literary novels, as yet unpublished. "I am only a minor science fiction writer," he said.

Later, I found he had already written and published eighty-five short stories and five science fiction novels—*Solar Lottery*, *The World Jones Made*, *The Man Who Japed*, *Eye in the Sky*, *The Cosmic Puppets*—and he was finishing *Time Out of Joint*, but in those days science fiction was in a literary ghetto and Phil was embarrassed that he wrote it. He was struggling to be a "mainstream" success by writing literary novels, most of which wouldn't be published until after his death.

I told Phil and Kleo that Richard, the girls, and I had moved to Point Reyes Station in 1955 to get away from the city. We wanted to own some land where we could raise plants and animals, and Richard wanted to devote his time to his poetry. He had never had a job; he was too nervous, and luckily his family had the wherewithal to support him.

Phil and Kleo told me that they had wanted to get back to the land and garden and raise animals too. To supplement their income, Kleo was commuting to Berkeley three days a week to work in the administrative offices of the University of California.

Phil described their house and the area in a letter to a friend: "…[W]e… bought a house in a small dairy-farming town up in North West Marin County called Point Reyes Station—it's on State Route One. We have a plot of land 100 x 160, and we're raising two ducks and one tomcat. The area is full of wildlife—deer, rabbits, almost three hundred species of wild birds—more than any other place in California. Including flocks of wild swan. Deer come right into our yard. All the men wear genuine Western hats and boots—they work on the nearby ranches."

I checked my watch. "Oh, dear, I have to get back to the girls," I said. "I wish we could go on talking. Can you come over tomorrow? I have some books you'd be interested in. You'll like the sheep, and our collie dog, Drift."

"Oh yes, we'd love to," said Kleo.

As I left, Phil insisted on loaning me some books: Franz Kafka's *The Castle*, Herman Hesse's *Siddartha*, and James Joyce's *Portrait of the Artist as a Young Man*. On the drive home I thought happily that the new couple had exceeded my expectations. I had stopped feeling miserable and was looking forward to tomorrow.

The next afternoon I showed Phil and Kleo around my house. Richard and I had furnished it with a combination of antique and modern pieces, Eames chairs, a Noguchi lamp, an antique New England pine table, Navaho rugs—that sort of thing. A clay sculpture I was working on was on the dining room table. The children and I had been eating buffet style in the living room while I worked on it.

"I'll bet this place costs a fortune to heat," Phil said, looking at the forty-five feet of floor-to-ceiling windows that ran the length of the house's southeast side. He thought that perhaps the welded steel fireplace in the center of the living area might help with the heating expense.

"It has resistance electrical wire in the floor," I told him. "We bought this house for $16,000, nothing down, $101 a month, on a 4 1/2 percent GI loan." We looked at the black-faced sheep in the field and at the large, rounded green hills across the valley. A flock of quail flew up. "There are dozens of meadowlarks around, and last night a fox walked by the corner of the living room."

Phil and Kleo browsed in Richard's collection of modern poetry. "Can I borrow this?" said Phil as he picked up a copy of Henry Miller's *Tropic of Cancer*, which a friend of Richard's had smuggled into the United States. It was illegal in the United States under the censorship laws of the time. Phil and Kleo stayed for dinner, and afterward we played games with the children. When the children went to bed, we talked and talked.

Phil said that he and Kleo had been invited by their neighbors, June and Jerry Kresy, to a "flying saucer group that met at 'Claudia Hambro's' house in Inverness." (Claudia Hambro was Phil's fictional name for this real woman in *Confessions of a Crap Artist*.) I had already heard about this group. It first met to talk about philosophy, but soon these otherwise sensible people came to believe Claudia's ideas about flying saucers. Claudia told them that soon the world was going to come to an end, but she was in touch with beings from outer space who were going to save a select number of people, among them, her group. When the last days came, her house would turn into a flying saucer. This would happen early next year on April 22, 1959.

Claudia told Phil that she perceived that he was from somewhere else. "In some way," she told him, "you will help the poor lost people from Earth when the last days come."

Phil wrote about Claudia in *Confessions of a Crap Artist*:

[She] was quite small, with a huge black pony tail of such heavy hair that I thought she must be a foreigner. Her face had a dark quality, like an Italian's, but her nose had the bony prominence of an American Indian's. She had quite a strong chin and large brown eyes that stared at me so hard and fixedly that I became nervous. After saying hello she said nothing at all but smiled. She had sharp teeth, like a savage's, and that also made me uneasy. She wore a green shirt, like a man's, out at the waist, and shorts, and gold sandals.... [I]n some respects [she] seemed breathtakingly beautiful, but at the same time I was aware that something was wrong with her proportions. Her head was slightly too large for her shoulders—although it may have been an illusion due to her heavy black hair—and her chest was somewhat concave, actually hollow, not like a woman's chest at all. And her hips were too small in proportion to her shoulders and then, in order, her legs were too short for her hips, and her feet too small for her legs. So she resembled an inverted pyramid. Her voice had a rasping, husky quality, low-pitched. Like her eyes it had a strong and intense authority to it, and I found myself unable to break away from her gaze. Although she had never seen me before—laid eyes on me, as they say—she acted as if she had expected to see me, as if I was familiar to her.

Phil told me that after his first "flying saucer" meeting he was terrified that Claudia was going to come to his house and "get him" and he wouldn't be able to keep from being involved with her and her group. When later she did come and knock on his door, he hid. Kleo and I laughed together at the thought of Phil hiding in his own house. The rest of the evening we talked about books and ideas. It was after midnight when the couple left. It had been a wonderful evening.

After that, they came over almost every day. We ate together and played soccer, baseball, and board games with the children. Sometimes Phil came over alone when Kleo was at work. I found him to be the best conversationalist I had ever met. I even stopped talking long enough to listen to him. We found we had endless ideas, attitudes, and interests in common. Both of us were shy, though we hid our shyness. Both of us were trusting to the point of gullibility and very romantic. Both of us had been expected to be big achievers by our parents. Both of us loved animals, books, and music, though Phil's tastes ran to Baroque music and opera and I liked modern classical music, "moldy fig" jazz, and folk music.

Both of us had been cherished children. Phil's mother, father, and grandmother had doted on him. I had been affectionately spoiled by my father, mother, our housekeeper, and my two much-older brothers. Both of our mothers were rather domineering. Phil's mother had wanted him to be a writer, mine wanted me to be a college professor. Both of us had lost our fathers at an early age. Mine died. Phil's mother divorced his. I told Phil about my two big brothers who had carried me around on their shoulders when I was small, about my brother who had died suddenly when he was only thirty-eight, about my father who had died suddenly when he was only forty-two. Phil told me about his twin sister who had died three weeks after his birth and how he felt guilty about this. He said that he carried his twin sister inside him.

When I read about twins later to learn more about Phil, I found out that it isn't unusual for a surviving twin to feel that he or she carries the dead twin inside him or her.

"And she's a lesbian," he told me seriously.

I hardly had been able to take in this remark, much less respond, when he topped it. "When I was a teenager, I had 'the impossible dream.' I dreamt I slept with my mother."

I was taken aback. Why would he tell me this?

"I won my Oedipus situation," he continued. When Phil spoke, a pleasant lilt in his voice, it was easy to go along with whatever he said. In the past I had always had a retort for anything that anyone would say, but I have to admit that some of the things that Phil came up with were so far outside my mental framework that I was struck dumb.

When I talked, Phil paid flattering attention. His responses were quick, detailed, and imaginative. It seemed as if we could go anywhere in the universe as we talked. Phil was unselfconscious, funny, delightful. I never had met anyone I enjoyed so much. I told Phil about Richard—that he hadn't been very happy in the luxurious environment he'd been brought up in. His father had made a fortune in the scrap-metal business, and after he died his mother had married another millionaire Jewish "junk dealer," as Mr. Handelsman, her new husband, jokingly called himself. I told him that Mrs. Handelsman, despite her fashionable clothes and her diamonds, was warm-hearted and kind.

I had met Richard, a stocky, handsome man with a wry sense of humor, when he waited on a table where I sat with my college friends. He was a partner in Little Bohemia, a unique bar located on the St. Louis waterfront, with painter Stanley Radulovich and his best friend, Jay Landesman. As he poured wine into our glasses, he recited bits of Baudelaire and Rimbaud's poetry.

I told Phil about hand-setting type for Richard's little poetry magazine, *Inferno*, while standing in puddles of water in the basement of a house on San Francisco's Potrero Hill and printing it on an old anarchist press. I collated the pages, put on the cover, and sent the magazines on consignment to small bookstores all over the United States. Once in a while we would get a very small check back. I had become very tired of these, to me, fruitless labors. Richard's continual depression made me depressed too. I had gone into that marriage a bouncy, energetic female just out of a happy college life. I wondered, "Is this what adult life is supposed to be like?"

In those days before women's lib, women were told that marriage was their vocation. Most women, with only a few exceptions, didn't pursue professions.

At one time in college I had thought about being a doctor, but there were no role models. I married because I was expected to marry. Richard pursued me, he had interesting friends, he wrote poetry. I had never met anyone who wrote poetry before. In those days, poets and writers and painters were rare.

Richard had been diagnosed by psychiatrists as having an anxiety neurosis. No wonder—his mother had been sending him to psychiatrists since he was a young child. Recent discoveries suggest that his symptoms may have been due to an allergic condition. He was depressed and withdrawn at times, and when he drank, like many heavy drinkers, he had a personality change and didn't behave well. In those days, women were held responsible for everything that went wrong with the family. I was supposed to make our marriage harmonious and happy, and I thought I was a failure.

It made Richard very anxious when he had to go to the barber. Men kept their hair short in those days and he felt he had to get his hair cut every six weeks. Every six weeks there would be an unpleasant incident in our household. Finally, Richard's psychiatrist, Dr. A, insisted that Richard submit himself to in-patient therapy. There weren't rehab and detox facilities everywhere in those days. Richard's family came to California to accompany him to the Yale Psychiatric Institute. Two months later, on Yom Kippur, the day of atonement, the most holy day of the Jewish year, he dropped dead.

Phil was fascinated with everything he heard about Richard and based Charley Hume on him in *Confessions of a Crap Artist*, but he didn't get him right at all. That character was also partly based on his friend, Mike Hnatt.

Richard's family and some of his friends never spoke to me again after they read that book. Some people draw incorrect conclusions from fiction that is only partly related to the author's life.

Phil told me his life story in great detail, presenting himself as a member of the working proletariat, a self-educated person dedicated to his work. After his father and mother had divorced, he hadn't seen much of his father. His mother and he moved to Washington, D.C. for two years. After they moved back to Berkeley, he dropped out of the last year of high school and had a home tutor. He had a decade-long job with University Radio and later worked for Art Music, both record stores. He was enthralled when I called him a "Berkeley beatnik." He thought this was an accolade.

One afternoon two weeks after we had met, Phil came over to visit me. Tandy was taking her afternoon nap and Hatte and Jayne were at school. We sat on each end of the couch talking. Suddenly, Phil grabbed my hand and said in a low, intense voice, "You represent everything I've ever dreamed of."

I was so surprised I almost fell off the couch. I sat there and stared at the floor like some Victorian maiden. I had absolutely no idea of what to say or do next. Phil drew me toward him and kissed me. After a moment's hesitation and without conscious volition, I kissed him back. We kissed and talked and talked and kissed. Ah, a whole new topic, our mutual attraction. Each of us had endless words to say.

I told Phil about the experience I'd had when I first met him; it must have been love at first sight, a phenomenon that I hadn't believed existed. I certainly never thought it would happen to me. I felt like one of those mythical heroines who has been awakened out of her enchanted slumber by a hero leaping over a ring of flames. Phil was enthralled when I told him this; he adored Wagner. The next time he came over, he brought the entire *Ring* and played excerpts from it. He said we would listen to the whole thing later on.

My emotions were in a turmoil. When he left I realized that this man I had fallen for was married, and I shouldn't be feeling the way I was feeling. I made an appointment with Dr. A. I thought of him as a kindly uncle and trusted him implicitly.

I had gone to Dr. A the previous year. Richard had been his patient, but Dr. A told me in those prefeminist days that he believed in treating the wife when the husband had problems. I didn't mind. It was fashionable to be psychoanalyzed—to have the imprint of the couch on one's back. In fact, psychoanalysis was the popular religion of the times. Of course, Dr. A was a psychiatrist, not a psychoanalyst, and when I visited him I sat in a chair, but still—it was almost like psychoanalysis because Dr. A didn't talk much and I did. While waiting out in Dr. A's anteroom, I skimmed through the medical magazines on the coffee table, noticing that all the illustrations advertising the new heavy tranquilizers showed women—bitchy-looking or depressed-looking women.

"Why don't they show any men?" I thought idly.

When I finally got in to see Dr. A, I asked him, "What shall I do? I'm in love with a married man."

Dr. A advised me not to worry about Kleo. He said, "Kleo is Phil's business, not yours. Don't get involved with Phil's relationship with Kleo." I tried to take this advice, but my feelings of guilt didn't go away.

Dr. A wanted to meet Phil. When I told Phil, he said, "Fine, I want to meet Dr. A." Dr. A was quite taken by Phil. In fact, Dr. A fell completely under Phil's spell and later was drawn into his delusional system and consequently was not helpful to him as a therapist.

I was caught up in a whirlwind relationship. Phil salved my conscience by telling me that Kleo refused to have children and that even the ultraconservative Roman Catholic Church granted annulments in that kind of marital situation. I had fallen madly in love, hook, line, and sinker. Even Phil's telephone number seemed to have a mystical beauty. Phil lavishly praised my character, my looks, my ideas, and the way I raised my children: "You treat them as if they were adults." He was continually affectionate. He did the dishes and mopped the floors.

"I always knew true love would be like this," I told him.

We walked, hand in hand, on the beaches, in the forests and up and down the hills of the Point Reyes peninsula. I drove—Phil liked me to do the driving—to the old lime kilns, to the historic graveyard, to the oyster farm. One minus-tide day we drove out to Pierce Point and climbed down the cliffs to the abalone rocks. Later I learned that Phil was quite apprehensive but finally mustered up his courage and climbed down the dripping rope.

He describes this in *Confessions of a Crap Artist*:

Now Fay had come to some rocky projections. Past her he saw what appeared to be a sheer drop, and then the tops of rocks far below, and the surf. Crouching down, Fay descended step by step to a ledge, and there, among the piles of sand and rock that had slid down, she took hold of a rope attached to a metal stake driven into the rock.

"From now on," she called back, "it's by rope."

"Good Christ," he thought.

"The girls can do it," she called.

"I'll tell you honestly," he said, halting with feet planted far apart, balancing himself with care, "I'm not sure I can."

"I'll carry everything down," Fay said. "Throw the packs and the fishing poles down to me."

With care, he lowered everything to her. Strapping the packs on her back, she disappeared, clinging to the rope. After a time she reappeared, this time far below, standing on the beach and gazing nearly straight up at him, a small figure among the rocks. "Okay," she shouted, cupping her hands to her mouth.

Cursing with fright, he half-slid, half-stepped down the rock projections to the rope. He found the rope badly corroded, and that did not improve his morale. But for the first time he discovered that the cliff was not sheer; it had easy footholds, and the rope was merely for safety. Even without it, in an emergency, a person could get up and down. So taking firm hold of the rope he stepped down, foot by foot, to the beach. Fay, when he got there, had meanwhile gone off and was seeking a deep pool in which to fish; she did not even bother to watch him descend.

I had no idea that he had such a problem about climbing down that cliff.

The girls were a little confused by Phil's presence but they couldn't help but like him and soon got used to his being around. They knew something was going on though not quite what. Kleo seemed to have disappeared. Phil adored the children and often went with us to the beach. I was shocked that Phil had never learned to swim and was afraid of the water. I wanted him to take swimming lessons so he could get over this fear, but he wouldn't. He said he only wanted to stand on the shore and watch. Phil took the children to dance class, cooked breakfast for them, and organized excursions to the zoo, a redwood forest, and an amusement park. The four of them invented a game, monster. The girls ran away shrieking with joy, while Monster Phil, dragging one stiff leg after him, a ghastly expression on his face, claws instead of hands poised in front of him, chased them around the house. All the neighborhood children came to play monster. After Phil got tired of being a monster, we'd play baseball, soccer, or volleyball out in the field. Sometimes Phil would hold one of the children on his knee while the others clustered around, and he would tell them a story he made up for the occasion.

Evenings, Phil built a fire in the welded-steel fireplace in the middle of the living room. After dinner we got out the card table and played Scrabble, Kimbo, or the Game of Life. Phil never took the path that went to college. I tried to teach Phil how to play charades, but he didn't like it at all. I hated Monopoly. I kept landing on Phil's hotel on Boardwalk, but Phil and the girls loved it. For his token Phil always chose the old shoe.

The whole town was shocked by our affair. Normally sensitive to what the neighbors thought, I hardly noticed. June Kresy was stunned. "I've never seen people behave like that," she said.

But finally in early December, in spite of my strong feelings for Phil, I tried to break off the relationship. Regardless of what Dr. A had said, I felt it was wrong. Phil and I had gone on an excursion, without the girls this time, and were walking on a rocky beach in Sausalito. I remember how the round stones of the beach felt under my feet. I had trouble keeping my balance and put one hand on Phil's shoulder as I faced him.

"Phil," I said, "I can't continue with our relationship. It isn't serious enough for me and I feel very guilty about Kleo. I love you but our affair is a mistake. You're a married man and that's that."

Phil took both my hands in his. He said in a tone of desperation, "Anne, please don't abandon me."

I realized in that moment that he needed me. After a pause I said, "All right—but we'll have to get married," and Phil agreed.

Dr. A was angry with me. He said harshly, "A nice Greek girl like Kleo may never marry again."

I didn't say anything. After all, Dr. A was a psychiatrist. But I thought it was strange that earlier he'd told me not to take any responsibility for Kleo and now he was telling me that I was seriously at fault. Well, it was too late now. I wasn't going to give up Phil for anything.

Dr. A wanted to see Phil again. When Phil came back he was chuckling. "Dr. A said, 'If Anne wants a husband she'll go out and find the best one available, just like she buys a box of soap at the grocery store.'" I didn't know how to respond to this, so I didn't say anything. Phil would say things that were completely out of my range of experience or bring up matters involving his past—cans of worms that seemed better left unopened.

Phil asked Kleo for a divorce. She agreed and moved back to Berkeley. Avis Hall, who lived across the street, remembered Kleo driving away at "a hundred miles an hour." Phil tells about her departure in *Confessions of a Crap Artist*.

Phil applied for a Mexican divorce as well as a California divorce so we could be married in Mexico that spring while waiting a year for the California divorce to be final, the divorce law at that time. However, the Mexican divorce would not be legal since Phil would not be legally divorced yet in California. I ignored these aspects of our legal or illegal relationship—foolishly—for although I was practical about everyday things, I wasn't practical about major life decisions.

Before I'd met Phil, the girls and I had planned to go back to St. Louis at Christmas to visit Richard's family. Phil encouraged me to make this trip. He wanted me to work out a financial arrangement with the Handelsmans for an income to supplement the $575 monthly amount I was getting from Richard's Social Security and from rent from a building back east that the girls and I had inherited from Richard. But any effort to do this couldn't possibly succeed. The Handelsmans had kept Richard on an allowance of $570 a month and wondered why we didn't drive a Cadillac and why we didn't outfit the three girls with new clothes every month. Meanwhile huge dress boxes of Mrs. Handelsman's "old clothes," thousands of dollars' worth of European designer clothes, some never worn, would be sent to me periodically. I don't think any of us had a realistic focus on money matters.

While my daughters and I were in St. Louis, Phil wrote me:

Dear Anne, That strange old lady who cleans up your house evidently descended on it as soon as you were out of the driveway—when I got back there to turn off lights and lock doors I found the front door locked and that big outdoor light off and the various small messes indoors cleaned up. Right in the middle of the dining table, in its paper bag, terribly visible in the cleaned-up ascetic room, was my pair of blue pajamas. A sort of chanting reminder that they who sin will be found out by the Others. However, that old woman has her own defects, since I found water running in the bathroom bowl and a spoon on the floor.

[On the way home from taking us to the airport he stopped by his mother's house.]

I went upstairs to my family's place and bummed a meal from them and told them why I was in town (i.e., that I had driven you and the children to the airport or spaceport, whatever it was). Thereupon my mother and I had a long discussion about breaking up a bad marriage (mine, and the one she had with my father).... I wiped off the windshield carefully and set off. Actually the trip was easy. The rain had almost stopped, and the...Christmas shoppers had gone home to eat. But about halfway along the route, about at the intersection with U.S. 101, I really started getting the shakes. I know damn well that it had nothing to do with the drive as such, it was simply that I was beginning to get back onto the part of the route that we five had taken coming in, and I was subconsciously contrasting the driving in with this driving back.... Marin County seemed shut down. Deserted. As if nobody lived there, like those half-ruined wartime housing developments that are now crumbling away and covered with weeds. By the time I got near Woodacre I was beginning to wonder if I could go back to Point Reyes

Station and spend the 13 days. Anyhow, I did get back and I intend to live through the 13 days, which proves that an ordinary human being can do almost anything if he puts his mind to it—which is your theory.... Here's how you can represent me to your rustic but well-placed family and friends. "He's well known in Russia and England...in fact, in Germany & Italy and France—also in South Africa and in Argentina (in translation of course)...and he's just beginning to become known here in the U.S. Lippincott is bringing out a novel of his next spring."

In a second letter he wrote:

You have no idea how much your phone call affected me. For an hour (more like two) afterward I was in a state of what I would in all honesty call bliss—unlike anything I've ever felt before. Actually the walls of the house seemed to melt away, and I felt as if I were seeing out into time and space for an unlimited distance. It was a physical sense, not a mere intellectual thought. A genuine state of existence new to me. Evidently my not having heard from you for a couple of days had had the effect of starting into motion a sense of separation from you—quite natural, but all I was conscious of was that I felt gloomy and lonely and at loose ends. As a reality you had begun to recede—not that my feelings toward you had changed, but that as an actual fact in my life you had in an obvious physical sense receded quite a distance. Then when you called, this distance was abolished, and the return of you as a physical reality caused a genuine transformation in me, as if I had stepped from one world to another.... There is a direct relationship between my hearing you, and the religious person, who, after the traditional isolation and fasting and meditation, "hears" the voice of "God." The difference is that you exist, and I have some deep doubts about that fellow God.

As soon as the girls and I returned to Point Reyes, Phil moved in with us, bringing his possessions with him. All his clothes, cheap to begin with, were old and shapeless. Phil didn't care about visual appearances or household objects at all. The only things he treasured were his Royal Electric typewriter, his Magnavox record player, his books and records, and his set of the *Encyclopedia Britannica*.

Among his favorite books were *A Crock of Gold*, by James Stevens, and *Miss Lonelyhearts*, by Nathanael West. His library included complete files of *Astounding Science Fiction*, *Amazing Science Fiction*, and *The Magazine of Fantasy & Science Fiction* magazines. He had a large collection of H. P. Lovecraft stories and novels, and other horror tales. He also had a collection of literary works, and at the time was especially interested in Camus, Kafka, Beckett, and Ionesco.

Hatte loved Phil's collection of old comic books, especially *Mandrake the Magician* and his complete file of *Mad Magazine*. She went from reading fairy tales to reading Phil's *Cosmic Puppets* and the other science fiction stories and novels in his collection.

Phil brought his two-drawer file cabinet, stuffed with papers. He'd kept a carbon copy of every letter he'd ever written.

"I suppose you're saving all those letters for your future biographers," I kidded him. He smiled his pleasant smile but didn't reply.

I gathered all of Phil's own novels and stories together, and in the evenings after the girls had been tucked in their beds, I sat in our bed reading them while eating an artichoke, dipping the leaves in hollandaise sauce and turning the pages. Phil kept coming in the bedroom to watch me read his books.

He said, "You remind me of Samuel Johnson; you drip hollandaise on your nightgown like Johnson spilled egg on his vest, and you have an acerbic wit like Johnson's." Then he added, "If you're Johnson, I guess I'm Boswell."

I smiled at him and went back to my book, thinking, "Everyone knows science fiction writers don't write biographies." As I read all his novels and stories during the next few days, I commented delightedly on each story and novel. I especially loved "Human Is" and told him, "'Human Is' is your best story."

Our reading tastes were eclectic. Phil and I both owned copies of *Winnie the Pooh* and *When We Were Young*. Both of us knew the texts well enough to quote whole sections and poems, to the children's delight. I tried to get Phil to read *Murder in the Cathedral*, but instead he dived into Richard's three volumes of Sandburg's *Lincoln*.

"I'm a Civil War buff," he said. "The Centennial's coming up and there's going to be a lot of interest in the Civil War." He thought he might write a novel based on that war. He also began reading intently the many volumes of Freudian psychology I had collected, as well as my *Treasury of Jewish Folklore*.

After he unpacked and shelved his books, he set up his personal apothecary in a closet next to the study. He had a large collection of pills and medicines and loved to prescribe for the girls' runny noses or bandage their skinned knees. He showed Jayne all his medicines, told her what each one was for, and said, "Adults are sick almost all the time." Phil couldn't believe that my medicine cabinet didn't even have aspirin in it. "It's beyond belief," he said, "that you can have a medicine cabinet with nothing in it."

I had been brought up by my Christian Science mother, didn't take any pills of any kind and seldom went to a doctor. "I never get sick so why should I?" I told him.

Phil took two Semoxydrine pills a day. "These were prescribed for me years ago," he said. He didn't tell me what for and I wasn't interested enough to ask. He got an attack of tachycardia not long after he had moved in. He told me, "My heart can beat rapidly for days and I run the risk of dropping dead unless I take quinidine." Then he added, "Quinidine is dangerous. I might drop dead from taking quinidine." I felt he was overly nervous about these sorts of things. He looked fine to me.

Phil's cat came with him, an ear-torn, dingy grey-and-white tom from some Berkeley alley. He adored cats and had always had one or two. He doted on "Tumpey." If this cat didn't show up for a meal, Phil would say mournfully, "Tumpey's dead again." I preferred beautiful pedigreed animals but Tumpey reminded me of the stray cats I had brought home as a child, and I tolerated him. Besides, Phil loved him.

We had hardly unpacked all of Phil's belongings when it was time to celebrate the first birthday of the year, mine. Phil bought me a fossil hammer. I was enchanted. How could he have known that was exactly what I wanted? We drove to Drakes Beach and collected fossil whale bones embedded in the cliffs there.

Phil was just finishing *Time Out of Joint*, his first book to be published in hardcover. He gave my name to a minor character in the last part of the book. Sometimes he worked in the study at my house, sometimes he went over to his old house to write. He wrote until all hours, but finally I protested that his schedule didn't fit in with family life. He immediately put himself on a nine-to-five schedule and came home every day for lunch. At lunchtime, we became so involved with our conversations that I usually burnt the first two melted cheese sandwiches that I was toasting in the broiler. We talked about Schopenhauer, Leibnitz, monads, and the nature of reality. Or Kant's theories as applied by Durkheim to the culture of the Australian aborigines. Or Phil would hold forth on the Thirty Years' War and Wallenstein—light topics like those.

Germanic culture had a great attraction for Phil. He told me he was one-quarter German and a "sturm und drang" romantic. He adored Wagner,

Goethe, Schubert, and Bach. He loved Pope John and hated the Berkeley Co-op, Edward Teller, Alan Watts, Alan Temko, and radio station KPFA, which he said was filled with communists. He hated old men passionately, especially old men drivers. He told me about the Gegenearth, the hypothetical hidden planet on the exact other side of the sun from Earth. It was impossible for us to ever see it. He gave lectures on countertenors, the castrati of the Middle Ages, and dwarves in jars.

One noon as we were eating lunch together, he said calmly, completely out of the context of our discussion, "I had a perfectly good wife that I traded in for you."

All my life I had been very direct and outspoken and never at a loss for words before, but this man could come out with statements that I couldn't figure out how to answer. He was so sweet and calm that I couldn't possibly get mad at him.

In March, Phil went to court to get his interlocutory divorce decree. When he came back home, he was upset and a little angry. I was puzzled because up until then he'd told me continually about how happy he was regarding the change he had made in his life. The next day we took the children to the amusement park at Lake Merritt, Oakland. We bought tickets for the little train that ran through the park. The children and I got on one of the cars but there wasn't enough room for Phil. The conductor put him in another car with a bunch of Cub Scouts.

He wrote about his thoughts at the end of *Confessions of a Crap Artist*:

> Probably she will make me a good wife…. She will be loyal to me, and try to help me do what I want to do. Her passion toward controlling me will ultimately subside; all of this energy in her will fade. I will make substantial changes in her, too. We will alter each other. And someday it will be impossible to tell who has led who. And why.

At the end of March, we drove to Mexico to get married. When we got to Tijuana I persuaded Phil that we should continue to Ensenada; Tijuana was too ugly to get married in. Phil was apprehensive on the lonely, mountainous ride down the Baja Peninsula. We stayed in a motel on the beach at Ensenada—I remember the large, rough-beamed room, the beautiful handmade blue-tiled floor, and the delicious, fresh-caught sea bass we had in the motel restaurant that night.

I had wanted to wait until April 2 to be married, but Phil was anxious to get back to Point Reyes for Jayne's birthday on April 8, so we hurriedly walked out on the streets of the town to find out what to do; we had no idea what the procedure for getting married was down there. Although I had taken five years of Spanish in college, I couldn't communicate with anyone. We weren't taught to converse in the forties, only to learn to grammar and how to read. Finally, we found an English-speaking marriage broker who would prepare the proper legal papers. The judge adjudicated in an ancient Spanish fort that looked like a small medieval castle with linoleum on the floor and chickens running here and there. Beautiful Mexican ladies with babies in their arms waited on the wooden benches placed around the walls to see the judge.

The marriage ceremony sounded beautiful in Spanish, and Philip K. Dick and I were married on April Fool's Day, 1959.

We went shopping in the local bazaar for presents for the girls. As we drove north toward the California border, Phil said he had to tell me something terrible about himself. He was embarrassed about this matter and felt it would make me stop loving him. He was sure that it showed how inadequate and defective he was. It turned out that he had a hernia.

"Why don't you get it fixed?" I said.

He said, "I'd have to go to the hospital and I couldn't do that."

This didn't seem like a good decision to me but, after all, we were on our honeymoon, so I didn't say anything.

In Ensenada we had bought a gallon of tequila (for thirty cents, I recall), and Phil decided that he wasn't going to pay duty on it at the border. I was quite apprehensive when he hid it under our luggage. He looked right at the border guard, smiled, and said we had nothing to declare. Twenty miles into the United States we heard a siren. It was the U.S. Customs police. Phil turned pale. I thought he might faint. He thought they were after him for the tequila. However, they passed our car and went on. He was extremely relieved.

When we got back to Point Reyes, we had been gone only three days. The announcement of our marriage was in the local weekly newspaper, the *Baywood Press*, on April 16, along with such news items as "Lavinia Adams Motored Sunday to Novato" and "Giant Mushroom Found by Warren Merritt." There were also mentions of the Ladies' Garden Club Primrose Tea Flowered-Hat Contest, along with the usual drownings, people falling off the cliffs, etc.

On the drive back we had decided that the girls should call Phil "Daddy." The children had no problems with this. When they spoke of Richard they called him their "first father." They were happy with Phil. Besides reading to them and playing monster, he let them eat hot dogs in bed. I wanted Phil to adopt the girls, but he felt he would then have to be totally financially responsible for them and he didn't have enough earning power. I was disappointed, but he pointed out to me that if he were to adopt the children he would be, to some extent, cutting them off from their paternal grandparents and he didn't feel that this would be in the children's best interest. After he explained this I could appreciate his position. After all, he was a good father and we had a great sense of family unity. These were the important things.

Now that we were married I felt comfortable introducing Phil to my friends. Once in a while I introduced him as "Richard." "One husband is the same as another," I kidded him. We went to dinner at the Okos. Adolph Oko was the local realtor. In 1948 he had been captain of an Israeli ship during the War of Liberation and ran the British blockade, taking seven thousand refugees from Bessarabia to Israel. Oko's wife, Gladys, was a sweet, pretty, somewhat vague woman who drank a lot. Phil created a not-very-sympathetic picture of them as the Runcibles in *The Man Whose Teeth Were All Exactly Alike*, and in this book he recounted some of the terrible, sacrilegious "Easter jokes" that Captain Oko liked to tell.

Captain Oko was a friend of Admiral Nimitz and a moving spirit of the Drake Navigator's Guild, which sought to prove that Sir Francis Drake had landed not in Tiburon, but on the shores of West Marin, where the "plate of brasse" had been found in the 1930s. Oko had reproductions of it made and gave us one to hang on our wall. (Years later the plate was proved to be a fake.) Phil wove all this lore into *The Man Whose Teeth Were All Exactly Alike*.

We became friends with our next-door neighbors, Pete and Joan Stevens, and they often came over for drinks and dinner.

In 1983 when I was working on this book, I contacted Joan by phone in a town in Arizona. Chris Stevens, one of her grown children who still lived in Point Reyes Station, told me that she didn't have a phone but that she could be reached at the local bar Wednesday evenings. I did reach her and we had a great talk. She remembered Phil with great affection and nostalgia and was rereading all his books.

Pete and Joan no longer lived together at that time (although they did again later on); Pete lived somewhere in the Bay Area. I was lucky to run into him in front of the Palace Market meat counter when he was visiting in the area and to be able to talk with him briefly. Pete enjoyed hearing that he was the model for the inventor in several of Phil's books and stories, among them The Zap Gun *and* The Man Whose Teeth Were All Exactly Alike.

Pete was a brilliant inventor and technician who worked for Walter Landor, a well-known San Francisco product designer. He commuted daily to a remodeled warehouse on the San Francisco waterfront. Phil and Pete became quite fond of each other.

I introduced Phil to Bob Allen, the slightly plump, five-foot, four-inch popular science teacher at the West Marin School. He took the two of us on a dig at Limantour Beach to excavate a fire lens, the remnants of hundreds of years of Indian campfires. We found obsidian arrowheads, bird points, pieces of an Indian pipe, and shards of Ming pottery that had been washed up from a shipwreck from Spanish Colonial times. Bob donated all our finds to a museum in Sausalito. Phil put Bob Allen and these events in *The Man Whose Teeth Were All Exactly Alike.* Bob was a prominent figure in *Dr. Bloodmoney,* also.

After Phil met Bill Thompson, the president of the Lions Club and the local butcher, he put him in *The Man Whose Teeth Were All Exactly Alike* as Jack E. Vepp. Dr. Plattes became Dr. Terance, and Joe Gomez, a local contractor, became John Flores. Flores was the name of an old Berkeley friend of Phil's who had died some years ago, so perhaps both of them occupied this character. Phil often melded two or more people into one character.

Lois Mini, the bouncy red-headed gym teacher at the West Marin Elementary School, had known Phil in Berkeley. Her ex-husband was Norman Mini, a close friend of Phil's. She became a good friend of mine, too.

Phil was extremely frugal, whereas I had holes in my pockets. Phil tried to teach me to be careful with money. He told me, "Save up errands and do them all at once to avoid wasting gas. Shop at more than one supermarket, buy loss leaders, and stock them up, but only if they are something you use a lot. Use discount stores for everything you need to buy. Never, never impulse buy." I tried, I bought a pair of white shorts from Sears Roebuck instead of going to Peck and Peck. I had to buy some decent clothes for Phil; this was a necessity. I bought him a few good-quality casual clothes, the sort that Richard used to wear, and new underwear.

Phil was happy with his new wardrobe. Then he said, "I'd really like to grow a beard."

"Great." I told him. He kept thanking me because I'd allowed him to grow a beard. I couldn't figure out why he felt he had to thank me. With the beard and the new clothes he looked quite distinguished.

Phil was the perfect husband. Almost too good to be true. If all my fantasies of a mate had been realized they wouldn't have come to one one-hundredth of life with Phil. He was a wonderful companion, lover, and husband, as I told him frequently. He told me in detail how beautiful, intelligent, wise, and kind I was. We hugged, kissed, and held hands off and on all day long. The children teased us about how mushy we were. When we all went to the zoo together and saw two capuchin monkeys twined together on a branch, Hatte pointed at them and exclaimed, not unkindly, "Look. Mother and Phil."

Phil was generous with his time and energy. He comforted the children when they had problems, but he didn't spoil them. He was a good disciplinarian, too. He talked to the children and reasoned with them. He helped fold the laundry. There wasn't anything he wouldn't do. He never sat around while I was working. He was the most considerate as well as the most lovable person I ever met.

That's what I thought back then.

In addition to all Phil's other charms and virtues, it turned out that he knew how to make frozen daiquiris. He had a talent for martinis too, and made me two every evening. He, himself, drank only one glass of wine. On one of our excursions with the girls, we went to the town of Sonoma to visit the Buena Vista Winery. Phil fell in love with a zinfandel that Buena Vista Winery bottled, a wine made from a mysterious grape of unknown origin. In the evening when we returned, he opened one of the bottles and sat in the living room sipping wine. He said, "In vino veritas," and then, "Whom the gods would destroy, they first make mad," followed up by, "That's the way the cookie crumbles," and then he talked of "hubris."

"What do you mean?" I asked him apprehensively. He laughed and laughed, and never did explain.

We had brought back duck eggs that Phil found under a bush in the Sonoma town square. We put them on a heating pad in the study in order to hatch them. Ten days later the eggs started to smell. We opened the windows to air the room out, theorizing that all the eggs couldn't be bad, and turned on the radiant heat in that room in case it was too cold. Three weeks later the smell became really bad and we had to give up. We took the eggs outside and threw them against the apple tree in the front yard. The sky was instantly full of turkey vultures, twenty of them, circling above the apple tree. The electric bill for that month was $135, astronomical for those days.

We used to buy ducks to cook from an old codger who raised several different kinds of birds in a marshy area on the other side of the Bay. He charged 25 cents a pound, but we had to do the plucking ourselves. It was disconcerting to buy a bird from him. He would chop off its head on a stump which he used for a chopping block and the head would fall on the ground and quack a little. Phil, the animal lover, described himself as originally a farm person on those days and was totally unperturbed. After our duck egg hatching failure, we bought some live ducks from the old codger, a Rouen and a Muscovy. A little boy who had to move away gave us his pet duck, "Alice," a wonderful white Pekin duck who was very intelligent and laid two hundred eggs with large yellow yolks every year. We bought a pair of guinea fowl, and they hatched their eggs somewhere off in the bushes without any attention from us. Soon we had twelve guinea fowl running around continually making loud, clacking sounds. The children and Phil trooped out to the former dog runs to feed all these fowl creatures twice a day.

We bought a half-dozen banty chickens in Petaluma, Phil had always wanted some. He loved to watch the colorful little roosters hopping around with their wings outspread herding the females. "They're just like me," he said.

Somehow we ended up with four roosters and no hens. All four roosters would perch on the fence outside of the study window where Phil was trying to write and crow for hours, much to his irritation. Soon we gave them away. We acquired a guinea pig as a pet for the girls. It looked to me as if it was always cowering in terror but it did let itself be petted.

Richard's friendly, sixteen-year-old bay quarter horse was still out in our field. Phil acted like he was a little afraid of him although he wouldn't admit it. He would drive the horse away with a broom when he went out to feed the ducks.

Phil wanted an owl for a pet. There were dozens of owls in the cypress trees surrounding our house. They hooted all night long. Once we saw a large owl taking a shower bath in the first rain of the year, turning, twisting, even raising his wings and washing his wing pits. At night when we heard the owls, sometimes we went outside and hooted back at them and they would always answer.

In mid-April, I brought in a newborn lamb who was too weak to get up and nurse. We warmed him, gave him some milk, and kept him in the bathroom overnight. Phil wrote about this in *Confessions of a Crap Artist*.

On April 22, Claudia Hambro and her two daughters went out on a hill to wait for the flying saucers to come and pick them up. Shortly after this the flying saucer group broke up. Claudia cut off both her long hair and that of her daughters and moved away.

As spring progressed and the irises and roses started blooming, Phil began to spend more time at his old house, gardening. I wanted our house to be his main concern, and we had our first quarrel. I am assertive. When I get angry, my voice gets louder and I talk fast. I thought this was just a little argument and was shocked when Phil went back to his old house to stay. I went over with the girls and we all sat on the front steps. Finally, Phil came out on the porch and said, "All right, all right," and came back home with us.

After thinking about this incident, I came to the conclusion that it would be better for our marriage if Phil sold his other house. He agreed and put it on the market and it sold almost immediately. When he received payment for it he said, "I know I should give Kleo half of this money, but I'm not going to." It disturbed me to hear him say this, but his relationship with Kleo was his business. The money from the sale of the house went into our bank account and was spent on living expenses.

That year we planted a large vegetable garden and bought a large freezer. I made jams and jellies, and froze fruit that we bought in bulk from nearby orchards. When summer came, I sunbathed naked on the patio. At first, Phil thought this was wonderful. Then he became apprehensive and kept hurrying to the front of the house to see if the milkman was coming. After that I put on a bathing suit although we were so isolated it didn't really seem necessary.

Phil listened to music all day long: Orlando Gibbons, *The Flying Dutchman*, Bach, Beethoven, Handel. He might as well have been plugged in to his Magnavox or my hi-fi. He knew so much about recorded music he could have made a career as a music critic, and in fact some of his Berkeley friends became music critics for the *New York Times* and the *Village Voice*.

His musical tastes were eclectic. He bought Marais and Miranda records because I liked folk songs. When Marais sang, "Oh how lovely is my wife...."

I will love her all my life," I thought, "Just like us." He also bought records of Paul Robeson singing old American songs for the girls. He played almost his entire collection of records for us, giving wonderful lectures as the music played. He played the Fisher-Diskau recordings of Schubert's songs so frequently that I learned them by heart. He taught me about Gilbert and Sullivan, whom I came to love, and that it was okay to like Tchaikovsky whom I secretly liked anyway. Our favorite record was the small-orchestra, Dublin version of Handel's *Messiah*.

Not long after we met, Phil took me to meet his mother, whom he called Dorothy, and his stepfather, Joe. The Hudners lived in a modest 1920s bungalow on Hearst Street in Berkeley with Joe's twin teenage children, Lynne and Neil. Lynne and Neil were Phil's stepsiblings as well as cousins, as Joe had been Dorothy's sister's husband. When Phil was in his early twenties, a year after Marion's death, Joe and Dorothy had married.

Phil was still disapproving of this match and regarded the circumstances of Marion's death suspiciously.

He never had a good word to say about his mother but sometimes, when they were together, I could see such a closeness between them that it was as if one nervous system were directing both bodies. Dorothy doted on Phil and was very proud of his writing. After he sold his house she and Joe gave him a vacation cabin they owned in Inverness, thinking that he might need a place away from home to write in.

Dorothy was fifty-two, but looked much older. She was a thin, white-haired lady who walked with difficulty, having had the nerves in her legs crushed by an operation that was in vogue when she was younger. It was supposed to improve circulation in people who had kidney ailments. Eventually she would die from the results of this operation. Dorothy had Bright's disease as a young girl and all her life she had suffered from kidney infections.

Like her son, Dorothy was verbal and had great charm. She was intelligent and gentle, although others said that there was iron inside her velvet glove. I, personally, never saw this. Her manner was a little melancholy. She spoke of Jane, Phil's long-dead twin, as if Jane had died only yesterday. She was loving and kind to me and enjoyed my children.

Joe Hudner was a muscular, small man, a second-generation Irishman with a brogue he had cultivated that was thicker than if he had just stepped off the boat from Dublin. He had been a blacksmith and collected old Indian recipes for forging and tempering steel. He dressed like a laboring man, but he was also an intellectual and an excellent carpenter and cabinetmaker. A warm, kind man, he built Philippine mahogany desks for all three older girls, a little footstool for me to sit on in the bath when later I became pregnant, and a rolling bookshelf for Philip.

Dorothy wrote; Joe wrote, engraved guns, and had made a large body of interesting sculpture. He had been in the labor movement and worked as a welder in the shipyards during World War II.

The couple kept a comfortable, orderly, modest household. When they moved they always had money enough to buy another small house for cash. The two of them were liberal, leftist, and pacifist but too independent and individualistic to be members of any particular organization or political party. They read widely, and followed all the current trends in political and philosophical ideas, and kept up with current trends in art and literature. Neither Joe nor Dorothy had gone to college; they were completely self-taught.

I hadn't taken the negativity Phil expressed toward his mother seriously. I was family-minded and initiated a lot of visiting back and forth. The Hudners responded to my invitations, and we enjoyed many pleasant family times and holiday celebrations together. Phil took part seemingly without any reservations. At holidays and on birthdays, Joe and Dorothy gave the children lovely presents, often books. The family relationships seemed to be stable and normal, there to last forever. Dorothy told me, "You and Phil are so well matched."

Like Phil, Dorothy doted on cats. At her house, her two cats sat in chairs at the dinner table with the rest of the family. Joe and Dorothy talked to these cats with great respect and affection. The cats had more status than anyone else in the household.

After Phil finished correcting the proofs for *Time Out of Joint* and sent the manuscript off to his agent, he would read avidly the book-review sections of *Time* magazine and the *New Yorker* when they came, hoping to find a review of this book. All his previous novels had been issued in paperback, some back-to-back with another writer's science fiction novel. For these piggyback editions he received only $750 in royalties.

He told me, "Most of my novels have been published by Ace, the lowest of the pulp publishers." It surprised me that Phil was so embarrassed about writing science fiction. When we invited the children's modern-dance teacher and his boyfriend over and were driving around sightseeing, they asked Phil,

"What kind of writing do you do?" He absolutely would not answer them. Later, when we were all having dinner together, Phil insulted them in such a cold and sarcastic way that they never spoke to us again. Phil didn't even read science fiction at that time except for Kurt Vonnegut's novels. He said, "I'm really a fantasy writer." He referred to his novels as "borderline surrealism" and styled himself "a proletarian writer." When he said this he would stand and look exactly like a proletarian writer should look. Later he told me, "I really want to be a literary writer."

"Why don't you write what you want to, Phil?" I responded. "Successful literary writers have a lot of prestige and make a lot of money." I saw Phil's talent and drive and expected great things from him: fame—worldwide of course—and lots of money.

We talked about how we could manage on my small income and Phil's meager earnings. At that time, Phil was writing two science fiction novels a year that sold for $750 to $1,000 each. Once in a while he would get $1,500. Earlier novels would sometimes be reissued and pay a second $750 or $1,000. Tiny sums came in from foreign rights. I remember how pleased Phil was when the Japanese edition of *Eye in the Sky* came in the mail. He got $30 for it. It was an attractive, small, shiny white book and read from back to front. I was to receive $10,000 from my late husband's estate and the girls would inherit an additional $10,000. Phil thought we could make this money last for the next twenty years. I was dubious.

I tended to worry about money, a trait I inherited from my mother. When I was growing up during the Great Depression we lived with Oriental rugs, mahogany furniture, and old silver and china that had survived from better days. My mother worried about money and feared a further reduction in status. She seemed to think that we were imminently going to a poorhouse just like those in Dickens's novels.

Phil told me, "It takes twenty to thirty years to succeed as a literary writer." He was willing to make this long-term effort. I thought his attitude was terrific. However, the word *budget* wasn't one I understood.

I wanted to invest the money I had inherited in rental property and persuaded Phil to look at apartment buildings in lower Marin County. We looked at an eighteen-unit apartment complex in Mill Valley that we could have bought for $20,000 down (the building is worth many tens of millions of dollars now), but Phil didn't want to be a landlord. The capital I'd inherited was used for living expenses over the next two years, and we were right back where we had started from.

To work out Phil's writing plan, we agreed that while Phil wrote I would run the house and keep up with my outside activities, the Bluebird troop, the PTA, the school library, and a political group that was trying to get a new high school located nearer the center of population rather than in the middle of a faraway cow pasture. I would work on my sculpture when I was at home. Every day I drove carloads of children to lessons, clubs, and other after-school activities. In summer, I daily drove the children and their friends to Shell Beach—where all the mothers gossiped with each other and the children played together and swam. During August, Red Cross swimming lessons were held there. My daughters attended and one year I helped the instructors teach in the very cold water while the dense August fog swirled around us.

One afternoon not long after the discussion about Phil's career, we were lying on the bed in the study, our arms around each other. We had just made love and I was feeling happy and relaxed. Phil started laughing and laughing. He said, "I have a great idea for a novel. It's about this guy, Jack Isidore. I'm naming him after an early encyclopedist, Isidore of Seville, who collected weird bits of knowledge. The novel will be in the first person. The opening line Jack Isidore says is, 'Let me tell you about myself. The first thing is: I'm a pathological liar.'" (In the published version it is, "I am made out of water.") And Phil laughed and laughed some more. For some unknown reason I felt a little chill of unease, but nevertheless I smiled encouragingly. Phil began working on this novel, *Confessions of a Crap Artist*, during the honeymoon period of our relationship.

Two
HONEYMOON FOR FOUR

"One of the sheep had a lamb!" Bonnie shouted, as he got out of the car. "She had a lamb just a couple of minutes ago!"

"We saw it through the window!" Elsie shouted at him. "The Bluebirds saw it; we were baking bread and we saw four black feet and I said, 'Look there's a lamb,' and it was. Mommy said it's a female lamb, it's a girl lamb. They're out in back on the patio looking at it." The girls skipped and raced along beside him as he went through the house and opened the back door to the patio.

—Philip K. Dick, *Confessions of a Crap Artist*

PHIL TOLD ME, "The function of the writer as a chronicler is very important. The chronicler creates the culture he writes about. A culture without a chronicler doesn't exist." He was a fluent writer, and his work came easily to him. He said that the idea for a novel came to him in one intuitive flash, but he couldn't tell it "in under sixty thousand words. The words come out of my hands, not my brain. I write with my hands. I type 160 words a minute, the rate of a really good legal secretary, and I'm accurate." One day he told me that he had typed sixty original manuscript pages without an error.

I learned with surprise when I interviewed Phil's friends Jerry and June Kresy, and Lois Mini after his death that back in the sixties, Phil was telling them that he felt pressured by me to write, and was exhausted from working so hard. He never said anything like this to me or showed any signs of fatigue. He seemed to love his work. He set his own schedule and the rate at which he worked was completely up to him. He actually didn't write as much as during the years he lived in Berkeley. I would have never dreamed of telling him how he should work, or how much he should do, except that I wanted him home in time for dinner.

Phil's plan was to write two novels a year, spending three months on each. During the three months between he would think about his next novel. The first draft of a novel took him six weeks to write and six weeks to revise. (Later in his life, he once wrote a novel over a long weekend.) In between novels, Phil worked in the garden, read, and listened to music. He didn't take many notes. His memory was so good he didn't need to. Very occasionally, at 3 a.m., he would switch on the bedside lamp and write a few sentences in a small notebook. When I first saw him sitting in the big armchair in the living room in the middle of the day looking vague, I asked him, "What are you doing?"

He replied in a very definite and slightly annoyed tone of voice, "I'm working."

I tiptoed away.

Some days, he'd take a chair outside and sit under the walnut trees for an hour gazing at Black Mountain. He hated being interrupted. "Beware of the person from Porlock," he told me, and recounted the tale of how Coleridge had been interrupted as he was writing the most perfect poem in the English language, "Kubla Khan," by someone knocking at the door and asking, "Can you tell me the way to Porlock?" He discouraged friends or neighbors from dropping in and could be quite rude if someone unexpectedly came to our door.

After he finished a first draft he liked to do all his own rewriting. His first drafts were virtually complete and needed such a small amount of revision that I suggested that he hire a typist for his second draft and use his energy for creative work. He wouldn't hear of this "I don't want anyone else to touch my manuscript."

Phil had an enormous store of recondite knowledge. He skimmed through research books quickly, picking up the main theme and remembering everything. He didn't read much but he browsed a lot. He loved his never-updated *Encyclopedia Britannica*, which he had bought as a teenager. When he wrote, he blended together a complex network of disparate parts. His talent for mimicry created dialogue that brings the people we knew in the early sixties back to vivid life when I reread the novels of those years. He said that he wrote about "little" people and small events and saw himself as a "nice little fellow." I saw him as brilliant, talented, and dashing. Phil would discuss his characters with me when he was planning a new novel. He talked about the people he was imagining and what was happening in their lives, but the completed novels never read at all like what he'd told me.

It didn't matter what sort of spot he got his characters in, he could always write them out of it. Although he produced great quantities of rapidly written first-draft material, he also mined old material, patching in bits and pieces. He was a master at making invisible bridges, and the text flowed as if it had all been written at the same time. He used events, artifacts, characters, and names from everyday life, scrambling names and people. There often would be a complex train of associations that linked the name to the person. For example, Emily Hnatt in *The Three Stigmata of Palmer Eldritch* was based partly on me. Phil was part of Richard Hnatt, her husband. Richard had been my previous husband. Mike Hnatt, a friend, was the model for Charley Hume in *Confessions of a Crap Artist*. Charley was Fay Hume's husband.

Phil amused himself with his work as well as using his novels for therapy. He used them to communicate his political, philosophical, sociological, psychological, and theological ideas. He attracted attention, entertained, and made some money with his writing. His novels were dream fantasies of what he would like to do, what he would like to have happen, or what he thought had happened. I suspect he even used his novels to make things come true—like a form of sympathetic magic or else he had precognition. More than once he wrote about the events of his life before they occurred.

His novels are an autobiography written in the language of dreams. When he felt he was revealing too much about himself, he would switch to another theme or change the sex of a character. I don't think he realized how much he was telling in the novels of the early sixties, or perhaps he thought he was such an obscure writer that no one would connect what he was saying with his personal life. Maybe he didn't care. Maybe, even, he would have liked his more perceptive readers to know everything.

Phil never let me read his work-in-progress, but the day he finished a first draft of a novel he brought it to me to read. I was pleased and excited to be the first person in the world to read this new work of his. He liked me to copyedit as I read and to note small faults of logic or inconsistencies of time, place, or character—but actually there was very little for me to do. I had been a "bookoholic," all my life, sometimes reading more than one novel a day, and I brought this reading experience to my editing job for Phil.

Phil encouraged me with my own creative impulses. I had become interested in doing welded sculpture, and he didn't mind that I kept my welding tanks in the dining room and burned holes in the dining room table. I would stop working when he came home for lunch and make him a hamburger and some kangaroo-tail soup while I would sip Metrecal, a horrible diet drink in vogue back then. Afterward, he would trim a Corina Lark or perhaps an Anthony and Cleopatra cigar and smoke it while we talked. He had become enthusiastic about cigars and might give a dissertation on how cigars were made. Luckily, I could soon get him on other topics. We would discuss cybernetics, astrophysics, natural science, music, or game theory. Phil became fascinated with cars and read every *Road and Track* and all the other car magazines and "droned on" (his own words) for months about the merits of various car models. At the time we were thinking of buying a second car. Finally, we bought a used Peugeot. Phil claimed it was the best car buy of that year.

Even before we were married we had decided that we wanted to have a child. When I became pregnant after trying for one whole month Phil was excited and worried. He continually urged me to eat brewer's yeast, wheat germ, soy protein, and other Adelle Davis food recommendations. We had just read her first book. He stuffed me like a Strasbourg goose, so that at the end of my pregnancy I had gained fifty pounds and weighed as much as he did. He himself went on a vitamin regime, tossing large quantities of every kind of vitamin down his throat. His tongue turned black. A physician friend told him that this condition had been caused by an overdose of vitamin A. After that, Phil never took another vitamin in his life, and began saying that all health food "nuts" were "fascists."

Phil took me to the doctor at monthly intervals. One day, in the waiting room, he said to me, quite seriously, "I wish I'd become a gynecologist; if I'd only realized…"

Phil finished *Confessions of a Crap Artist* at the end of that happy first summer and brought it to me to read. When I finished it I sat for a while with the book on my lap, feeling puzzled and uneasy. "What a strange, uncomfortable novel," I thought, "so close to reality in some ways, so far in others. Was I really like Fay? I hoped not, because I didn't like her at all. No I wasn't like Fay. I guess this is what fiction writers do." I swept any problems the novel hinted at out of my mind. I had tremendous faith in Phil as a writer and tremendous faith in our relationship. Call it denial if you will, but perhaps faith is the other side of the denial coin and faith can move mountains.

The setting of the novel, the house, the sheep, the children, the details of our lives (like my sweeping up the scattered children's toys with a broom) are accurate. In the novel, Fay sweeps Nat off his feet, not vice versa, as in real life. I wondered why Phil wrote it that way. Like Fay, I was put out that Phil cooked big breakfasts that made me gain weight. My late husband's ashes really were sent to the Palace Market. I was outspoken and direct, but not that crude, and not devious. I'm afraid that Phil was the devious one. If Fay was a portrait of me, it was not one of warts and all, but all warts. Phil portrayed Fay as needing a husband for herself and a father for her children, so she acquired Nat. He had internalized Dr. A's idea. It never seemed to occur to Nat that Fay loved him.

In spite of my confused and uneasy feelings, I could see that it was a good novel, well written, unusual, and full of color. I told Phil this and then asked him, "Why didn't you tell me you didn't want to when I asked you to go to the store to buy some Tampax?"

Charley Hume wasn't at all like Richard. Richard was quiet and withdrawn, an anxious, sensitive person although he had an athletic, healthy look. Phil had more sympathy for Charley than for Fay, a typical fifties male attitude. In his novel, it was Fay's fault that Charley hit her. I guess she was supposed to have some mystical control over his motor nervous system.

I was amazed many years later when I read the introduction to the Entwhistle Press edition of Confessions. *Phil goes on at length about what a wonderful fellow Jack Isidore is, obviously identifying with that weird, provincial, sexless fellow whose head was filled with fantasy. The Phil I knew was as much like Jack Isidore as a bird of paradise is like a bat. The French movie,* Barjo, *portrayed the dark side of that novel, and it did a great job portraying Jack. It was fun to see a beautiful French movie star playing a role that had been based on me even though the woman portrayed in the movie was a cold, demanding, manipulative bitch—and not like me at all.*

Confessions of a Crap Artist didn't sell. It wasn't published until 1975 and then *by a small private house. The editor's introduction states, "Shortly after completing it, he married the woman who had inspired him to create Fay Hume, and they lived together for the next five years." I could have sued him if I were a litigious type of person.*

A friend called me from Los Angeles in 1976 and said, "Phil sure got even with you by writing that novel." She didn't know that it had been written during our blissful honeymoon. A young fan of Phil's said to me, "Confessions of a Crap Artist should have been a warning to you." But it wasn't like our everyday life at all. Some readers have taken this novel literally. Several Philip K. Dick fans have been surprised to learn that I was already a widow when I met Phil. Two Philip K. Dick scholars from Switzerland came to Point Reyes to visit me and talk about Phil. One of them was struck dumb as he sat in the living room staring at me. Finally he told me he was fascinated by meeting "the real Fay Hume." "Thanks a lot," I said. It turned out that he actually liked Fay Hume!

Perhaps if back then I could have understood the dark side of Phil's nature, that underlying mistrust and fear, things might have turned out differently, but I had no idea that anything was wrong, surrounded as I was in everyday life with this man's love. He had as great a talent for loving as he did for writing. I believed completely in the self that he presented to me and still do. In those days I thought his novels were fiction.

Phil's agent submitted the *Confessions* manuscript to Knopf. Alfred Knopf personally wrote to Phil saying he was interested in publishing the novel if Phil would rewrite the last third to make the female character more sympathetic. He compared Phil's writing to that of Salinger, Roth, and Mailer, the three top novelists of that time. We were both thrilled—but Phil said, "I *can't* rewrite this novel. It's not that I don't want to, it's that I'm not *able* to." This is a big clue to Phil's writing. At the time I was disappointed that Phil wouldn't or couldn't take advantage of this fantastic opportunity, but it was his novel, his career, his decision. Of course Knopf didn't buy the novel.

Phil went to work on a new novel and again wove it around his everyday life. We had read about Leakey finding the skull of Nutcracker Man in Tanganyika. We got into a great discussion about Neanderthal Man, Peking Man, and the Piltdown Hoax, a discussion that turned into a friendly argument that lasted weeks. I brought home various books from the library to prove my point. (Phil never went to the library.) The gist of the argument: was Neanderthal Man a vegetarian or a meat eater? Phil contended that he was a vegetarian. He said "The way Neanderthal Man's teeth were formed proves it. Those were teeth formed to crack and grind seeds and grains, not tear meat."

I was quite sure Phil was wrong. "What about all those weapons for killing animals? What about those animal bones in their caves?" I said. Phil was sure he was right anyway. He told me crossly, "Be quiet, or I'll unplug you." I laughed so hard I almost fell off the couch.

The next day I found a book at the library that stated definitively that Neanderthal Man was a meat eater and brought it home and read it out loud to Phil. He was furious. He denigrated the authority of the writer. Then he started on his new novel, *The Man Whose Teeth Were All Exactly Alike*, about a modern-day throwback to Neanderthal Man. In the novel Neanderthal Man was a vegetarian. He continued to make this point in later novels: the Neanderthal-like "chuppers" in *The Simulacra*.

We had a number of arguments like this one, competing with each other to be the authority on some subject or the other. I thought of these arguments as a friendly competition, a game like the ones I had played with my much older brothers. Phil didn't seem to mind when I won. He was proud that I was well read, and he liked to argue, discuss, and theorize with and against me. He made his points and won his share of these discussions.

Phil finished *The Man Whose Teeth Were All Exactly Alike* and soon brought me another novel to read, *In Milton Lumky Territory*. "Phil, you are so incredibly productive," I told him, and sat down and read it.

"A strange novel, like a dreary tempest in a teacup," I thought, "but well written, imaginative, and like other current literary novels, downbeat."

A nice responsible, hard-working, intelligent, and attractive young man (whom Phil named after our next-door neighbor's little boy) is seduced by a flaky older woman who is wearing my clothes. The young man has a tremendous mistrust of this older woman but he sticks with her and works hard in her business. He is ingenious, patient, and takes initiative, but she controls and screws up everything in an aimless manner. Although Phil presented the novel as one that he had just written, it really was one of a group of literary novels that he had written in Berkeley before he moved to Point Reyes Station. The main female character was probably based on his favorite high school teacher, Mrs. Wolfson, whom he'd had a crush on. He revised the novel somewhat in 1959, blending me slightly into the lead female role.

That fall, my late husband's family, the Handelsmans, came on one of their yearly visits. Part of the time, they stayed in a suite at the Fairmont Hotel in San Francisco, and the girls went into the city to stay with them. They came loaded with presents: Chicago kosher corned beef and my favorite Pratzel's Jewish rye bread from a St. Louis delicatessen. Phil describes all this in *Martian Time-Slip*. Phil charmed the Handelsmans, and he and Maury Handelsman drove around the area looking for real estate; Maury was always looking for profitable investments. Phil based Leo Rosen in *We Can Build You* and Leo Bohlen in *Martian Time-Slip* on Maury. Maury was a father figure to him.

After the Handelsmans left, Phil and I attended a school-board meeting with a group that was trying to get a kindergarten started. The members of the board, mostly ranchers who dominated the local political scene, regarded a kindergarten as an unnecessary extravagance. There was a tradition of yelling at political meetings in this rural area and the school-board chairman yelled at me for circulating a petition to get a kindergarten started. I had violated their trust. I should have consulted them first. When we got back home and went to bed that night, Phil put the fossil hammer on the floor by his side of the bed. I thought his reaction to the school-board meeting was a little extreme but he pointed out to me that it wasn't terribly long ago that the windows were shot out of the house of a person who disagreed with the local political machine. I had heard this story before, it really had happened, but it seemed to me that this was in the distant past. No one would do that sort of thing now.

That year we cooked a big Thanksgiving dinner and invited the Hudners. We couldn't have any cranberry jelly, though. That was the year the entire cranberry crop was seized by the federal government because it was contaminated with insecticide. Such a thing had never been heard of before and we never expected that anything like this would occur again. Even without cranberry sauce, we had a great holiday family gathering.

In January 1960, Phil was awarded a contract for a new novel with Harcourt Brace on the basis of their interest in *Confessions of a Crap Artist*. Harcourt Brace wanted Phil to fly to New York to work with one of their woman editors, but Phil said he wouldn't think of it. I wanted him to go. It was a great opportunity. I was disappointed to hear him say, "A few years ago I was asked to go to New York to write episodes for the *Captain Video* show for $500 a week, and I didn't go then and I'm not going now."

"Why not?" I asked, wondering why he hadn't gone to New York to write the *Captain Video* series. What a great opportunity. Why hadn't he told me about this before?

"I can't," he said in such a definite tone of voice that I didn't want to pursue the topic further.

He worked with the woman editor by mail, but later that year she got pregnant and quit and Harcourt Brace merged with Jovanovich. Phil's novel got lost between the cracks, and it wasn't published for many years.

Phil arranged his writing career cleverly in regard to that contract. He wanted to help with the new baby, due in February. Instead of writing a new novel he had sent Harcourt Brace a revision of a novel that he had written in the fifties, *A Time for George Stavros*, which he retitled *Humpty Dumpty in Oakland*. I thought it was the best literary novel that he had written. Neither Harcourt Brace nor I knew that *Humpty Dumpty in Oakland* was not a new work. Phil told me that *Humpty Dumpty in Oakland* was exceptional because it was a novel about the proletarian world from the inside, whereas most novels about the proletarian world were written by middle-class writers who didn't really understand the proletarian life.

As my pregnancy came near its end, twice, because of false labor pains, we had to drive at breakneck speed to Kaiser Hospital in San Francisco, a thirty-five-mile drive. After the second trip, Phil, emotionally exhausted, insisted that I stay with his mother in Berkeley, where I would be closer to the hospital. Reluctantly, I agreed and stayed with Dorothy and Joe for the next ten days. They were lovely to me. Their home was peaceful but somewhat melancholy. When I left, Dorothy was sad. She told me seriously that she wished I could continue to live with them in Berkeley. This was a nice thing for her to say, but a little odd, too. What about Phil and my three daughters?

On February 25, 1960, Phil and I had an eight-pound baby who popped out into the world like a cork out of a champagne bottle, a beautiful, blonde baby girl. Waiting at the hospital was hard on Phil. After the baby was born he told me, "I was terribly afraid something would be wrong." I laughed at him, "Oh, Phil, you're so morbid. Look, isn't the baby darling?"

He leaned over the hospital bed and looked into the baby's face, and said, "Now my sister is made up for." Well, that was Phil, always saying off-beat things.

We decided that Phil could name the baby, and he decided on Laura, Laura Archer Dick. Phil and the three girls came to pick me up the day after Laura was born. Phil was in a state of utter enchantment. When we got home he sat entranced, watching me nurse the baby. Joe and Dorothy drove up from Berkeley to see their first grandchild, but Phil would only let them look at her for one minute. Literally one minute. Then he rushed them out of the room. I couldn't believe it. "Maybe he's afraid of infection," I thought. I was too busy with the baby to worry about this, however.

After Laura was born my weight sank to 135 pounds and stayed there. Phil said sadly, "All my wives get fat." He let on that he really liked thin, dark-haired women, but that I was an exception.

At that period Phil stopped writing every day and helped me with the house, the other children, and the baby although he didn't have the rapport with the baby that he had with the older girls. A few weeks after Laura was born, Phil started having terrible pains in his chest. We were afraid that he was having a heart attack. I left the baby with Hatte and rushed him to Kaiser Hospital in San Francisco. Phil was put in bed in an emergency room and a doctor ran in with an electrocardiogram machine. My heart sank. I thought, "Oh no. Not another husband dying."

Phil said cheerfully, "I think I'm either going to die or else I'm going to have a baby." It turned out that he was having pyloric spasms. The doctor told him to drink less coffee and read and meditate more to stimulate his parasympathetic nervous system, which was out of balance with his other two nervous systems.

Taking care of the new baby didn't keep us busy enough. We managed to get involved with a project that was to cost us a lot of money and a lot of conflict. The Peugeot Phil had bought wasn't performing well, so we jumped from the frying pan into the fire and bought a 1953 Jaguar Mark VII saloon, a beautiful curvy white car with a mahogany dashboard, complicated instruments, tucked gray leather upholstery, and a sun roof. We paid $2,000 to the owner, the head mechanic at British Motors, for it. Phil looked elegant driving this car. It was in beautiful shape except for the carpeting, so we bought the best-quality royal blue plush wool carpeting that we could find. We took it out and drove it ninety-six miles an hour on the Nicasio highway. Later we found it still had its original tires, retreaded seven times. They were so soft we could almost poke our fingers through the sidewalls.

We'd only had it for two months when the mechanic at our small, local garage made an adjustment to the idle mechanism. Later that day on White's Hill, the car, full of children, blew a valve. No sooner had we had the valve fixed than the axle broke. After we had a new axle installed, something else happened, and something else, and something else. We needed a British mechanic under the hood to keep that car running. When it started raining that fall, a steady heavy rain that went on for days, the sunroof leaked and the blue carpet started to grow small white mushrooms. I wanted Phil to help me build a shelter for the car but he wouldn't, so I took the car into San Rafael and traded it in on a new Volvo. Phil was furious. He was still talking about this twenty years later. I think he really liked that Jaguar, but wouldn't admit it. He probably liked the mushrooms growing on the carpet, too.

That same fall we saw an advertisement in our local weekly newspaper, the *Baywood Press*, for a repossessed spinet. We decided to look for a musical instrument for our house, perhaps a piano, or Phil thought he might want one of the new electronic organs. Finally, we bought a Baldwin acoustic spinet and Phil went to Berkeley and bought a lot of sheet music. Phil used the spinet advertisement we had seen in the newspaper in the novel *We Can Build You*.

I started on a new project that was to have a big effect on Phil. While Laura was napping, I would visit our neighbor, Lorraine Hynes, and we would chat about this and that as we drank coffee. One day we decided that we were tired of just sitting around talking; we wanted to do something worthwhile.

I had been fascinated with all the accidental metal shapes and splashes that were produced while I was working on my welded sculpture. Lorraine and I thought we could turn them into an interesting form of jewelry. Phil encouraged us and bought me an anvil, a drill press, and a polishing motor. He built a well-constructed workbench in the utility room where I kept my welding tanks. He told me, "I don't like to do carpentry. I made this bench extra strong so I won't ever have to make it over again."

Lorraine and I worked out wild new techniques for making jewelry using a tiny welding torch. We forged black iron bracelets with pearls set on them, made jewelry out of fire-glazed red copper and textured bronze, and learned to weld bronze rod into various shapes. About the same time I began to tile the master bathroom in our house. I bought different colored small tiles and made a mermaid, several fish, a cosmic eye right over the toilet, a boat, and a large sea serpent. It felt like you were under water when you were taking a bath. Phil wrote about this mural in *We Can Build You*. In that novel the bathroom tiling project is done by Pris Frauenzimmer, a horrible woman.

We had been having louder arguments. Phil claimed that he loved it. "We're like a Mediterranean family, everyone waving their hands and yelling," he said with great relish. A couple of times I threw a few dishes to punctuate my point. Later, I would be sorry that I had become so angry. But Phil said to me lovingly, "You can do anything you want, as long as you don't bore me."

Afterward I could never figure out what those fights had been about. In our everyday life we seemed to get along well, even have an exceptional understanding. The fights seemed to have no identifiable source. One day I threw many more than just two dishes. One crashed through a narrow window by the front door. I threw the penny bank, too. Tandy picked up the pennies as we continued to yell at each other. Afterward, I was very upset. I had scared myself with my very angry outburst.

I had an idea that would make everything better. We would all, except baby Laura, go to Disneyland. The next day we took the girls out of school, left Laura with our neighbors, and drove to Los Angeles. We walked around Disneyland all day, going on most of the rides. I loved the Rocket to the Moon. Phil was fascinated with the Lincoln robot. When we got back home the following day, we were exhausted and had forgotten all about the fight. Later, I made a stained-glass window of a monk raising his hand in blessing to replace the broken window by the front door. We never did deal with the unknown source of those fights. Years later Phil described himself as an emotional terrorist. He certainly knew how to push my buttons; I had many at that time.

Phil told me about his out-of-body experiences: "I walked in the living room and I saw myself already there." Another time he said, "I was lying in bed and I saw myself standing by the bed getting dressed. Suddenly I was in the body that was getting dressed, looking down on the body that was in bed." Another time he told me, "I saw a ghost walking around, an elderly Italian gentleman. It may have been the ghost of the man who used to live on the farm that was once here." At night when the wind blew he thought he heard a train, the ghost of the narrow gauge train that came through Point Reyes Station in the early 1900s. But I could hear it, too. It was only the wind.

I'll bet he wished he could have had an out-of-body experience when he had to knock the yellow-jacket nest off the eaves. At first it was just a little nest, and we watched it grow with interest. Suddenly it was as big as three basketballs. Hundreds of yellow jackets were zooming around our patio and we were afraid to go out of the house. Phil put on a long yellow raincoat, a strange hat, and boots and draped himself with mosquito netting. The girls and I nearly died laughing at his appearance. He knocked the nest down at night and sprayed it with insecticide. We all told him how brave he was. He loved this.

That fall, we bought a bird book to identify the many species of birds that migrated through the West Marin area every year. The book listed only red-shafted and yellow-shafted flickers, but ours were orange-shafted. We watched the Kennedy-Nixon debates. Phil wrote in Martin Luther King's name for president. Later he felt bad for Nixon, as much as he disliked him, when Nixon cried after he lost.

The Search for Philip K. Dick

In spite of faithfully using birth-control techniques, I became pregnant again. I felt that I didn't have the resources to raise a fifth child. In fact, I could barely manage with the four children and Phil. At first, Phil argued against my getting an abortion. But I was determined to do what was best for the family. It made me furious to be faced with two such bad choices. I fumed, dumb scientists. They could put a man in space but couldn't figure out a reliable method of birth control.

After a great deal of carrying on with psychiatrists, trying to get a legal California abortion, we went up to Seattle to have an illegal operation. When we came back, I started taking the new oral contraceptive, Enovid, a pill that the newspapers said was going to change the world and revolutionize the relationship between the sexes.

I believe Phil's extremely dark novel *We Can Build You* reflected his mood at the time of this abortion. He was far more disturbed than he let on. This novel was the last of his attempts to write a literary novel. He added a space-port and a real-estate project on Mars for its publication in 1972 to make it into science fiction.

Bob Bundy was based on our neighbor Pete Stevens. Maury Frauenzimmer was based on Phil's friend Maury Guy (who had begun to study the New Age belief system Subud and was soon to change his name to Iskandar Guy). Phil punned on Maury's name change in the novel when Maury Frauenzimmer decides to change his name by consulting the encyclopedia volume indexed as "Rock to Subud." Sam K. Barrows was based on William Wolfson, Phil's attorney. Phil was Louis Rosen, Leo Rosen's son. Leo was based on Maury Handelsman. Louis/Phil says in *We Can Build You* that he is exactly like Lincoln. They are as alike as two peas in a pod. He diagnoses Lincoln as a manic-depressive or schizophrenic, and one of the deepest, most complicated humans in human history.

We Can Build You is notable for the first appearance of Phil's beckoning unfair one, the first "dark-haired girl," Pris Frauenzimmer. Pris was a real rotter and schizophrenic to boot. I'm afraid Pris was at least partly based on me. (She was tiling my bathroom, anyway). He wrote:

Suffering was part of life, part of being with Pris. Without Pris there was no suffering, nothing erratic, unbalanced, but also there was nothing alive. Only small time slots, schemes, a dusty little office with two or three men scrabbling in the sand.

I told Phil how delighted I was with the Stanton simulacrum and how thrilled I was at the moment in the novel when the Lincoln simulacrum comes to life: "Why, Phil, he's more real than most real people."

Phil was at his most funny and his most serious when he wrote about Dr. Horstowsky giving Louis Rosen hubrizene, "a pill that hums the opening of Beethoven's Sixteenth Quartet. A person can almost hum this drug." Louis now wants a pill of Beethoven's Ninth Chorale. "If God exists, the angels say 'yes.'" The doctor offers an alternative, a lobotomy.

As Phil worked in the study in the mornings, I did housework. My natural habit was to be in either a comatose or a meditative state at this time of day. Phil would emerge from his study frequently to read newly written paragraphs to me or talk about something in the news or something he'd just read. He was delightful but it wore me out. I needed some time to myself in the morning. I said, "Maybe you should get a place to work away from the house." Phil thought that this was a fine idea. We found a beat-up old wooden building, ten by thirty feet, down the road a quarter mile away. Phil named it "the Hovel" and it really was. The ground showed through the floorboards. We rented the Hovel from Sheriff Bill Christensen, who lived around the corner. The first of each month Phil took his $30 rent money to Bill's house and stopped to chat with him. They were both great talkers and enjoyed each other's company. Bill was an interesting man who had fought in the Spanish Civil War and had a silver plate in his head to prove it. He was the only law enforcement person in the large area of West Marin, and some of his stories were amazing.

Phil hauled his Magnavox, some of his novels, his typewriter, and his desk over to the Hovel. He bought a stock of chocolate bars to give to the children when they came by on their way home from school. The minute he had finished moving, I was sorry that he was gone. But although I urged him to, he wouldn't move back.

He said, "My mother taught me to take the consequences of my actions. I never chew my cud twice. Never look back. Something might be gaining on you."

Three
FAMILY LIFE IN THE COUNTRY

In her hillside home in West Marin County, Bonny Keller...emerged from the bedroom, wiping the water color paint from her hands.... And then through the window she saw against the sky to the south a stout trunk of smoke, as dense and brown as a living stump. She gaped at it, and then the window burst; it pulverized and she crashed back and slid across the floor along with the powdery fragments of it. Every object in the house tumbled, fell and shattered and then skidded with her, as if the house had tilted on end.

—Philip K. Dick, *Dr. Bloodmoney*

By 1961, MY small inheritance and the money from the sale of Phil's house were gone. I worried, "How are we going to manage?" Phil was concerned about money too and didn't want to write any more literary novels. The five he had written in the past two years had been rejected by every publisher in New York. One day his New York agent sent them, plus six Berkeley literary novels, in a large box. When Phil opened it, I was impressed. "Some day these will all be published," I told him as he put the manuscripts in the top of a closet in his study.

He thought for several weeks and came up with several different ideas for his career. Fascinated with the Eichmann trial, which was going on then in Jerusalem, he thought he might write a novel about another Nazi, Martin Bormann, who was thought to be hiding in South America. He made a brief outline and then abandoned the idea. Then he thought of writing a historical novel about the Middle Ages, a period when, he said, the port of Marseilles had been closed for a hundred years. He did some research but soon abandoned this idea, too.

About this time I started reading some of Carl Jung's writings. Dorothy Hudner had been deeply influenced by Jung's works, and when she heard about my interest she sent us one of the beautiful Bollingen editions. Both Phil and I read it and soon we acquired and read the whole set. I thought of going to

Zurich to study with Jung. I dreamed about cooking dinner for him. In the dream, I opened the refrigerator but it was filled with rotten meat. I guess it's just as well I didn't go. We listened when BBC interviewed Jung arriving in England for a visit. They asked, "Dr. Jung, do you believe in God?" We were awed by his answer: "I do not believe. I know."

Phil studied Jung's volumes *Alchemy* and *Transformation Symbols in the Mass*. He was interested in Jung's idea that a New World religion would soon arise, a religion based upon a quaternity instead of a trinity. The fourth force will be, Jung said, the force now regarded as demonic. This statement had a big influence on Phil.

I read Jung's introductions to the *I Ching, The Book of the Golden Flower,* and *The Tibetan Book of the Dead* and bought these three books and some others: a book about the Hindu vedas, *The Bhagavadgita*, and some volumes about Zen Buddhism.

Phil became interested in the *I Ching* and Linus Pauling's theory of synchronicity, which Jung describes in his introduction to *The Tibetan Book of the Dead*. Phil began to use the *I Ching* as an oracle several times a day. Once he asked it if we should sell our old Ford station wagon. The oracle replied, "The wagon is full of devils," so we sold it and bought that Peugeot, which also turned out to be full of devils. Phil was quite chagrined when one day the oracle told him, "The learning of the self-taught is cumbersome." He dreamed about an elderly Chinese sage with many outlines. He believed that this dream represented the many sages who, over the centuries, had written the *I Ching*. He thought the *I Ching* was alive, like the Bible, and that the *I Ching* had sent this dream to him.

I disagreed. I saw the *I Ching* as a sort of super "Dear Abby" with an Asian flavor. Finally, one day I asked the *I Ching*, "Is there a better oracle than you?" It replied something like this, "You yourself are a better oracle for your time, because I am very old and was written a long, long time ago. You are part of your own times, and with sufficient intuition, you can make out the seeds of the future better than I." So I closed the *I Ching* and never consulted it again. Phil used it to the end of his life, although at times he became angry with its advice. Eventually he began using yarrow sticks instead of coins.

Many religious themes interested Phil. At that time many new translations of the Bible were coming out. He liked a book entitled *The Desert Fathers*. He quoted a Russian proverb, "Break a stick and there is Christ."

We read the *Tao Te Ching* and at the same time, coincidentally and synchronistically, a book on cybernetics by Norbert Weiner, which described machines of eight different orders. A machine of the eighth order would be one that would create its own matter. Weiner believed that Taoism described a universe like the one in cybernetics theory.

I had found a beautiful book on Japanese landscape gardening that Phil liked. He used the concepts of *wu wei* and *wabi sabi* from this book. He didn't like *Zen and the Art of Archery*, a popular book of that time, at all. After he had finished it, he dropped the book over his shoulder and kicked it up in the air with his heel, saying, "So much for Zen Buddhism."

Everything wasn't always so super-intellectual. We watched the Rose Bowl Parade on TV, *Sherlock Holmes*, *Cyrano de Bergerac*, and *The Rocky and Bullwinkle Show*. We played Go, canasta, chess, Scrabble, and verbally threw "Tom Swifties" at each other like the following:

> *The book business is hidebound.*
> *Plants are taking over the world sporadically.*
> *The operator let me off the hook.*
> *The discovery of atomic energy electrified the world.*
> *The Senate inquiry into the modern use of sidearms was muzzled.*
> —Philip K. Dick, *Galactic Pot-Healer*

That spring, Mamie Eisenhower—that was the name we had given our oldest Suffolk ewe, she had bangs like Mamie's—had triplets. On Good Friday afternoon, Phil played the Dublin version of Handel's *Messiah* on the record player while working just outside on the flowerbeds around the patio. He came running back in the house: "I saw a great streak of black sweeping across the sky. For a moment there was utter nothingness dividing the sky in half." There was no doubt in my mind that he had seen something. Perhaps it was the great spiritual black hole symbolically re-created on Good Friday when the churches in the world were commemorating the crucifixion.

I thought it would be good if the house were legally in both of our names instead of only mine. A man and wife should both own the domicile where they were bringing up their children. Phil agreed and so we went to the title company and made the change. The property had been listed in "joint tenancy" instead of "community property" because Richard's family's lawyer had advised Richard to have it listed this way in case we got divorced. Then I wouldn't automatically get the house as was usual in California at that time. Although I didn't realize it then, not only were Phil and I not legally married but Phil now owned half of the house. We were both happy that we had taken this step. It put Phil in the high mood that produced *The Man in the High Castle*.

Phil had suggested that I read Ward Moore's novel, *Bring the Jubilee*. I borrowed it from the library and read it with delight. *Bring the Jubilee* is an alternate-reality novel set in a world in which the South has won the Civil War. A footnote in it refers to a novel written by a Northerner about a world in which the North has won the Civil War. It wouldn't be our North, but a North that a Southern writer living in a victorious South would imagine. I told Phil, "I wish Ward Moore had developed that fascinating idea further. I wonder what that world was like?"

It wasn't long after this that Phil started working on his new novel, which was set in a universe where Japan and Nazi Germany had won World War II. Phil's typewriter was being rebuilt. Tandy had dropped it, so he wrote the beginning of *The Man in the High Castle* on a $10 1936 Underwood typewriter that we had bought for the children to play with. One key didn't work. It didn't seem to faze him.

While Phil was writing, I was making jewelry with my partner, Lorraine Hynes, but we weren't getting along well. Phil went back and forth between our neighboring houses, supposedly mediating, but somehow everything between us kept getting worse and worse. Soon Lorraine quit and I was working alone in my small laundry-room workshop.

To keep me company, Phil starting making some molten globby metal forms. He loved doing this. He made an irregular silver triangle and polished it for an hour on the buffing wheel. He described this object in *The Man in the High Castle*: "a single small silver triangle ornamented with hollow drops. Black beneath, bright and light-filled above."

He took off a couple of days from his writing to go to Frazier's, a fine store in Berkeley, to make my first sale to Mrs. Hom, the buyer there. (She continued to buy from me for the next fifteen years until Frazier's was forced out of business by the street people who lined the curbs with their merchandise and scared away the upper-middle-class shoppers from the Berkeley hills with their odd costumes and weird demeanor.) Phil created a jewelry display in small baskets. He cut a design in an art-gum eraser and printed handsome cards on the children's toy rotary printing press using handmade paper an artist friend, Inez Storer, had given us. He wrote about all this in *The Man in the High Castle*, exactly as it happened.

Before I knew it, Phil was taking over the whole jewelry business. Finally I had developed something for myself besides housework and raising kids, and he wanted it. He already had his writing. It was my business. I didn't want him working in it if he was going to completely dominate it. Huffily, I asked him not to work in my small shop anymore. He withdrew without a word, and I thought he understood.

That evening we went downtown to visit Jerry Kresy. When we were ready to leave, Phil took the silver triangle out of his pocket and asked Jerry if he'd like to have it. "Sure," said Jerry, "I've got a fine place for it right on the front door," and he picked up a hammer and a nail and nailed right through Phil's silver triangle. Phil winced as the nail pierced his cherished ornament. Suddenly I felt bad. What was happening? Phil was being hurt—but it was too late to do anything about it, wasn't it? I brushed my thoughts away. It was, after all, only a little piece of metal.

That summer Phil became involved with local water politics. The one-inch-diameter pipes bringing water to our house were so old and rusty that in summer when the pressure dropped, the only way I could wash dishes was to go out on the ground-level concrete front porch at midnight and use the hose. There wasn't enough pressure in the lines for the water to rise to the level of the kitchen sink.

Phil decided to do something about this problem. He went around the town asking people about their service and was quite amazed when homeowners would tell him, "They're pumping nothing but mud to us." He couldn't believe that people "were so mute" and hadn't complained about this problem. He wrote letters and attended meetings. It wasn't long before two-inch-diameter pipes were being laid up the two-mile hill to our house at the very end of the waterline. Phil was mild mannered, even humble, not at all pushy—but he had a way. I told him, kiddingly, "It's lucky you're a reclusive person or you'd be another Goebbels."

It was a wonderful summer. The children pushed Laura around in their doll buggy on the patio. Jayne had a pancake-eating contest with Phil. She won, eating twenty-three pancakes in one sitting. Phil and the girls collected "shaky grass" in the field and put it in a vase on the dining room table. We went downtown evenings to watch the local townsmen play donkey baseball. Phil bought a huge two-handled lumberman's saw and a giant axe to cut firewood for the winter—which he never used.

Iskandar Guy (then, still Maury Guy) came to visit bringing his beautiful new girlfriend. We took a picnic of cold guinea fowl to Stinson Beach and ate with our hands, not using any utensils, a style that was part of Maury's new Subud religion. The sun, the sky, the ocean, the beautiful young woman, and the delicious food combined together in a way that made me feel that something cosmic was breaking through that day.

In late summer, we decided to have the lambs slaughtered for the freezer. We had far too many sheep for the size of our pasture. All the ewes had had lambs, some of them twins. Our next-door neighbor, an old-time rancher, offered to slaughter them. Phil said he was going to hold the lambs for Mr. Hendron. I thought I should watch and give moral support.

They were beautiful big animals. Phil held them while Mr. Hendron cut their throats. It was horrible. I didn't eat mutton again for years. Phil didn't seem to be disturbed. It was surprising since he loved animals and was so sensitive. He said, "Remember, I come from a farming tradition. All my father's people were ranchers."

Phil brought me the manuscript of *The Man in the High Castle* to read. He said, "I don't think I'll even send this off. I'm afraid it isn't any good."

I loved it. I was pleased that, for a change, Phil had based a female character on me who was really a heroine. I totally identified with Juliana. Suddenly, naked, she went into a schizophrenic fugue and cut a man's throat. It was horrible, even if he was a Nazi SS killer.

As I read, I became totally absorbed. I thought, "Frank, how could you give way to despair at the moment that your artistry was being recognized? Of course Juliana believed in Abendsen and his world, a world of hope, a world without oppression. There was Abendsen with his arms crossed, rocking back on his heels just like Phil did. For a moment, contemplating the blobby silver triangle, lovely, sensitive Mr. Tagomi came into our universe—but he was disoriented here and returned to his own world. Betty Kasoura was cooking one of my menus for Robert Childan. Those complicated feelings of pride and inferiority that Childan had. For a short time he rose above his own nature and experienced the grace of God. Ah, Phil, are we all doomed to commit acts of cruelty, violence, and evil?"

"Phil, it's the best thing you've ever done. Send it right off." He was pleased but still dubious. But he retyped it with only a few changes and did send it off.

Every time I read The Man in the High Castle, *I find another level of meaning that I didn't see in previous readings. I had to laugh when I found out, while working on this book, that one of the thugs Tagomi killed has a calling card in his wallet that reads "Jack Sanders," which was the name of an old friend of Phil's from Berkeley in the fifties. The intensity, the daring, the delicacy of feeling, and the playfulness of* The Man in the High Castle *bring back the spirit of Phil more than any of his other novels—but still it is only a pale shadow of the man I knew.*

When it came time for publication, Phil sent his publisher the most awful picture of himself from the early fifties that had ever been taken. An old friend of Phil's, John Gildersleeve, said, "That picture showed every bad character trait that Phil had ever had, and none of the good ones."

Phil dedicated the novel to me: "To my wife, Anne, without whose silence this book would never have been written." I wasn't sure I liked this phrasing. I never did quite understand it.

After writing *The Man in the High Castle*, Phil rested for a while and did his thinking thing. We went out more. We took a trip to San Francisco to buy some books. We had dinner in town. Driving up the Olema grade at night, we saw in our headlights an owl with his claws caught in a dead skunk's body. It was too heavy for the owl to fly away with. The skunk had also sprayed. I said that perhaps we shouldn't interfere with nature's ways, but Phil stopped the car, got out, and freed the owl. I had to agree that it was the right thing to do. Phil smelled for weeks and we had to throw out all the clothes he had been wearing.

In January and February of 1962, the rains were especially heavy. Phil was beginning to work on a new novel, *The Game-Players of Titan*. I found some shaggy-looking mushrooms growing under our cypress trees and wondered if they were good to eat. I took them to a mushroom expert, Dr. Robert Orr, at the Academy of Sciences in San Francisco, who told me they were shaggy manes. The Orrs came out to visit us on several occasions, and with their expert guidance and several reference books we became fanatical mushroom hunters, tramping daily during the rainy season through the mist-covered slopes of the mixed bay and oak forests on Inverness Ridge. We were usually the only people there. "We're comrades, marching shoulder to shoulder," I told Phil.

Sometimes Lois Mini and Tandy went with us. It was a treasure hunt, looking for those exotic little bits of color, texture, and form that were also delicious to eat: chanterelles, bluets, oyster mushrooms, boletes, *Agaricus augustus* and more. Of course Phil was fascinated with the red and white *Amanita muscaria* which, he read, was used by the Eskimos for religious reasons because of its hallucinogenic properties. We were almost the only people gathering wild mushrooms in the area at that time except for a few Italian Americans. A few years later all the counterculture folk were gathering and eating wild mushrooms, and some of them eating *Amanita muscaria* with no bad or even, disappointingly, hallucinogenic results. Mushroom hunting is a great activity during the wet winters of Point Reyes. The daytime temperature is in the fifties. It's perfect mushroom country (everything, in fact, molds). The torrential rains of winter instead of being depressing become an asset.

We joined the Mycological Society and went to meetings in San Francisco. Along Bear Valley Trail we found a geoglossum, a little black, leathery "Earthtongue." I was fascinated with the slime molds on the rotten logs, tiny plants that move. Phil put all these fungi in his novels. I became tired of my own mushroom recipes and asked Phil if he could think of any new way to cook the wild mushrooms. He invented several excellent seasoning combinations although he said he really didn't know how to cook.

Phil was excited when we went to the Mycological Society banquet and ate a dish made out of edible *Amanita caesareas,* the tasty edible mushroom that looks similar to and is closely related to the deadly *Amanita phalloides.* It was scary, but I ate a little anyway. We sat with a young black man who was later to take a vow of silence and walk around the world playing his guitar and writing poetry. That night he was still talking. At one point, out of the blue, he told me he loved me. I didn't know what to say, so I didn't say anything. About twenty years later I ran into him and acknowledged the kind remark that he had made at that Mycological Society dinner. He wasn't talking still but he laughed and laughed in a wonderful way.

The Game-Players of Titan was a bit of a letdown after *The Man in the High Castle,* although imaginative and well crafted. The game was patterned on our bouts of Monopoly. The society Phil described in this novel was obsessed with getting its females pregnant. I think Phil used some material from his Berkeley days.

Next, Phil told me about his new idea for a novel: "I'm going to write about the plumber's union and the Berkeley Co-op. I'm going to put them on Mars." This became *Martian Time-Slip*.

As I look back on those days, sometimes I wonder if I am only imagining how happy our life was, but Lynne Hudner, Phil's cousin and stepsister, remembers, "Phil loved the girls and loved being a part of a large family. His marriage of that period was like a marriage between two adults." When I interviewed my friend, Inez Storer, for this book, she said, "I saw a couple with a balanced relationship. Phil was domestic, hovering around the kitchen. There were dogs and children around. Phil took a lot of interest in the children. The family was the most interesting and erudite family that I knew."

I found June (Kresy) von Schucker in Arizona, still living with the chiropractor she had run away with years ago. We talked for a long time. June recalled, "Back then you two were so happy, getting along real well. I remember everyone laughing all the time. Everything seemed to be just fine."

I contacted Jerry Kresy by phone in Oakland in 1983. He had become a recluse and was suffering from a serious heart condition. I felt warm toward him for old times' sake and wanted to meet him for lunch but he didn't reciprocate my feelings. He gave his emphatic judgment about the relationship between Phil and me over the phone: "When he was married to you, Phil came out of himself for the first time in his life. He loved you, Anne he loved you.... He came out of himself for a while and gave and gave.... [Phil was] a totally selfish person, [and you] were one of the few persons he cared for.... [He] was a little man, violent, had a little life.... [He] was a selfish computer.... [H]e loved [you], Anne.... He loved you. [angrily] You and Phil had what everyone wants, and you ruined it."

I was blissfully happy. Everything in our lives was running smoothly, nothing dramatic, it was an everyday life. We drove the kids around, had big family meals, and worked in the garden. Phil was interested in everything that was going on, listening intently, asking questions. It seemed to me that our love was expanding, deepening, evolving. We shared everything. We were equal partners in a total relationship. There was no hint of any shadow. We told each other that each of us was to the other like father, mother, brother, sister, and uncle.

Our love life, which had been perfect, became even better. Phil was an adoring lover, totally at home with physical and emotional intimacy, affectionate, other-directed. Our everyday life was so rich, so full, that sex, even though wonderful, was only a small part of the gestalt (as Phil would say). I remember one night when he seemed for a moment to be a transcendent being.

Phil continued to be very funny. One day a flock of bluebirds landed in the cherry-plum tree just outside the living-room window. Phil quickly put on the record "The Bluebird of Happiness," the corniest song ever recorded. He loved to hang around the kitchen while I was cooking dinner and talk. Sometimes he would make desserts with the children, creamy fudge, or lemon or chocolate soufflé, or a chocolate cake. Other times Phil and the three older girls would drive to the Inverness Park store after dinner to buy the makings for root beer floats. He started getting a little pudgy. He told me he'd been fat in high school and had a kind of transient diabetes. I put both of us on a diet. He lost ten pounds in a week. I didn't lose any weight at all.

Although we got along beautifully most of the time, currents of conflict did exist. One source of conflict in our marriage was my desire for equal status. I saw Phil going off to write, having a prestigious career, while I was stuck with the housework. Although he always did the breakfast dishes, sometimes mopped the floors, and helped much more than most husbands, he wouldn't agree that, in principle, housekeeping was partly his job. We had a number of bitter arguments about this. Betty Friedan's book, *The Feminine Mystique*, had just come out and, of course, I'd read it, but I'd already thought of a lot more than she wrote about.

Although we still argued, I didn't throw dishes anymore. Phil loved to make authoritative pronouncements, and sometimes he was completely wrong and I would tell him so instead of listening respectfully as females were supposed to do in the early sixties. In fact, everybody in our household argued and discussed various issues continually. Phil said all the girls should become lady lawyers. He was right. Phil was good at arguing, too. He was never at a loss for words. He could get angry. He was not the poor beaten-down little man that he portrays in his novels. But as I bustled around the house yanking the Electrolux vacuum cleaner along behind me (I hated vacuuming), I remember Phil saying, "I feel like that vacuum cleaner."

Then, changing the subject, he went on to tell me how people in Berkeley kept tarantulas as pets on strings and how wild tarantulas would jump six feet high out of the bushes on the University of California campus.

Phil felt the children should take the consequences of their own actions, and when Hatte and Jayne fought, Phil told me, "Don't interfere, let them work it out by themselves." Phil was anxious about the girls' futures and especially concerned that they speak proper English. He was worried that they were picking up poor phrasing and back-country colloquialisms that would be handicaps for them later on in their lives.

On April 1, Phil came running in from the field with Hatte, Jayne, and Tandy close behind him. All of them were jabbering excitedly about the flying saucer that had just landed. I was almost convinced until I remembered that it was April Fool's Day. Our third anniversary. That evening we celebrated with a roast beef dinner followed by a lemon meringue pie that Phil and the girls made.

On another occasion, Tandy remembers Phil saying to the girls, "The Martians are landing. Come on," and he grabbed the salt and pepper shakers and ran out the door as they trailed excitedly after him. I think their idea was that if you shake salt on a Martian, he becomes tame.

He really got us all going about the meteorite, or whatever it was. We were sitting in the living room talking and suddenly Phil rose to his feet, his eyes dilated, and pointed over my shoulder out the window. "Something glowing landed over there in the field," he said, excitedly. After much discussion we decided that it must have been a meteorite. We spent the whole next day searching for fragments and actually found some black glassy slivers, but I think they are indigenous to the area. After all, Black Mountain had once been a volcano.

I could never tell whether Phil's accounts were real or made up. The weirdest tales would often turn out to be true, and the most everyday, convincing account would turn out to be—well—a fabrication.

In addition to telling about events that turned out not to have really happened, Phil was occasionally "gestalting" (he would say) some scene that didn't exist. At night he would sometimes momentarily see a scene in the headlights of the car, like an animal that wasn't there.

Since *Sputnik* had been in orbit, we watched the sky hoping to see a satellite. Once we saw something wobbly going across the sky at twilight on the plane of the ecliptic. (This time I saw it, too.) Phil said it was a weather balloon. We became interested in studying the night skies and bought a book on stargazing. Soon we were lying nightly on our backs on a blanket out in the field, using a flashlight covered with red tissue paper and reading our new star map. We identified most of the constellations before we moved on to other things. We watched an eclipse of the sun through smoked glass that year, too.

Phil didn't believe in flying saucers. He thought the people who believed in them were kooks and lunatics. His idea was more fantastic and funnier. He thought that people were seeing some sort of gaseous, air-living creatures. "The movements that are described are more like the movements of living creatures than a ship from outer space," he told us.

On Hatte's twelfth birthday, May 26, 1962, we cooked a picnic dinner at Phil's cabin in Inverness for a group of girls including all ours. After dinner, Phil turned the lights low and read H. P. Lovecraft's "The Rats in the Walls." The girls loved every horror-filled moment.

Spring slipped into summer, and we planted fig trees, vegetables, and two hybrid tea roses that Phil fancied, Peace and Charlotte Armstrong. One day, Phil and I sat side by side on the edge of the patio each with an arm around the other's shoulders. We didn't speak. We were part of a moment of such perfection that it is with me still. Even after all that happened later on I still believed in this moment—for a very long time. As well as being my husband, Phil was my best friend.

That summer, Phil's old friends from University Radio days, Vince and Virginia Lusby, came to visit. Virginia remembers, "I was surprised to see Phil doing all those domestic things so happily. I remember him running out in the meadow to bring little Laura away from the sheep. Then he was helping the older girls out in the kitchen. I liked Phil so much better than when I had known him in Berkeley. Phil brought in a head of broccoli from the garden and showed it to us proudly—complaining how much more it cost to grow than to buy. He was the perfect country squire."

Frequently on sunny weekends we entertained either the Hudners, friends of Phil's from Berkeley, or old friends of mine. The science fiction writer Poul Anderson came with his wife and daughter to play croquet. Phil's ex-mistress, Janet Feinstein, came to spend a weekend at the Inverness cabin with her two daughters. The way Phil carried on in advance you'd think the Queen of Sheba was coming to visit. We got along fine, though. I felt so secure that this situation was no problem for me. Allen Ayle, an old friend of Phil's, was deeply involved with yoga, and when he came to dinner he drank only a glass of water. Lois Mini brought over her ex-husband, Norman. When another old Berkeley friend, Alan Rich, came to visit, Phil showed him how to use the *I Ching*. When I interviewed him twenty years later, Alan remembered how impressed he was with what a happy family we were.

During that summer Bill Christensen, the sheriff, conducted a campaign against the packs of dogs that were killing local ranchers' sheep. We'd had problems with dogs and our sheep, too. At 4 a.m. we would hear the sheep running, and we'd tear out of the house in our pajamas, waving our arms and yelling to drive the dogs away. Phil bought a .22 rifle to protect our small flock—but he didn't wait for dogs to chase our sheep. He would run outside and start shooting if a dog even walked by on the road. I was terrified he was going to shoot a child. He didn't look or aim; he just shot. The gun lay on our bedroom closet shelf, loaded. I was really afraid of what might happen. I told Phil, "I'm going to get rid of that thing," and gave it away. He didn't say a word.

Hatte remembers the late summer day two-year-old Laura picked all the tomatoes on the tomato plants. When Phil went out to reproach her, she looked up in the sky, raised her hand as if something up there had come and told her to pull those tomatoes off the vine. Phil told Hatte, "Look how early girls learn to lie."

Tandy went to Berkeley to stay with the Hudners for five days. She had a little tantrum the third day she was there and the Hudners packed her in their car and drove her back to Point Reyes Station. Phil and I were indignant that Tandy had been treated this way. This incident created a breach between our families.

About this time, Phil's mother, Dorothy, decided to move with her family to Mexico again. (The Hudners had lived there in the fifties.) Phil became desolate and angry that his mother would think of going to Mexico, "abandoning" him. I was amazed to hear him use the word *abandoning* when he claimed that he didn't like his mother. Dorothy gave up her idea of moving to Mexico, but soon afterward she became ill, and Phil thought she might die. He told me that if his mother died, he wanted Joe to come and live with us. Dorothy, however, recovered.

Phil's Great-Aunt Lois's husband died in early fall and I went down to San Jose, about seventy miles south of Point Reyes Station, to stay with her for a few days. Phil, alone in Point Reyes, became so nervous about the possibility of a grass fire—it was the time of the year that the grass was driest—that he made all the girls sleep fully dressed so they'd be ready to run out of the house at a moment's notice. There had been a grass fire earlier in the summer on the hill across the valley from our house.

The next time we left to go on a small excursion, Phil unplugged all the electric cords. He told me he was afraid that rats might chew them and start a fire. Every time we took a trip after that, Phil would unplug all the electric cords. I thought this was odd and was impatient waiting for him. I'd never heard of anything like this happening, but he sounded so convincing.

That fall, a rat did get in the walls of our house. I had read Ruth Stout's new book about organic gardening and decided we should compost our garbage. We started burying it in a pit. Instead of making compost, we drew dozens of rats from the nearby dump. The rat who came to live in our wall was a busy fellow. One night, he stole all the cat food and hid it under the dishwasher. In one night he moved almost the entire contents of a ten-pound bag of cat food. We put out poison and the rat died—in the wall—and we began to smell a horrible stench. The stench prompted Phil and Pete Stevens to happily tear out the wall to remove the rat's decaying body. They loved every moment of this loathsome job. Afterward, Joan Stevens came over and we made the new Italian dish pizza and daringly put artichoke hearts on it. Phil and Pete made frozen daiquiris to celebrate their brave deed.

Then another rat chewed a hole in the laundry room wall. We put out poison, and it ate all the poison we put out and kept chewing bigger holes. We set a trap for it. It sprang the trap several times before it was finally caught. When we found it in the trap, it was very much alive. Phil tried to drown it in a laundry tub full of water. It kept swimming around dragging the trap with it. It simply would not drown. Phil fished it out, took it outside, and hit it with a hatchet, finally killing this almost immortal rat. Phil dug a hole to bury it in, started to fill the earth in over the rat's body, paused for a moment, fished in his shirt for his St. Christopher medal, and dropped it in the hole on top of the rat.

The Cuban missile crisis occurred in late October. We heard large groups of planes overhead all night long. We were frightened. What would we do in our glass house if nuclear bombs started dropping in San Francisco? We sat out on the patio and tried to figure out where to hide. We realized there wasn't any place. We decided to walk downtown and buy a stock of groceries to try to survive. By the time we got to Harold's Market we changed our minds. We ended up buying one carton of Pall Mall cigarettes to barter with should there be a holocaust. We had read that cigarettes serve as currency when civilization breaks down.

Books continued to play a large part in our lives. I read *The Lord of the Flies* at Phil's recommendation. Phil was reading Nabokov; he disliked *Lolita*. Dorothy sent books for the girls and we all read *Charlotte's Web* and *Stuart Little*. Where did we get hold of that horrible illustrated book about teratomas? I think I brought it home from our neighbors', the Hyneses', library. There were pictures of cysts with fingers in them and some with bits of vertebrae. There was a horrible something that had once been a twin that remained as a cyst in the surviving twin. Phil was fascinated and used ideas from this book in *Dr. Bloodmoney*. At this time, he was also reading with much admiration Norman Mailer's *Advertisements for Myself* and *The White Negro*. Then I brought home a book from the library that had a profound influence on Phil, *Existential Psychiatry* by Ludwig Binswanger, a Swiss psychiatrist who had based his psychiatric theories on Heidegger's phenomenology.

Phil became overly involved with the case histories in this book, overly involved with Binswanger's concept of the psychological realities: the world of the street, the aethereal world, the tomb world. He continually talked about the awful case histories, I can remember them still. They cast a morbid, somber atmosphere over our entire household. This book was a major influence on *Martian Time-Slip*, in which Phil put forth his ideas about the nature of schizophrenia.

Binswanger's book wasn't at all good for Phil, although *Martian Time-Slip* is regarded by some critics as one of Phil's best novels, one that married mainstream writing with science fiction. The anti-hero of *Martian Time-Slip*, Jack Bohlen, fights his tendency to slip into schizophrenia. He describes the onset of this disease in high school. Jack Bohlen remembers the morose, silent brooding mood that he fell into at a party; he felt paralyzed, his gaze fixed on a matchbook cover. (I would have told him, "Hey, you're just having a low-blood-sugar attack.") Jack is sure that something is wrong with him. He moves to Mars because of his schizophrenia and because of the crowding on Earth.

In his twenties, Jack suffered a horrible psychotic episode. He saw people as robots, made up of cold wires and switches. He lost touch with time. Now, on Mars, he's having these symptoms again but fighting them.

He won't be isolated like Manfred and end up mute and institutionalized. One of the ways he can fight schizophrenia is to have an extramarital affair.

For him:

> ...it is vital to maintain intimate contact at almost any cost....
>
> The first step in schizophrenia is isolation: the utter alienation of perception from the objects of the outside world, especially the objects which matter—the warm hearted people there. And what takes their place? A dreadful preoccupation with the endless ebb and flow of one's self; the changes emanating from within which affect only the inside world. It is a splitting apart of the two worlds, of inner and outer, so that neither registers on the other. Both still exist, but each goes its own way. It is the stopping of time, the end of experience of anything new. Once a person becomes psychotic, nothing ever happens to him again. And he realized, "I stand on the threshold of that, a coagulated self, fixed and immense, which effaces everything else and occupies the entire field."

Jack Bohlen describes the state he is trying to keep from slipping into as "monumental selfishness."

When I read *Martian Time-Slip*, I was disturbed by the little boy looking out of the window like Phil when he was a latchkey child in Washington, D.C., waiting for his mother to come home. Phil became quite cross with me when I continued to worry, probably a little obsessively, about that child, but I couldn't get him out of my mind. Phil said, "You don't have to worry about him. He was all right. He ran off with the Martian 'Indians.'" At the end of *Martian Time-Slip*, Manfred ends up an old man on a life-support system after having had a stroke.

Life on ramshackle, dreary Mars is humdrum, not like it was promised to the immigrants. Silvia Bohlen, Jack's wife, is disturbed by the noise of children, the radio, and the fact that her husband is away from home so much. She takes Dexedrine to wake up and phenobarbital to go to sleep. (Was Phil doing this?) The neighbors have four little neglected girls, the ages of ours. Phil put in such everyday details as the teaching machine a door-to-door salesman tried to sell us, and the Sunday *New York Times* that we read. Where did Phil get the model for Arnie Kott, a brutal redneck union leader? Arnie had a brother named Phil who graduated from the University of California as a milk tester, the profession of our Point Reyes Station friend Jerry Kresy. In my previous husband's small book, there was a poem, "Arnie," about a friend of his who died. The portrait of my ex-father-in-law, Maury Handelsman, as Leo Bohlen, bringing corned beef and rye to Mars was a good one. Of course he would be preoccupied with looking for real estate, taking up options, looking for a deal. Our friend Alys Graveson *was* Anne Esterhazy; Phil mimicked her patterns of speech perfectly.

Yet this somber novel didn't cast a shadow over our everyday life, which went on merrily. When Christmas came we had a huge tree thickly covered with lights and ornaments. We had shopped for two months before Christmas, driving all over the Bay Area to get just the right presents and spending far too much money. We stayed up until 2 a.m. Christmas Eve wrapping the last presents. The children awakened at 5 a.m. to get their stockings. When we had the ceremony of the tree later that Christmas morning, a foot-deep layer of gifts covered half the living room floor. There were games to play and puzzles to work. Phil had bought a chemistry set for Hatte and an antique electric train that circled the Christmas tree. Later we had a big Christmas dinner with a turkey stuffed with chestnut dressing at one end and oyster dressing at the other. I was exhausted, but Phil loved every minute of the day.

"Just like Bob Cratchit and his family," he said happily.

Four
DISASTER IN POINT REYES STATION

...one day, while lifting out an electric corn popper from under the sink, Arctor had hit his head on the corner of a kitchen cabinet directly above him. The pain, the cut in his scalp, so unexpected and undeserved, had for some reason cleared away the cobwebs. It flashed on him instantly that he didn't hate the kitchen cabinet: he hated his wife, his two daughters, his whole house, the back yard with its power mower, the garage, the radiant heating system, the front yard, the fence, the whole fucking place and everyone in it. He wanted a divorce; he wanted to split. And so he had, soon.

—Philip K. Dick, *A Scanner Darkly*

DURING WET WINTERS in coastal northern California, relentless heavy rain continues for weeks. In San Francisco, people have to stop their cars on the freeway until the downpour returns to being merely heavy rainfall and they can see to drive again. In West Marin, rains are sometimes accompanied by gale winds. On the point itself, hurricane gusts of up to 105 miles an hour frequently occur. It gets so windy near my house that it's dangerous to take the garbage out to the garbage cans beside the road. They sit under a long row of cypress trees, and tree limbs can suddenly break off in the high winds.

The winter of 1962–63 was marked by this kind of rain. Our pasture turned into a sea of mud. The acre-size hollow in our field, which we christened "Lake Dick," filled with water, and in the lulls between storms the children paddled around in galvanized washtubs and caught tadpoles.

A frog symphony enriched our nights. Almost every day we put on slickers and boots and went to hunt the mushrooms growing on Inverness Ridge.

I have such a vivid memory of driving into our driveway after dark on a cold evening, seeing Phil throw the door open, stride out to meet me, and help carry in the groceries. We started talking as we walked to the house and continued while unpacking the bags of groceries. All the lights in the house were on, and

Phil had started a fire in the fireplace. He always wanted to know everything that had happened that day. He had been staying home more, too busy with his work to go out in the community much. I'd tell him about the volunteer work at the school library, what the Bluebirds had done, all about the local politics, and all the latest gossip.

We would talk about the children, Phil's writing, the music on KPFA, our dreams and our interpretations of them. While I cooked, Phil would help Hatte with her English or Jayne and Tandy with their math or science. Phil's relationship with Hatte had become special since she had become old enough to share some of his interests. After dinner we'd get out the Monopoly set and roll for tokens. Phil, with the old shoe, would build a hotel on Broadway. I would eventually land there and be forced out of the game.

The many people and events we talked about during those early-evening hours appear in *Dr. Bloodmoney*. The school-board meetings headed by Orion Stroud are like the ones Phil and I went to when we were trying to get a kindergarten started. *News and Views*, like the *Baywood Press*, had a reporter there. I hate to say it, but Bonnie was probably based on me. She is living in my house, anyway. In the book Phil dropped the H bomb on her. Phil had a crush on Jan Stratton, the principal's wife, who was part of the character of Bonny, too. George Keller was the principal of the West Marin School in the novel, while Jan's husband, George Stratton, was the principal in real life. George replaced another short-lived principal whom the school board was "out to get." Phil and I and others rushed to his defense, but it turned out that before enlisting community support to save his job he had already secretly signed resignation papers.

Mr. Austurias was based on Bob Allen, the science teacher. (The school board "got him" the next year, too.) Mr. Austurias picks chanterelles and cooks them with our recipe. That rascal, Phil, has him making love to Bonnie. Then he kills him off. Dr. Stockstill in the novel has a house in West Marin and a boat in Tomales Bay like Dr. A's. A local contractor had the name Stockstill in our real world. Phil was scrambling names and people as usual.

The mad atomic scientist who created the holocaust (this is the only novel of Phil's in which the bomb drops) was based on the physicist Edmund Teller, the prime mover in the creation of the hydrogen bomb. Phil hated Teller. Mr. Tree, a.k.a. Dr. Bluthgeld—Dr. Bloodmoney—is paranoid. He has an attack of vertigo (as Phil had had in high school), the street tilting away from him. Mr. Tree has blotches, or thinks he has blotches on his face and can't ride in a bus or go to the opera, ballet, or symphony, as Phil couldn't as a young man. Mr. Tree believes he is disfigured. Foolish Bonnie likes evil Dr. Bloodmoney. She is promiscuous. In the end, she leaves her husband, deserts her children, and moves to Berkeley: "Her marriage is over and everybody realizes it." Phil steps in and out of his characters regardless of gender.

In *Dr. Bloodmoney* there's a big discussion about how good mass production is, the opposite idea to the admiration of handcraft discussed in *The Man in the High Castle*. I, of course, was deeply involved in making handcrafted jewelry.

Phil put some of his old friends from Berkeley in *Dr. Bloodmoney*. Phil and Maury Guy (Iskandar) share the role of Stuart McConchie. Jim Fergesson was inspired by Phil's old boss at University Radio, Herb Hollis. Dean Hardy and Ella Hardy are based on Phil's friends Vince and Virginia Lusby. Hoppy Harrington was created from Phil's memories of the many eccentric radio repairmen who worked over the years at University Radio. Hoppy used the timer from our RCA washer-drier combination for repairs to the essential machinery of that post-holocaust society. There was a little of Pete Stevens and Tony Morris, another local friend of Phil's who was an appliance repairman, in the character of Hoppy, too.

In *Dr. Bloodmoney*, Walt Dangerfield is cut off from Earth, stuck in a rocket that goes round and round in its orbit. It never got off to Mars the day the bomb fell, because the second-stage rocket never fired. Dangerfield's wife, who accompanied him, has died, and he is all alone up there. Dangerfield has Phil's ulcer. Heroically, he acts as cosmic disc jockey to the people struggling to survive on Earth. He soothes, entertains, educates, and keeps the world community together but, alas, he becomes ill. Is he dying? I was worried about Walt/Phil.

Was Phil also little Bill, a teratoma, living in his twin sister's side, in touch with the voices of the dead? I was hopeful when little Bill got "born" out of his twin sister's side but worried when he ended up in the impaired body of Hoppy. It was good that Hoppy/Phil wasn't going to take over the world through his psychokinetic control of Walt. It looked as if he would for a while. In the end all ends well—I think. At any rate, it was more hopeful than *Martian Time-Slip*. Phil put together some of the strangest kinds of feelings in this novel. *Dr. Bloodmoney*, in some ways, is really horrible. But it's also charming. Is there such a thing as charmingly horrible?

As the spring of 1963 approached, we were quarreling more. Phil pushed all my buttons regularly. Provoking arguments had become his new indoor sport.

I continued to compete with him and tell him straight out when he was wrong. But years later, my oldest daughter, Hatte, told me that she remembered a new note in our arguments. In one, Phil yelled, "You killed Richard and now you're trying to kill me." Back in those days, I couldn't process this information. I didn't even hear it. I do remember Phil saying on a number of occasions, "You don't love me, you just wanted a husband and a father for your children," repeating over and over the idea that Dr. A had verbalized to him during their first meeting. No answer I gave carried any weight with him. I tried many times an indignant, "I do too love you," but when I couldn't ever get him to acknowledge this avowal, I finally sarcastically replied, hoping to shake him out of this negative litany, "Well, of course, I just wanted a husband and a father for my children. Why else would I marry you?" No doubt he believed this.

One afternoon, as we were driving out of the field after hauling some lumber to the barn, Phil got out of the car to open the gate. As he was opening the gate, I slipped the clutch, gunned the motor, and inched the car forward, preparing to drive the car out on the road. Suddenly Phil flung the gate open and ran off in the field. I thought, disgustedly, "What is he doing, now?" After I had driven out on the road, he came back and got into the car. I didn't even ask him what he thought he had been doing. Everything was too discouraging. My defense was denial. (But the other side of this coin was that I had a staunch unyielding faith in our love for each other and in our marriage. Yet, I was also annoyed.)

Looking back, I wonder how Phil interpreted my annoyance; he might have thought I was angry because I hadn't been able to run over him with the car.

Then Phil began sending the children off to their rooms for no reason. One day, one of the girls left the freezer door open and Phil took privileges away from all three girls. They felt he was being unfair, and so did I. I called a family meeting to try to solve this problem. "Great idea," I thought, "We'll solve our problems with family meetings." But during a discussion of some domestic problem, the girls all agreed with me and each one said that she thought Phil's viewpoint was wrong. Phil stalked furiously out of the living room, and there were no more family meetings.

Phil took up snuff instead of smoking Egyptian cigarettes. He might as well have taken up chewing tobacco and spitting on the floor as far as I was concerned. He often had snuff in his beard. Yet, he was funny, too, when he enthusiastically discoursed on the different brands of snuff, the history of snuff, and so on.

We sought some counseling with Dr. A and saw him alternately once a week, hoping that this would help our marriage. But Phil wasn't really having therapy. He was playing games, gathering material for his writing, getting prescriptions, and preparing for a coup.

Next time Maury Guy came out to visit us he and Phil had a falling out. Maury was studying Subud and the *I Ching*. Phil told him, "The *I Ching* is a bunch of bullshit. I'm going to write a novel about it and show it up," although at this time Phil consulted the *I Ching* at least once daily. Maury was deeply offended on the *I Ching*'s behalf. Maury had also gotten terribly tired of Phil's litany about me: "Anne's marvelous, she's terrible, she's marvelous, and she's getting more terrible by the moment." Maury said, "It was all so confused that I thought perhaps Phil was dabbling in drugs."

June Kresy, Phil's former neighbor, remembered that Phil came over to her house several times "expressing great fear" of me. Phil had told June that he felt that he wasn't contributing financially to the marriage, and June noted that this feeling of Phil's was turning into a strong resentment of me, but she couldn't understand the fear of me he expressed.

I had absolutely no idea that Phil felt like this until June told me many years later.

Once Phil and I quarreled so furiously that furniture was thrown, and Phil struck me. The children were upset and frightened. I called Bill Christensen to come and intervene. When Bill drove into the driveway in his official car, Phil walked out to talk to him. I expected Bill to tell Phil that he shouldn't be hitting his wife.

But Bill said to me many years later, "Phil was so good with words. I had observed him being so loving and charming to you. And there was something about him that made you want to help him. I should have talked to you, Anne, but there was Phil, calm, cool, and collected, and you were standing there angrily on the porch, your arms folded, your eyes shooting sparks, and Phil would say, 'You see, she's just about to go off again. And I love her so. Isn't it too bad?'" And so Bill drove off. I thought he had "talked to" Phil, but instead

Phil had convinced Bill that I was violent and crazy. He had evidently been laying the groundwork for these ideas with Bill all along, and possibly he really believed them. I was assertive and direct, and yelled at times, although by then I had stopped throwing dishes.

I continued to worry aloud about money. I didn't mean to put pressure on Phil and in my heart I always believed that somehow we would manage, but, looking back, I think Phil didn't perceive my faith. Perhaps I only expressed the negative side of my thoughts and feelings.

I continued to develop my jewelry business, opening up accounts in southern California by mail, and told Phil, "Maybe the jewelry business will grow enough to help our family finances." It never occurred to me to worry about Phil's ego in relation to my earning money. After all, he was a recognized writer. How could a brilliant and accomplished person like him have any ego problems?

Phil told me that he was going to sell the Inverness cabin that Joe and Dorothy had given him. I was sorry to hear him make this decision. I loved that place; we'd had some wonderful times there. But there were a few rotten boards on the front porch and Phil said that he didn't want to spend any time doing carpentry or house repairs. This sounded logical. He did sell the cabin. I didn't know that he had promised Joe and Dorothy that he would transfer the cabin back to them for the purchase price if he were ever going to get rid of it; nor did I know that he told Joe and Dorothy that it was my idea to sell it.

Next, Phil told me, "I'm tired of being a writer. I can't get what I want published, I don't earn any money for what I write. I want to go back into the record business." After a lot of conversation about writing versus having a record store, he convinced me that this was what he really wanted. I said, "So, let's mortgage the house and buy a record store." Shortly after this conversation, Phil's mother phoned. Speaking coldly, she told me it was improvident of me to believe that mortgaging one's house was a good way to finance a business.

The next time I saw Dr. A, he bawled me out and told me that I had "delusions of grandeur for wanting to mortgage our house and go into the record business." "But," I told him, "it was Phil's idea, I was just going along with what he said he wanted." Dr. A didn't seem to hear me. Behind both Dr. A's and Dorothy's comments was the implication that I was trying to make Phil give up his writing. Looking back, I think that I had missed my cue. When Phil talked about giving up writing and buying a record store, my role should have been to beg him to continue to write. I wouldn't have minded doing this at all. I *liked* that he was a writer. That was one of his big attractions. I could have cared less about owning a record store.

That summer I had planned a vacation for all of us, a week camping at Yosemite. I told Phil, "Going on a camping trip will be good for this family. It will bring us together." Phil wasn't enthusiastic. He didn't want to go, but I insisted. I was trying to find some way to improve our relationship. "Next year, let's go to Mexico or Canada," I said. I made all the preparations, food, equipment, clothes, but at the last minute Phil balked and refused to go. The girls and I were disappointed; we went to the Russian River just up the road twenty miles and camped in a tent for one night.

Then occurred the first of Phil's unpredictable actions that was to frighten and paralyze me, and also to make me very angry. I was eating a pleasant dinner with my family when Sheriff Bill Christensen came to the door. Bill had a bunch of papers in his hand that said I had to go with him to Ross Psychiatric Hospital for seventy-two hours of observation. The papers were signed by Dr. A.

It was easy in those prefeminist days to arrange psychiatric commitments in California in 1963. I wasn't the only woman this happened to. Only one doctor's signature was required. The laws have since been changed to prevent this kind of civil-rights violation.

Phil was perfectly charming to Bill, and calm as a cucumber. You'd think Bill was coming by to have a cup of coffee and gossip with us. Hatte remembered Bill's saying, "You girls will understand this when you're older."

But even as a thirteen-year-old girl, she thought to herself, "I understand as much as I'll ever understand; I know that he's wrong and I know better than he what's right."

Phil had been telling Dr. A that I was ruining the family with my outrageous expenditures; that I had a "grandiose" plan to mortgage the house for $50,000 and buy a record business; that I was planning trips to Mexico and Canada; that I had threatened him with a knife, and tried to run him down with the car. Phil had arranged for Bill Christensen to confer with Dr. A, too, after having primed the latter with the same stories. Phil used to say to me, as a commentary on human nature, "Everything I tell you three times is true." In this case, he got quite a bit of mileage with this technique. Hitler originated it.

Earlier, he had approached my best friends to persuade them to testify against me at a sanity hearing, but they wouldn't agree. They thought I was fine mentally. But Phil's big lie technique had left them stunned, and in those days it was taboo to get involved with husband-and-wife problems. Years later my friend, Missy Patterson, told me, "Anne, you were railroaded."

I couldn't believe what was happening; it was like a bad dream. One minute I was sitting with Phil and the girls at the dinner table, the next minute I was riding in the sheriff's car going to a psychiatric hospital. I gave Bill a piece of my mind in a deadly calm way. I knew I had to be cool but I would really have liked to hit him over the head with my purse.

Hatte was furious at Phil; this was something he didn't expect. She never felt really friendly to him again. During my stay in the hospital, Missy Patterson told me that Phil asked her several times to take the girls to the beach, but she refused. She didn't want to do *anything* for him. At one point Hatte bawled out Dr. A, but she was just a thirteen-year-old and had no power to change anything.

When I got to Ross Hospital, I told the head psychiatrist, Dr. S, my story. I began, "I was having normal fights with my husband; I used to occasionally throw a plate or two for emphasis...." At the time he led me to think he believed me. After talking with me, Dr. S talked to Dr. A. He was furious with Dr. A and wouldn't even speak to Phil (who had shown up at the hospital). His lips literally curled with contempt when Phil tried to talk to him that evening. Phil slunk away, looking ashamed.

Dr. S pointed out to me that I had the choice of going to a legal hearing with judges, lawyers, and witnesses or agreeing to going to Langley Porter Clinic for two weeks for an evaluation. At the end of that time, he felt, they would release me as a person who did not have the sort of serious psychiatric problems that would warrant hospitalization. I felt crushed and stigmatized. I had no spirit left to fight and to go through an involved legal hearing. I had no option but to take his advice and go to Langley Porter.

Researching for this book, I was able to obtain my medical records from Ross Hospital and Langley Porter Clinic under the Freedom of Information Act. In 1963, there were no such rights. But I was in for a surprise. Dr. S, who I had thought was sympathetic to me, wrote, "The husband was the more stable of the two.... [H]e would never lie." He must have talked to Phil later and, like Dr. A and me, been enchanted by Phil, the magical shaman of the twentieth century. Maybe Bill

Christensen weighed in there, too. I was brought up believing in male chivalry, but in many cases I've noted men bond together against a woman. I was amazed when I got older to realize that many men are quite afraid of women.

It was frightening as those heavy metal doors shut and locked behind me when I entered the fifth-floor ward at Langley Porter. But I learned something important. Now, I have a lot of empathy for the political prisoners of the twentieth century who were seized and carried off and imprisoned—often for good. I was one of them, but luckily one who got back home.

The doctor at Langley Porter prescribed a medication, Stelazine. I tried one pill but it made me so groggy and depressed that I held the next one under my tongue when the nurse gave it to me and shortly afterward quietly spit it out in the toilet. Taking this awful drug was mandatory, but no one in his right mind would take it. Every day after I was given one I surreptitiously spit it out.

When I looked around me, I found that in some ways this was going to be an interesting experience. The other people in the ward with me weren't crazies at all, as I had expected. They were just people—pitiful people with terrible problems. I wanted to help them. I listened to their stories and gave some encouragement and good advice.

Generally it was very boring there. I felt isolated from my busy life and insisted that Phil and the girls come every day to keep me company. They spent the entire time I was in the hospital driving back and forth over the curvy thirty-five miles between the hospital and Point Reyes Station.

Hatte was the valedictorian of her class for eighth-grade graduation and I couldn't go. Though she had been popular with her classmates, she was suddenly uninivited to all of the parties that were being given. On one occasion during the drive to the hospital, Phil told her, "I'm going to talk to the doctors today. I'm sure they're going to tell me that I'm the one that should be in there, not your mother." On the way home he told her, "That's what they told me."

Hatte reflected, "I already thought that, myself. Well, maybe it's true and maybe not, that's the kind of thing he'd say." The hospital records say Mr. Dick "was unhappy. He says that he has never seen his wife looking worse. Mr. Dick feels he is the mentally ill partner and should be hospitalized. He feels he may be schizophrenic." The doctor who wrote the record went on to say that he feels the problem is that Mr. Dick was "unable to control his wife." Well, of course not. That's not what marriage is about.

A few days later Phil and I took part in a group therapy session at the hospital. The psychiatrist in charge was amazed and entertained at the snappy dialogue, the complex interaction between us, and all the depressed patients momentarily woke up.

At that time Phil was writing *The Simulacra*. Part of the story is set in Jenner, a town like Point Reyes Station, described as a dismal, rainy, swampy, jungle populated by vegetarian "chuppers," throwbacks to Neanderthal Man. Richard Kongrosian, world-famous psychokinetic pianist, is falling to pieces. The beautiful woman president of the country, Nicole Thibodeaux, has turned out to be a phony, a simulacra of the real Nicole, who died long ago. The country has been taken over by the head of the secret police. To save Nicole, Richard Kongrosian uses his psychokinetic ability to send her to Jenner to stay with motherly but boring Mrs. Kongrosian and her five chupper children. From this time on a policeman has a major role in Phil's writing.

Langley Porter released me after two weeks. Phil insisted that I stop and see Dr. A on the way home from the hospital. As far I was concerned, Dr. A was a non-person: he didn't exist in my universe anymore. That afternoon, I remember Dr. A saying to me, "You fooled Ross Hospital, you fooled Dr. S, you fooled Langley Porter Clinic, but you don't fool me. I know you're a manic-depressive." And grumpily, after I had given him my coldest response, he said, "All manic-depressives drop their psychiatrists."

He advised me to switch over to a female psychologist, Dr. J, who was also a marriage counselor. She was there at his office to meet me, a skinny bleached blond with harlequin glasses, a designer suit, and high-heeled shoes. I had to agree. I certainly would never talk to Dr. A again, and she seemed warm and kind. It was arranged that Phil would come with me to sessions with her.

I phoned Dr. J, my ex-psychologist, and we met for an interview at her house in Mill Valley. She seemed awfully nervous at first. It was almost like she had a guilty conscience. She told me that she didn't like Phil; his magic and charm and her receptors "weren't in phase with each other." She said that Dr. A got a kickback from the fees I paid to her. After Phil left, I went to see her once a week for about two years. Often my second daughter, Jayne, would ride with me, and we'd grocery shop afterward while the family laundry was washing at a nearby laundromat. During our last session, Dr. J thanked me for coming to her and didn't charge me. I remained in touch with her over the years.

That afternoon in Dr. A's office, Phil's usual cheerful self appeared clouded over by bewilderment as he put his arm around me in a protective manner. But it was too late. He hadn't protected me from himself.

I thought I had just been through a horrible experience, but worse was to follow. The morning after we got back home, Phil told me that Dr. A had said I must continue taking the pills I had been spitting out in the hospital (of course, I had told Phil about this), that I was sick, and I must take these pills or he would leave me. So I took them. I wanted to keep my family together, and, in spite of everything, I loved this man and didn't want to lose him.

Stelazine, an antipsychotic drug fashionable at that time, has many side effects. Sometimes it is referred to as a chemical straitjacket or a chemical lobotomy. Some people taking it develop an extreme lethargy that can pass into a coma and death. It is helpful to about 40 percent of schizophrenics. It makes some people think more clearly. Phil was lucky; it affected Phil this way.

These drugs must have been much stronger that the ones I had spit out at Langley Porter because they turned me into a zombie. I had no energy, I couldn't think, and all I could do was lie on the couch. Once I had taken one of them I didn't have sense enough not to take any more. I took these horrible mind-dulling pills for two or three months. Later, in *The Ganymede Takeover*, written by Phil and Ray Nelson, a young woman is described as undergoing oblivion therapy. She loses her personality and keeps staring at ants building anthills. Unhappiness has been cured—but there's no one left in that psyche to be unhappy.

My friend, Sue Baty, the local judge's wife, told me in 1982, "You weren't sick before you took those pills; the pills made you sick. I was horrified, but I didn't know what to do. I had grave reservations about Phil's motives and felt Dr. A was acting unprofessionally." Unable to accomplish anything or even do much housework, I practically lived over at Sue's during the day that September. I read all her books but I couldn't remember a single thing that I read. I didn't know that Phil was also taking Stelazine. He told June Kresy how good it made him feel. She told me in our phone interview that she remembered him saying, "It doesn't have the same effect on me that it does on Anne, at all."

In *The Three Stigmata of Palmer Eldritch*, Richard and Emily Hnatt make a lot of money selling her ceramic pots and decide to take the expensive

Evolution Therapy (or E Therapy) from famous Dr. Denkmal in Germany. Richard evolves, his thinking becomes clearer, more subtle and creative, but Emily is one of the rare failures: she *devolves,* her features coarsen, she becomes rather simple, loses her creativity, and begins doing pot designs that she has already done before.

When I finally stopped taking those dreadful pills, I was very angry. I hadn't been doing anything for months and I was rested and strong. But I shoved the anger down where I wouldn't have to deal with it or even know about it. I wanted to put my life and my family back together, to restore it to a happy, normal condition. But in my brain, my whole past was a series of blurs: my grade-school friends; my favorite brother; the junior-high fudge club; my little dog, Spot. They all were like ruined frescoes in my mind, the colors gone, the outlines partly missing, the middles totally obliterated. I'd forgotten everything I learned in my favorite college courses about the Renaissance and invertebrate paleontology. I'd forgotten my children's infancy. I'd forgotten most of the good times with Phil.

We both went together to see Dr. J. Once, during a visit to her office, she told Phil that his aim had been to control me—in a novel, in a hospital, or with drugs. She pointed out to Phil that he had a problem that may have existed in his family for generations.

Phil replied agreeably, meekly, "You're probably right."

I told Phil, "You want a submissive wife who is an interesting intellectual companion. It's like wanting dry soup or warm ice. I can't be submissive. It's not my nature. My idea of a relationship is an equal partnership." I reproached him about the whole hospital-Stelazine episode.

He replied emphatically, "The whole thing was a mistake." But that didn't change how I felt or what I had experienced. I wasn't to forgive him for a very long time, maybe not ever.

At Dr. J's, Phil blamed me for a decision he had made. Earlier in the year we had discussed where Hatte would go to high school. Should she go to local Tomales High or make the long commute to one of the large suburban high schools in southern Marin County? Phil had made the decision that she should go to Tomales High. This topic came up at a therapy session with Dr. J, and Phil was bitter at me about it. I told him, "You decided, Phil."

He was startled and said, "Yes, I did, and that's just typical of me to blame you."

Dr J said, "Put away your rusty old weapons." Phil really liked this image and puts this idea into the hilariously funny *The Zap Gun*. In this novel, Lars Powderdry, weapons fashion designer for Wes-bloc, designs such items as a sixty-stage guidance system that is "plowshared" into a cigar lighter that will compose new Mozart string quartets when lit. Lars' Peep-East counterpart, Lilo Topchev, designs similar fake weapons. The political balance between the two superpowers depends on public belief that each side has military superiority, and that these phony designs are real. On his way to neutral Iceland to collaborate with Lila on real weapons to repel real invaders from space, Lars Powderdry, terrified of failure, buys a copy of the *Blue Cephalopod Man from Titan* comic book at the airport magazine stand and finds that all his "original" designs had already been printed there.

In the midst of some of the funniest writing Phil ever wrote, serious personal and theological tidbits and incredible political precognition surface. There is a Julian the Apostate satellite. Lars is almost killed by an overdose of drugs that Lilo gives him. Meanwhile, he is taking his own combination of Escalatium and Conjorizine in quantities that would kill an ordinary person but which only give him a post-nasal drip. Pete Freid, in this novel, is a dead ringer for Pete Stevens. In real life, Pete worked for Walter Landor. In the novel, Pete Freid works for Jack Lanferman. Walter Lanferman was a high school buddy of Phil's.

Pete Freid is the one who makes the actual weapons that Lars designs. Surly G. Febbs, typical man-of-the-times, dreams up a real weapon, a needle-eye converter that will turn an enemy into a bearskin rug. A fascist type, he has made the first *real* weapon in years and is planning to take over the government but falls victim to the hypnotic man-in-the-maze game, the prototype of Phil's famous empathy box. There are endless secret police in this novel. Phil probably finished this novel in 1965 while he was living in Oakland and added a lot of drug information that I don't think he would have known about when living in West Marin. He also added aspects of his new housemate Nancy Hackett to the portrait of Lilo Topchev.

Almost simultaneously, Phil was writing a novel about a woman who was a drug addict. Kathy Sweetscent, in *Now Wait for Last Year*, is probably Phil's most monstrous female character, a woman with malignant worms of the psyche. She is sadistic, self-destructive, and makes more money than her husband, dear, earnest Dr. Eric Sweetscent. She has whimsically addicted herself to a fatal hallucinogenic drug, an addiction that can't be cured. She surreptitiously drops this drug into Sweetscent's coffee. Good man that he is, he travels into the future and obtains a cure for both of them. In the future, he finds that she has deteriorated physically and mentally. In ten years, she will become unmanageable and violent and will have to be forcibly committed. Eric considers suicide, but in a touching conversation with an automatic taxi in Tijuana, decides to go back and care for her.

Phil didn't show either of these two novels to me. I didn't read them until after his death. The checks for these novels didn't go into our joint bank account, either.

In the midst of all these unhappy events, a happy event occurred. Phil won the Hugo Award for *The Man in the High Castle*. The *Baywood Press* sent a photographer to take a picture of Laura holding the Hugo and displayed it prominently in its next issue. We cooked a special celebration dinner. But that fall, one terrible thing after another happened. Our blue merle collie died. We bought a white borzoi, a living sculpture. Phil named him "Ollie," after *Kukla, Fran and Ollie*. I came to love this dignified, intelligent dog more than any other pet I had ever owned, but in retrospect, I don't think it was the right dog for a proletarian writer.

Next, President Kennedy was shot. Phil literally fell on the floor when he heard the news over the radio. He followed the events of the next several days closely and was terribly emotional about the situation. He remained depressed all that fall.

Tumpey, Phil's beloved tomcat, disappeared. Phil began muttering that the fates were out to get him. "We'll get some kittens, Phil," I said, "some darling Siamese kittens." We drove to Tiburon and bought two Siamese kittens, a boy and a girl, twins.

Shortly after we got them home they developed cat distemper. They wouldn't eat; they were dying. The vet came and said, "They probably can't be saved." But Phil was determined to save them, so the vet told him how to force-feed the kittens for a one-in-a-hundred chance of success. Phil stayed up all night and fed the kittens with an eyedropper for a couple of weeks. But they kept fading away. I told Phil I thought it would be more humane to put them to sleep. But he wouldn't. He just kept trying to keep them alive. He was terribly depressed when they died. I should have realized something was terribly wrong when Phil didn't want to get another cat.

Soon after this, we quarreled over some trivial matter, and Phil packed his suitcase and went to Berkeley to stay with his mother. I couldn't believe it. He went to his mother's! In my rule book, grown men did not run back to their mother's house even if they did become angry with their wives and leave home for a respite. I drove to Berkeley with the girls to bring Phil back. Near his mother's house, I saw him walking along the street. He got in the car with us.

"You mean you'd drive clear over here to bring me back to Point Reyes?" He was astonished.

"Of course, dummy," I said.

Seeking a way to help our marriage and our whole state of being, I had the family begin attending St. Columba's, the small High Episcopal church in Inverness. Tandy had been going to Sunday school, loved it, and had been trying to persuade us to come to church with her. The church was in a handsome old Craftsman-style summer mansion overlooking Tomales Bay that had been the vacation home of a branch of the Frick family. It had teak floors and heart of redwood walls and was located in a grove of oak trees.

Phil said, "If I could invent a church, I'd invent one just like this." He became quite excited when he found a hymn that was dated A.D. 496. He was fascinated with the High Mass, and became friendly with the vicar, Fr. Reade. Phil would visit him and they'd talk theology for hours.

We decided to join the church, go to confirmation classes, and become baptized. Every Sunday Phil got dressed up, wore a suit or a sport coat, and all of us in our best clothes went off to church—"religiously," kidded Phil—every Sunday.

One Sunday, we met an interesting woman, Maren Hackett, who was church hopping. The three of us soon became best friends. She'd visit us or we'd go to dinner at her place in San Rafael. She was a double-dome intellectual, a member of the Mensa Society, an ex-policewoman, and an ex-pile-driver operator. Honestly! We discussed theology and church history with her as well as other topics. She was not only theologically well informed and devout, but a sophisticated, knowledgeable person.

Once, Maren brought her nineteen-year-old stepdaughter, Nancy, with her, when she came to visit at our house. Nancy was an attractive girl with long dark hair and bangs, but she hardly said anything—she just sat on the couch during the entire visit, almost as if she weren't there. I had never seen such a quiet teenager. I didn't pay much attention to her and, of course, I never had any inkling that one day she would be Phil's next wife and the mother of his second child.

One weekend night that fall, we went to a party at Jack and Patty Wright's house, which was near the top of Mt. Vision in Inverness. Phil drank several martinis, unusual for him because he wasn't a drinker. Unfortunately, he was driving that night, and as he came out of the Wright's driveway, he didn't turn the wheel sharply enough and the car went over the edge of road and hung there, nothing underneath its front end.

The neighbors came with a rope and a truck to pull our car back on the road. While we were waiting for them to get everything set up, Phil took my arm and tried to forcibly lead me into the driver's seat. He said, "Get in, and I'll push." If he had pushed the car it could have gone over the side of the mountain. Of course, there were trees to stop it from going terribly far—I think. I pulled away from him, annoyed—and as usual, immediately put this incident out of my mind. I was very good at denial—or was it faith—or bourgeois family values—or an excess of loyalty?

On a happier note, the Wrights invited Phil and me to go hear Harry Partch, the composer, give a world premiere of one of his symphonies in an old warehouse in Petaluma. The huge room had thirty of Partch's sculptured wood instruments and glass "cloud chambers" in it. As well as musical instruments, they were beautiful as sculptures. Partch and his assistants ran from one instrument to another to perform the symphony. Partch used a forty-nine-tone scale, and his music was unique and lovely. Phil mentions Partch in his novel *The Crack in Space*.

That Christmas, Tandy was the Virgin Mary in the Christmas play at St. Columba's, and Hatte was the archangel Gabriel, her blue eyes flashing as she told Mary, "And you will bear a child."

Phil was excited, he told the girls, by his choice of a gift for me: a garbage disposal. I was furious when I opened the package on Christmas morning. It wasn't at all the kind of thing I wanted. It wasn't at all the kind of gift that he had usually given me. Ungraciously, I told Phil he'd have to take it back. The girls got Barbie dolls and clothes, and even a Ken doll. Hatte remembers Phil measuring the Barbie dolls and trying to figure out their proportions. He said, "They couldn't exist in the real world. Their heads are much too small for their bodies." Phil started working on a new novel around this time. "It's about the Barbie dolls," he said. "It's going to be named *The Three Stigmata of Palmer Eldritch*."

Phil was fascinated with the theology that we were learning at confirmation classes, but it didn't stop our having another argument and his running off to his mother's again. I phoned there and after we talked at length, he came back home.

A few days later in a session with Dr. J, Phil complained, "Anne doesn't pay enough attention to me; she loves the dog more than she loves me."

Dr. J told him, "You experience Anne moving away from you emotionally, but, actually, you're moving away from Anne." Phil looked thoughtful.

We still hugged all night, sleeping like spoons, and our sex life was as loving as ever. I tried to be more affectionate during the day, but when I would hug him he would push me away, saying angrily, "You're only being dutiful." Later, he told Dr. J his mother had been "dutiful" and he had hated it.

Dr. J had arranged for Phil to see a new doctor, Dr. P, because she felt he needed to talk to a man, that the therapy situation in which he had to deal with two women wasn't productive for him. After seeing Phil a few times, Dr. P told Dr. J that he was afraid that Phil was going to kill me.

I was surprised and disturbed to hear this from Dr. J in 1982.

Back in 1963, although struggling with feelings of anger and confusion, I still thought Phil was a wonderful, brilliant, talented man. I believed that, as my husband, he had made a commitment to me as deep as the one I had made to him and that even though we were having problems they would somehow all work out. Along with the quarrels and the trips back and forth to Berkeley, like a whole parallel life, we still enjoyed family life, working in the garden together, great conversations, and good sex.

Phil, the girls, and I were baptized together like one of those Northern European pagan tribes back in the dawn of Christianity. I had hopes that now we would stop burying each other alive in the peat bogs. As we drove home, Phil told me cheerfully, "At the moment of my baptism I saw, slinking out of the baptistery, his tail between his legs, a small red devil, the classic type, with horns and a spiked tail." Was this the day when, on the way home from church, Phil, seeing a dead cat in the road, pulled the car over, picked up the cat, and gently, almost reverently, laid the little cat body on the grassy shoulder?

A month after our baptism, in early February 1964, we were confirmed, kneeling together at the altar rail at St. Columba's Church. The vicar told us that when a man and wife were confirmed together at the same time, their marriage was blessed by the church. It was like a second marriage ceremony. Phil took an active part in his confirmation and this ceremony. I really believed it was not simply a routine he was going through—but he was such a complicated man.

At this same time he was working on perhaps his greatest novel, *The Three Stigmata of Palmer Eldritch*. Years later, he told friends that he had seen a terrible face in the sky, a face with stainless-steel teeth, slotted-metal eyes, and a steel arm—the face of "Palmer Eldritch"—but he didn't tell me. If he had, I would have probably said to him, "You probably ate something that didn't agree with you."

Phil was packing his clothes and going to his mother's "forever" and then coming back home to Point Reyes about twice a week. Our life was an emotional roller-coaster. I almost got used to this unsettled behavior. I thought, "Phil will be doing this forever. Well, that's the way it is. Sort of like being married to a sailor or a traveling salesman." But Hatte was resentful and remembered Phil disciplining her and the other children in an arbitrary manner.

When Phil was in Point Reyes, he would come home from working at the Hovel in the late afternoon and flop down in his big armchair. His face would sag. He would look like he was half-dead.

"Phil, what's the matter?" I would ask.

"I've got the flu again," he would say in a nasal voice. Every afternoon he would have the flu. Phil started "carrying on" about our neighbor, Lorraine Hynes, as if he were in love with her. I regarded this as terrible disloyalty and it evoked no end of battles. Actually, Phil could have flirted with anyone if he had made me feel like the special woman in his life as he used to, but, insecure, I could give him no freedom. He gave Lorraine a hundred of our books. Then he gave away my unabridged dictionary to a casual guest, an antique decoy duck that I'd had restored to another guest, and an autographed first edition of an e. e. cummings collection of poetry to a third.

One day, after a quarrel, he was packing to leave again, walking around the bedroom in his underwear—and suddenly he sat down heavily on the bed and said, "You're the great love of my life."

"But Phil, if you love me and I love you, why are you leaving?" I asked. He didn't answer. He sat there for a while, and then got up and continued packing.

I ran around the room after him asking him over and over, "But why are you leaving?" But he wouldn't answer.

Now, when he came back from his mother's, he'd say, "I'm afraid that I'm going to kill myself with the drugs in Dorothy's medicine cabinet. She's going to kill me, the way she leaves those drugs lying around."

When I interviewed Lynne, Phil's stepsister, she told me, "Dorothy's medicine cabinet was like a minipharmacy. She had everything! Phil would come to the house and open the cabinet and just start taking pills. He would take whatever he happened to pick up. It was amazing that he didn't make himself ill."

Bill Christensen remembered an earnest one-and-a-half-hour conversation he had with Phil at the Hovel one evening. Phil paced the floor. "Anne is the great love of my life," he told Bill. "A writer is the worst one in the world for this to happen to. I'm at my wits' end." Bill said, as the evening went on, it seemed as if Phil were repudiating the way he'd described the situation between him and me at the time of my forced hospitalization. Bill said, "I realized I was dealing with a guy who was getting slightly off his rocker, but then he got right back on…. He could be so cool and intelligent and charming."

I had long ago made my peace with Bill Christensen, retired now and still a neighbor. A great raconteur, his memories of the 1960s were detailed and clear.

He was to die of Alzheimer's a few years later. It was a tragedy that no one had been able to interview him about the time he fought in the International Brigade and about the many incredible police situations he had been involved with when our area was like the Wild West and he was the only lawman. He had kept copious notebooks, but his wife thought all that old, bad stuff should be forgotten.

Then, in the middle of an argument, Phil suddenly started pummeling me. We were just having an ordinary argument and, totally unexpectedly, he started hitting me. This happened on two different occasions. I tried to talk to him. His face was set. He looked like he didn't hear me. I wasn't there, just a punching bag. Then he grabbed me and hugged me and cried. It was all too much. I began to feel as if I were ninety-five years old and half-dead. The third time this happened, I clenched my fists and stood up and moved in his direction, preparing to hit him back. He looked almost happy and ran away from me and out of the room.

To add to my depression, everything in the house was breaking. The dishwasher broke, the oven broke, one of the burners on the range broke, the washer-drier broke (although it was always breaking), the couch springs suddenly sagged to the floor—the whole house was falling to pieces.

Then, one day, just before going to church, Phil said he had something serious to tell me, something that would explain why he couldn't function properly in life. Before he even spoke, I knew I didn't want to hear whatever it was he wanted to tell me. He could function just fine. Why did he have to go on as if he couldn't? I was rushing around trying to get myself dressed and yelling at the girls to hurry up and get themselves ready.

Phil said, "When I was quite small I was homosexually molested."

Confused thoughts flashed through my mind. "It's probably not true," or "It was probably a neighbor," or "Things like this just don't happen." "Why is he telling me this? I can't do anything about it and it's just too horrible."

But all I could say out loud was, "You should tell this to your psychotherapist." It is possible that at that moment I had an opportunity to help Phil and I really blew it. I just couldn't process this information. In the ambience of those days even homosexuality was exotic. Pedophilia was hardly believed to exist. I had never ever heard of a case of it. I was trying to hold a middle-class marriage together and this information was far out of my range. His timing was hardly propitious either. His admission went unresolved.

Now when Phil left, he wouldn't come to the phone at Dorothy's when I called. When very occasionally he did, he was cruel. Cruel. He had never been like this before. Dorothy was cold and unkind over the phone, also. I felt pure hatred emanating from Berkeley. I had read about this emotion in books but never observed it or experienced it in real life before. It struck me as a very strange emotion to have. What good is it?

At one point Phil got in a terrible state of rage with Dr. J in a telephone conversation. She let him rant on for a half hour and then hung up on him and never spoke to him again.

Dr. J told me unapologetically that she had a hard time with anger and she absolutely wouldn't deal with it. That seemed very strange to me. Wasn't it a psychologist's job to deal with difficult emotions?

The next time Phil came back home and we tried to make love, he was impotent. I reassured him, "It's okay, you'll be fine next week." In *Now Wait for Last Year*, he wrote, "He couldn't. This, too. Miserably, he moved from her, sat on the edge of the bed…. He stroked her hair…. 'Too bad,' he thought, 'I wasn't able to make love to her.'"

Then Phil brought *The Three Stigmata of Palmer Eldritch* to me to read. I probably failed Phil again when I failed to understand this novel. Was it because our life was so disturbed, or had my intellect really been impaired? I didn't like reading about Emily devolving. Her mind was muddy. She was drawing the same pictures and making the same pots that she had already made last year. She couldn't think creatively anymore. We had just joined the church, and here was this novel telling about something like a Black Mass or perhaps worse. Whoever ate the wafer that has been brought back by Palmer Eldritch becames Palmer Eldritch. Wasn't this a blasphemous distortion of the symbol of the wafer and the body of Christ? I was baffled, uneasy, upset.

I am aware that there are many interpretations of *The Three Stigmata of Palmer Eldritch*, considered by some Dickian scholars to be one of Phil's finest novels. My small personal encounter with this novel was not on a literary level. There was something almost demonic in this novel of Phil's, while at the same time he seemed to love the church services, the confirmation class, the ancient hymns, and talking with Fr. Reade about theology.

I think Phil started out to write about the wafer of worldly pleasure, Can-D, as opposed to the spiritual wafer, Chew-Z, brought by a being from the skies. Phil didn't know about LSD at this time. He based his ideas on his reading about hallucinogenic mushrooms. Chew-Z was made out of a fungus. In the beginning of the novel, Palmer seems to be a good spirit; in fact, perhaps he is God. As the novel progresses, there is great confusion as to whether he is good or evil. Good and evil seem to be all mixed up together. The novel got away from Phil, like his life got away from him at that time.

Sadly, I didn't see then, in the shocking strangeness of this novel, how much the protagonist Barney Mayerson loved Emily Hnatt, how much he wanted to get her back, how guilty he felt that he had abandoned her so selfishly.

I didn't see, then, how terrible Barney felt that he hadn't responded to a call for help from his friend and employer, Leo Bulero, when Leo was imprisoned and forcibly drugged by Palmer Eldritch. Barney hated himself; he felt he was rotten, evil. He always put himself first. To expiate his sin, he was going to exile himself to dreary Mars, a trip from which there was no return. He was going to infect himself with deadly Martian epilepsy; he was going to eat Chew-Z and be taken over by Palmer Eldritch. When Ronnie Fugate, a precog who also worked for Leo, looked into the future, she saw Leo murdering Palmer Eldritch. Barney remained on Mars but became like Palmer Eldritch. He tried to get back to Emily. He had a chance but he ruined it, making the same mistakes he made when he lost her the first time.

I didn't see, in the midst of the great spiritual and emotional confusion and upheaval both in our lives and in the novel, that Barney acknowledged responsibility for his actions. He didn't blame them on Emily or some other female. This novel told it like it was. In later years, Phil disavowed *The Three Stigmata of Palmer Eldritch*. He said he wished he hadn't written it and didn't want to hear anything about it.

I believe now that Phil was trying desperately (and failing) to work out a major inner conflict in this novel. He was trying to become whole, as he writes years later in *VALIS*. In the confirmation classes and at church he had looked inside himself and found not Christ but Palmer Eldritch. He got the idea of Christianity all right but couldn't make it work for himself; he couldn't integrate it. It became all twisted and evil. Or did it? At the end of the novel, at the last minute, Phil throws out a question mark about the nature of Palmer Eldritch. Perhaps he wasn't so bad after all; perhaps, instead of an evil thing he was just a weird creature that had been hanging out in outer space for countless eons.

Phil continued to travel back and forth between his mother's house and Point Reyes. I picked up the mail when he wasn't home and was surprised when I received a large bill from the West Marin Pharmacy for various pills and drugs: Sparene, Stelazine, Preludin, an amphetamine, and others. I hadn't known anything about any of these. I scolded the druggist for selling them to Phil.

Phil was writing, partly in Berkeley, partly in Point Reyes Station, *Clans of the Alphane Moon*, a novel with a theme of divorce and reconciliation. He produced a great deal of work that spring. Another novel, *The Penultimate Truth*, probably revised from a 1950s story, was written at about this same time. The plot involves a man emerging from underground after having been deceived by the government. *The Crack in Space* (I bet Phil got the idea when his muffler sprang a leak) was partly based on material left over from *The Man Whose Teeth Were All Exactly Alike*. The scary stories "What the Dead Men Say" and "The Little Black Box," and the novel *The Unteleported Man*, were also part of this output. None of the money from these works went into our joint bank account.

Also at his time Phil wrote a touching story, "Precious Artifact," about engineer Briskle, a man exhausted by his work of the past five years, transforming arid, dreary Mars into a garden. He was so tired that he doesn't even care that his wife and child were arriving on the next rocket. It's just as well; they weren't his wife and children, anyway, but the enemy, Proxers, disguised as members of his family. Briskle just wanted to go home to Earth, but, in fact, everyone and everything on Earth, even his cat, were Proxers who had destroyed Earth and covered up the devastation with an illusory human civilization and illusory people.

Phil left for Berkeley and filed for divorce on March 9, 1964. He rented a room near his mother's house. He phoned me from Berkeley in a week and told me, "It was a good try, Anne, church; too bad it didn't work."

Lynne Hudner told me, "Dorothy had a lot of guilt about the breakup of this marriage."

When we split up, it was as if we were receding from each other, both of us helpless to do anything about the forces that were moving us apart. I think that when Phil was feeling bad, he didn't want to come back, and when he was feeling better, he thought, "I behaved so badly I don't want to inflict myself on them."

It seemed to me more and more as I worked on this book over the years that what was happening inside Phil at that time had little to do with me. Later he spoke of having had a major "nervous breakdown" at this time. Even after he filed for divorce, Phil continued to return to Point Reyes Station, but at longer intervals. One time he brought his beloved Royal Electric typewriter and gave it to me. Another time he told me he wanted the girls and me to keep his beloved *Encyclopedia Britannica*. Then, as he left again, I would give him various books from our collection. He came back in early May, although, as I look back, I see that it was more like a ghost than Phil who arrived, bringing his new electric typewriter and his suitcase, planning to stay forever, but leaving again in a few hours. Perhaps by then, I was a ghost, too, with little left to give. Though I wanted him to stay, I no longer could imagine that he would.

Jayne graduated from eighth grade in early June. She couldn't believe that Phil wouldn't come to her graduation. She kept looking around the room for him, sure that he'd come.

Hatte reflected, "One day there was a family. The next day it was gone. The father left and never came back."

A Postscript to Part I

With some anxiety, even after the passage of eighteen years, I traced and found Dr. A. Over the years he had gained weight and looked like a great blond Buddha. He came to my house to be interviewed for this book, and we sat out on the patio. He tilted his chair against the side of the house. I hadn't seen him since the traumatic events of 1963. He wordlessly expressed a warm, apologetic approval toward me.

It was difficult to get him to talk, he was so tuned in to listening. He sat, quiet and alert in a listening pose, his ears even seeming to extend slightly. But it was a healing moment—to be able to forgive him and converse with him.

As our conversation developed, he began to talk about Phil in what seemed to me to be a nonfriendly way, speculatively labeling Phil with various psychiatric diagnoses and then saying he never could figure out what was wrong with him. I didn't want to hear this psychiatric slander. I had thought Dr. A liked Phil. But after all I had invited him over to listen to him and he was a guest in my house. He went on and on. I didn't know how to respond or even if I should respond. I listened for a long time and then finally managed to blurt out, "But I loved him." Dr. A looked very surprised and left shortly afterward.

PART II: 1964-82

*More and more of the past came back to me as I wrote about my personal memories.
Events I had never discussed with anyone were now down on paper, not still stuck
painfully inside me. Now, I wanted to know what had happened to Phil after his
life with me. Would I be able to find out? Where would I have to go to find the
people who knew him? Would they talk to me? How would I feel, learning about
things I had ignored while Phil was still alive? My oldest daughter, Hatte, warned
me, "Mother, don't get lost in the world of Philip K. Dick." There were times when
I felt like an intruder, times when I was shocked, dismayed, grieved—but once I
started, my bulldog self wouldn't quit.*

Five
BACHELOR IN OAKLAND

...a pulsating black presence beating like a huge heart, enormous and loud, going thump, thump, rising and falling in and out, and angrily burning out everything in me it disapproves of. And that seemed to be most of me.

—Philip K. Dick, *Counter-Clock World*

IN 1963, PHIL began a correspondence with Grania Davidson, who had written him an admiring letter about *The Man in the High Castle*. In 1969, Grania lived in Mexico with her husband, Avram Davidson, who was at that time the editor of *The Magazine of Fantasy & Science Fiction*.

As the correspondence developed, she wrote Phil:

The idea of your being in love with my margin notes puts me in such a good mood, that I've decided to write you an Enticing Letter.... If you would like to fall in love with me...I would be pleased;.... I like your writings.... If you do not wish to come down here, you can wait and fall in love with me up there. We could have clandestine meetings by the sea. We could hold hands together surreptitiously in basement Chinese restaurants.... I like you, I am frankly drawn to you through your letters.... I hope that perhaps I might be able to help you fill your void...and that you might help me fill mine (er, how's that for symbolism?).... I look forward to your letters, these days, with the excitement of a giddy schoolgirl. I close now with, not love...but with the hope that such a thing might be possible.... P.S. I asked the *I Ching* what might happen between us and the answer was:...Hexagram #45, "Gathering Together."

I'm glad I didn't know about this letter back then. I have to admit that it's a masterpiece of flirtation.

When Phil wrote Grania that the relationship with me was finished, she began writing to him in a more explicit vein.

In June 1964, she wrote:

> …should it happen that we develop a rapport between us, it can stew and simmer quietly until you are quite sure what is best for yourself and others…. I am in no hurry… that is why it is certainly wiser for me to live in Berkeley, rather than West Marin…. [I]n Berkeley I have friends other than yourself…and will not become bored or impatient… though eventually I'd like to live near the sea, somewhat isolated, but not at first…. I've been isolated for much too long down here and am much in need of a fling.

In mid-June of 1964, Grania came up to Berkeley to meet Phil. She stayed at the house of her friends science fiction writer Marion Zimmer Bradley and Walter Breen. Grania was intelligent, charming, verbal, and confident enough of her femininity to overcome a serious weight handicap.

Many more surprises were in store for me when I interviewed Grania Davis, who had been Grania Davidson in 1965. Grania invited me to her house in San Rafael and served me a glass of Greek wine. Now much thinner, she had written and published science fiction novels, worked in a travel agency, and traveled extensively. An accomplished woman of great charm and great determination, Grania had an unusual voice with a slightly quavering timbre that gave the impression of great sensibility and sympathy.

Phil was still living near his mother, but he asked Grania to find him a house to rent. She found one on Lyon Street in Oakland. It had a small cottage in the backyard where she and her little boy, who would be coming soon to join her, would live.

About this same time Phil drove to Inez Storer's house in West Marin in the secondhand white VW he'd just bought. Inez had asked Phil to write a piece of publicity for a show of her paintings. He had asked her in return to get a prescription for him. Phil told Inez that he was going to kill himself. He said, "I can't live with Anne and I can't live without her."

Ray and Kirsten Nelson, both good friends of Phil's when he moved back to Oakland, were both friendly and helpful while I was collecting the material for this book. I met with each one of them several times and have corresponded occasionally with Ray since. I was surprised to learn about Kirsten's romantic relationship with Phil.

Ray also recovered a dim memory of meeting Phil briefly much earlier when Phil was married to Kleo. The Nelsons kept a connection with Phil throughout the rest of his life and Kirsten remained Phil's confidant. Ray visited Phil in his Santa Ana condominium a few months before his death.

Ray thought that Phil was driven to despair by not being able to make money with his writing, even though he had won recognition for it. Ray wrote, "The key to understanding Phil's life is…the economics of a writer's life in these United States…. [Phil finally] having concluded that he could not make a living as a writer…saw his life as being dominated by an evil God."

While Grania and Phil were moving their possessions into the Lyon Street house, Phil went too fast on a curve, totaled the VW and seriously dislocated his shoulder. He was in a body cast, his right arm pinned to the front of his chest, and he was unable to write for most of the time that Grania lived with him. He told his new friend Ray Nelson that he had tried to commit suicide but was such a failure he even failed at this. Ray asked him anxiously if he would try again. Phil told him, "Suicide is for the living." He told Ray that, since he had made a serious attempt to die, he was actually dead even though the attempt had failed. He said he was a "walking corpse."

Ray Nelson and Phil became close friends and soon began collaborating on a novel. Later, when I visited Phil at his house in Oakland, Ray was friendly and warm to me and we immediately got along well.

Although Phil was telling everyone "monster" tales about me, Ray didn't buy them. He wrote me years later, "I knew that Phil had attempted suicide because he was convinced that he would never be anything but a drag and a liability to you and your children."

Phil phoned me and told about his injury. I hoped he would come home and let me take care of him, but he didn't give any indication that he was going to do this, although he wanted tons of sympathy. He gave me his address on Lyon Street and asked me to come visit him; I went almost immediately. The neighborhood was rundown, weedy, and filled with litter. It seemed incredibly dreary to me. How could he stand it after beautiful Point Reyes? Along the way there, though, I was cheered by the new ephemeral art form, the mudflat sculptures extending for miles along eastern San Francisco Bay. They were made of driftwood and other debris and were quite wonderful. Each time I drove by some of them had fallen down and new ones had spontaneously been built in their places.

Phil had furnished his house with his battered old Magnavox, a few pieces of Salvation Army furniture, and several sheepskin rugs that we had had made from our own sheep. To my dismay, he had acquired two cats, which made me think he was going to be living permanently at this location. They had already ruined the sheepskin rugs, which they evidently preferred to their cat box. I don't remember what we talked about, the mudflat sculptures, probably. I had become fearful of saying anything to him, he was so incredibly touchy. I didn't know about the little cottage behind his house or that Grania was living there.

In their life together, Grania found Phil caring and domestic. He bought her an old Chevrolet and a Philippine wooden salad bowl. She noted that he was disciplined and orderly about the physical setup of his house. He ate regular nutritious meals, kept his house tidy, did his laundry, and generally kept himself physically together, but she found him to be extremely volatile— "too many mood swings and craziness and carrying on." Phil never stopped telling her stories about his terrible ex-wife. He said he'd worked hard and written eighteen novels to make the money to support the sprawling household in Point Reyes. Later she wondered if Phil invented these stories in order to justify leaving his wife and four children. Phil also told Grania that he had been attracted to Hatte and he "was going to have to watch it." Phil asked Grania to marry him. Grania said, "Phil's idea was if you had sex with someone, you got married. He was serially monogamous."

Grania noted that Phil had a whole drawer full of medications and was taking Elavil and Stelazine prescribed by Dr. A and many other strong tranquilizers. At times he was so agitated he would walk the floor all night listening to opera on the record player at high volume.

Back in Point Reyes Station I was faced with a legal situation in which I had to answer Phil's divorce action or he would automatically get the divorce on his terms, which meant he would get half the house. Where would I raise my children? I felt very anxious about this, but still I couldn't bear to file for divorce, so my attorney, Anne Diamond, found a little-used legal alternative, and I filed "for reconciliation." This action surprised and dismayed Phil.

When I contacted retired attorney Anne Diamond after Phil's death, she invited me to have lunch with her. I met her in her beautiful home in Ross, which was filled with a collection of antique Asian art. Anne had always been quite fond of me and was helpful with my search, gave me new insights about the divorce, and instructed her office to supply me with all the relevant records. She told me that the Anne and Philip K. Dick divorce was the worst case she had ever handled and she now used it as a model to teach young divorce attorneys.

Phil's papers and manuscripts were still in the Hovel. My attorney asked me for a financial paper that happened to be there, and it made perfect sense to my pragmatic nature to go to the Hovel, saw off the lock, get the paper, and put on another lock. I was rather proud of the technical aspects of this small achievement. Phil; his attorney, William Wolfson (the husband of Phil's favorite high school teacher); my attorney; and my psychologist all became hysterical. "Why?" I thought. "It wasn't a paper of any importance." Because of this incident, Wolfson served me with a restraining order that said that I couldn't visit Phil anymore. Phil changed his phone and got an unlisted phone number; we were out of touch—until he phoned again a few weeks later.

To further complicate an already difficult divorce, my attorney, Anne Diamond, had been the attorney for Margaret Wolfson, William Wolfson's wife, during their recent divorce, and Phil's psychiatrist, Dr. A, and my psychotherapist, Dr. J, had a falling out over the monetary kickbacks. The divorce became a battle of the sexes. Unfortunately, Dr. A and William Wolfson believed Phil's tales instead of helping him. (Mrs. Diamond, the wife of famous forensic psychiatrist, Bernard Diamond, repeatedly moaned, "Too bad he isn't getting any decent psychiatric care.")

Over the phone Phil told me, "I asked Bill Wolfson twice to drop the divorce action, but he refused." I wondered what that meant.

My old enemy and now friend William Wolfson met me for a no-host lunch at a Larkspur Landing restaurant. I had the red, paperback Levack PKD bibliography tucked under my arm, and as soon as we sat down a beautiful dark-haired woman rushed over to ask me where I had bought that book. She wanted a copy for her ex-husband, who loved The Man in the High Castle, *had begun writing a script for it, and was trying to buy the movie rights. When I got back home, the ex-husband phoned me and later I met him for lunch. He was one of the inventors of Dolby. He let me read his great beginning of a movie script, a sequel to* The Man in the High Castle.

Vince Lusby, Phil's old friend and co-worker at University Radio, visited Phil at the Lyon Street house soon after Phil had moved in. Phil told Vince that the reason he was getting divorced was that I would buy every new car that came along and that he had to stop me before I lost the house. He told Vince that I had attacked him with a carving knife, that I had chased him around the yard with the white Jaguar (which we hadn't owned for years), and that I had murdered my first husband. Vince was surprised at all this since he knew me. Then Phil told Vince seriously, "Anne has wired up my old Magnavox so that she can listen and spy on me here."

When Vince told me this after Phil's death I was so shocked I didn't know what to say. We went on with the rest of the interview at his house in Richmond. At the end of my visit, Virginia Lusby gave me a bourbon and soda, and then I made the long drive back to Point Reyes Station. The next day I called Vince, still not quite believing what he'd told me. "Vince," I asked, "when Phil told you his Magnavox was wired up so I could listen to him there in Oakland, was he kidding?"

Vince told me somberly, "No, he was serious."

I asked Vince, "What did you say to Phil when he told you that?"

"I was shocked as hell. I didn't say anything."

I began to realize then that the situation back in 1964 was quite different than I had thought at the time—but then it's also possible that Phil was playing a role.

That spring Phil wrote "What the Dead Men Say," a story that I didn't read until after his death. Johnny Barefoot, the protagonist, hears booming voices over the radio, sees a blurred face on the TV, and hears gibberish and a far-off, weird babble on the telephone. Dead Louis Sarapis, from somewhere out in space, controls all the media and is planning to take over the country through his niece, Kathy Egmont Sharp, a psychotic amphetamine addict who is in a mental hospital for part of the story. When Johnny draws the straw that destines him to kill Kathy, his heart is leaden because once he had loved her. Sharp was my stepfather's name. Phil's protagonists had ex-wives named Kathy in several of Phil's post-Point Reyes novels. At first she is a horrible character, but as the books go on she becomes more positive.

Phil wrote the science fiction novel *A Maze of Death* about this time also, a unique novel that seems to tell about a psychotic episode from within.

I drove to the science fiction book store, the Big Cat, that Ray and Kirsten Nelson owned in Albany. It was located just off San Pablo Avenue. There, I met Kirsten, a slender blonde lady with a Norwegian accent. Still very attractive, she must have been a raving beauty in 1964. It was a cold day, cold even inside the bookstore, and Kirsten kept her powder-blue parka on. We sat down at a cluttered desk in an unlit utility room at the back of the store and I untangled the wires of my tape recorder. With a flourish, Kirsten handed me a photocopy of a love letter Phil had written to her. Surprised, I took it. I hadn't realized that she was such an important person in Phil's life.

Phil had written:

> I love you, without as Grania phrases it, carnal intent but with love…. [B]elieve me; I love several people but that does not mean I want to go to bed with them; I love my sister Lynne and I also, and this sounds crazy, love Al Halevy and Jack Newcomb and several others, including Carol Carr, but of all of them it's you I want to be with…. I just want to be where I can look at you and see that something in your eyes, that beauty and clarity (the trigram LI) and beyond that a thing about you I can't name, because I'm not a poet; I only know how to write prose…. There is, in my life, all the sex (pardon the word, dear) that I can use; in fact too much; I want, I guess, life itself. I believe I can get it from a woman, THE woman. You are the woman…. I wish I could hold you for a moment…. I don't want you to warm me; I want to breathe life into you, and Al, for all his faults, wants to, too. We love you together; others do, too; we love you in silence, unable to speak; as in Mozart's 'Magic Flute', "Zuruck. Zuruck. Hier muss man zuruck." ("Back, back; here one must go back.") But I won't, not until you say go away and leave me alone; not until you say, as Ottavio Rinuccini said in 1608 for Monteverdi's great five-line madrigal: "Lascia te mi morire." ("Now let me die. I suffer beyond hope of solace. Ah, let me die.")…. How can anyone as lovely as you feel bad? But maybe you don't feel bad; maybe it's only me, thinking about you, imagining you; I hope so; I want you not to feel bad…. If anything that lives is sacred to me it is you.

I told her, "My goodness, back in 1964, I didn't know anything about you." She was apologetic in her manner and explained that her relationship to Phil was "all drama."

She had met Phil at a party at her house soon after his car accident. He was in a body cast with his arm in a sling. "I found him to be romantic, exciting, fascinating, as did several other ladies there. He had fantastic charisma. He proposed to every woman he met. The jokes he would crack were so funny. Phil loved to fall in love; he was in love with falling in love."

Phil talked to Kirsten for hours on the telephone. He had a special long telephone cord sent to her house so she wouldn't have to sit on the cold stairs where her phone was located. He sent her a card saying "Happy Long Phone Cord Day."

Kirsten observed that Phil was moody, upset, and emotional about the divorce. She said, "Phil was having all kinds of battles within himself over the breakup. It was like a battle of good and evil. He was feeling guilty and torn up, and if you feel guilty towards someone, you're going to feel angry towards them. Phil felt inferior because of the beautiful, fancy house. Phil was writing all those novels and couldn't make any money.

"Also he needed to feel in the midst of things and have a lot of people about him, a lot of activity. He needed and wanted excitement. The more exciting he could make things the better it was for him. He told me it was too quiet for him in Point Reyes. He had incredible ups and downs. Sometimes I wondered, who was Phil? Was he real? When was he playing a role? No one knew. But certainly his feeling for women, that tremendous ability to set up a closeness, was quite unusual. There was no one else like him."

Two weeks after I had received the restraining order, Phil phoned and gave me his new unlisted number. I drove over to see him, still hoping to mend our relationship. On Sunday of that same week, the children and I went to a show at the Borzoi Club dog show in Oakland. On the way back, we stopped at Phil's house at his invitation and had a rather formal tea party. Unbeknownst to me Grania was hiding in the closet!

On July 17, 1964, Grania wrote her friend, Cynthia Goldstone:

I do not believe that things between Phil and I can go on too awfully much longer…not because of a lack of desire or a lack of trying or a lack of love on either of our parts, but because he is so sick…and something will soon happen that will separate us. He will, in a self-destructive mood, go back to his wife whom he hates…or kill himself…. [He] has begun to talk about it a lot…is showing all the signs; making symbolic suicidal attempts like slashing his hands with a knife…and has bought a gun, though I was able to dissuade him from getting ammunition (I think)…but who wants someone to stop him and show him another way out…which I have been able to do…SO FAR…

been able to take away the knife and hide it…to comfort and love him…SO FAR… but I am not always there…. His wife is serving him with various writs and doing other nasty things like breaking into his little office and stealing his financial records…. He is separated from his children…. He is in constant pain from his shoulder…and helpless in many ways, can't drive, can't write, can't wash, tie his shoes…. It is not all in his mind, you see…. [H]e has reasons…good mundane reasons for feeling as he does… except that there are the other things TOO…the things which ARE IN HIS MIND… which are added to his daily problems…. I can see symptoms growing…daily, growing and taking hold of him…until the dear, delightful, intelligent and interesting Phil turns into something utterly unrecognizable…MORE AND MORE EACH DAY…. This is what I fear…I don't really think he'll go back to his wife…I don't really think he'll commit suicide…these are just possibilities…. The real fear…the real PROBABILITY is that he is cracking up…possibly for good.

He looks to me for help…tries to deify me…. I really CAN'T help, the way he means…. I can only love and be sympathetic and try to understand and offer suggestions and smooth things…and as long as I can…but when I can't…he flies into…rages…. Then I soothe him and assure him and tell him that he has not lost me, and we go to bed and all is well for a while, because we have diverted him from his real problems into an artificial one of losing me…. Or else he becomes frightened…chokes on his food and paints huge, horrible pictures of what will happen and how he can't possibly go on and that the life is draining out of him…. And so it goes…and so it has gone for a couple of weeks now, lasting longer each day and getting worse…. [T]he only thing that can stop the cycle is sleep…[i]f he can be persuaded to go to sleep…. What I SHOULD do is leave for good…never come back…. But I love him…I really do, and I don't know what he'd do if I deserted him…but when Ethan comes…I cannot expose Ethan to this sort of thing…. I CANNOT expose Ethan to this…and I CANNOT leave Phil…. What to do???

This letter was so melodramatic that Grania decided not to send it; instead, she crumpled it up and threw it in her wastebasket.

This letter, heavily creased but flattened out again, was found in Phil's files after his death. He must have fished it out of Grania's wastebasket. I obtained a copy from the Philip K. Dick papers in Paul Williams's garage in Glen Ellen.

A few days later, Phil and I met in court to determine the amount he should pay for separate maintenance. My handsome blond older brother Arthur, then a vice president of Goodrich Rubber, had come west on business and appeared with me at the hearing in his three-piece navy pinstripe suit. Phil came into the courtroom in his rumpled jeans, an elderly shirt with one empty sleeve pinned up, and his arm in a sling. His body cast was rather dingy by then, too. I was amazed when he walked up to me and kissed me on the cheek. For a moment the image of Judas slid through my mind. I introduced Phil to my brother. They shook hands, smiled, and each told the other, "Nice to meet you."

The judge turned out to be a science fiction fan and was fascinated with Phil. My attorney was quite worried. But all the questions put by Wolfson seemed ridiculous to me: "Whose laundry was done in the washing machine, Phil's child or the three older children's? Who should pay for it?" I fielded these questions easily, adding counter-testimony to my answers. My brother was tickled. The judge awarded me $75 a month temporary support. Phil paid it once. I never wanted to pursue him aggressively for this picayune monthly payment, fearing it would drive him further away.

Back at Phil's rental house in Oakland, Grania, despite her doubts, did stay, and her boy came up from Mexico to join her. Phil was lovely to the child and built him a sandbox in the back yard, but Grania became even more disturbed when Phil bought a small derringer, "because he was afraid of Anne." Then he began to say that Ray Nelson was plotting against Kirsten and was going to kill her. Grania felt she couldn't deal with these problems. Phil was staying up all night; she didn't dare try to sneak the gun away, heaven knows what he might do. Finally, though, she did steal it and gave it to Ray to hide.

I asked Kirsten about this alleged plot of Ray's, and she laughed heartily as she told me, "Well, that was because Phil was trying to get me away from Ray."

Ray Nelson told me, when I interviewed him, that he didn't take any offense back in those days at Phil being in love with his wife. Phil was just having an "intellectual romance." He said, "Phil was just so darn charming you couldn't get mad at him." Then he asked me anxiously, "Do you think they had a real affair; did Kirsten say anything to you?" At the end of the interview, he asked, "Would you like to have an 'intellectual romance' with me?" Although we didn't have an "intellectual romance," we kept in touch in a friendly way over the years.

Kirsten continued, "Then Phil told me, 'I'm going to shoot myself,'" but she felt this kind of talk was mostly histrionics, Phil was amusing himself and his friends and fighting off depression and boredom. When Phil entered his house accompanied by Kirsten or other friends, he would search the house, saying, "The FBI and the CIA have bugged my cat box." It was hilariously funny but nobody knew if he was kidding or if he was serious. They thought he was kidding but they weren't sure.

In late summer, science fiction fans and writers came from all over the country to Oakland for the National Science Fiction Convention held on Labor Day weekend. Phil's house was not far from the Leamington Hotel, where the convention was held. In late August, fans and writers from all over the United States were hanging around his house and he was having nightly parties. A lot of science fiction political intrigues were going on, in which Phil had become involved. Then, suddenly he would chase everyone away, lock himself up, and go into a hermit state for a couple of weeks.

Once, when I phoned Phil while a number of people were in the room with him, he spoke to me in a cruel, mocking manner. Then they left while we were still talking and his manner immediately changed and became pleasant and civilized. I didn't understand why he would behave this way but was happy that at least he ended up being friendly.

Phil phoned me just before the convention and invited me to come over to Oakland and go to it with him. Ray Nelson wanted Phil and me to get back together. He believed that Phil still loved me. He was the one who suggested to Phil that he invite me. I was delighted, thinking this was all Phil's idea and hoping that a reconciliation was in the offing. The convention turned out to be a nightmare. There wasn't anything for me to do but sit around at tables with people I didn't know while Phil was off talking to other people. For years Phil had conditioned me to avoid the world of fandom, and here it was in all its glory. I drank too much. I wanted to leave and go off with Phil somewhere. He finally left with me at 2 a.m. As we walked out on the streets of downtown Oakland to go to the car, he suddenly got a terrible look on his face and walked away. He left me in the middle of the night in the middle of the street in one of the most dangerous spots in the Bay Area.

I was stunned. I couldn't believe Phil would do something like this. In my haste to get away safely I backed into a telephone pole. Back home I had hardly gone to sleep before dawn appeared. I decided to go back to Oakland and find out what had gone wrong. I took our four-year-old daughter, Laura, with me. When we knocked at Phil's door, he came out in his pajamas, his eyes wild, waving a small revolver in the air. I stood there paralyzed for a moment. Then I grabbed Laura's hand, backed up quickly, and left. I was terribly upset that she had been there and had been frightened by Phil's strange and hostile behavior.

I called up Dr. J and went to her office on the way home. She told me, "You mustn't ever go over there again." I had to agree with her. I had to give up.

My life had reached a turning point. That night I sat at home thinking, "Phil is destroying everything that I love most in the world—himself and our family." I couldn't believe my own thoughts: "I'm going to buy a deer rifle at the Palace Market tomorrow and shoot Phil." Then I thought, "No, I'll go buy a deer rifle and shoot myself." After a short while I decided neither of these ideas were worth anything. I couldn't do such a thing to my children. I'd end up in jail, or they'd have a mother who was a suicide on top of the present mess. This was the only time in my life that I ever found myself seriously thinking a murderous thought, but now, when I read about a killing associated with a marriage or a love affair in the newspaper, I can empathize with the feelings of the person who did such a terrible deed.

That night I had a dream that I was in a small rowboat with the four girls. I was trying to save Phil, who was in the water beside the boat, drowning. But each time I tried to pull him into the boat he would almost pull me into the water instead. Meanwhile, we were drifting toward an immense waterfall. In the dream I had to make a terrible choice. I had to row away and leave Phil in order to save the girls.

Not more than a few days passed before Phil called, and naturally I told him all about my thoughts and their resolution—I always told him everything.

Then, one day in mid-October, he called me to ask, "Can I come back home?"

"Yes," I said. "You can come back. The study is still set up for you."

I was making jewelry in my workroom with my first employee, Henryetta Russell (who worked for me for forty years). I decided that I wouldn't stop working when he came. I needed to go on with my separate life. By then I must have learned at least a little bit that I couldn't emotionally depend on Phil. When he arrived, I greeted him and told him we would get together at dinner time; I needed to work. I probably was somber and serious.

He carried his new typewriter and his suitcase into the study. An hour later, when I came out of my workroom to get a glass of water I saw Phil walking to his car carrying his suitcase and his typewriter. I felt very sad as I watched my husband walk away from my house—I knew it was for the last time.

Grania moved out of the Lyon Street cottage just before Halloween. She tried to keep a friendly relationship with Phil, but he was angry at her for leaving. When shortly later she went to the Lyon Street house to pick up her possessions, Nancy Hackett was there sitting on Phil's lap.

Maren Hackett, the friend we had met at church, had invited Phil over to her place because she, herself, was interested in him. She was surprised when the relationship that he formed was with Nancy, her nineteen-year-old stepdaughter.

After Grania left Phil, Jack Newcomb left his wife and moved into the cottage. Ray told me that there were a lot of illicit amphetamines around and rumors of drug dealing. Phil started taking amphetamines "recreationally" at this time. Ray Nelson said that Phil was better versed on drugs than Al Halevy, a pharmacist acquaintance.

Phil was writing me strange letters about an amphetamine salesman who ended up in jail and an Israeli gunman who was hiding out in his basement. I was shocked by these letters except that I didn't really believe them. Years later, Ray Nelson told me that everything Phil had written was true. Phil gave Jack the original manuscript of *The Man in the High Castle*. He told Jack, "I love you. Use this as an insurance policy." Jack told Phil, "I'll never sell this while you're alive."

In 1983, Jack Newcomb called me from Los Angeles to ask me to buy the manuscript of The Man in the High Castle *for $5,000. He said that Ray had told him I was "okay"; that's why he was speaking to me now. When I heard his name and that he was calling from a pay phone, I called him right back so that the charges would be on my phone and we could talk for a longer time. He remembered charging gas on my Texaco credit card and told me, "Phil spent most of his time putting you down." He thought I was rich, that I had $5,000 to give him for Phil's manuscript. (It would have been a good investment—but who knew at that time?) I referred Jack to the Eaton Collection at UC Irvine. (Kleo always thought I was rich, too. I have to laugh. I do own a very nice house, which I bought in 1955 for nothing down and $101 a month.)*

"It was a strange period," Grania recalled. "There was the diaper scandal. Someone stole diaper-service diapers from Marion Zimmer Bradley's front porch. Somebody resembling Phil was seen there. Phil and Jack got hold of a Klaxon horn, which they used to harass people they didn't like. They blew it over the phone at me. They drove by Marion Zimmer Bradley's house and blew it late at night. They were full of manic mischief."

Phil became furious with Jack and kicked him out. Kirsten went with Jack as a go-between to help him pick up his clothes. Phil was so angry at Jack that he even became furious at Kirsten.

Later that fall, Phil came out to Point Reyes to visit me and in the course of the conversation casually mentioned that Jack Newcomb had wanted to kill me. He had dissuaded Jack, he said. But I thought, "Where had Jack gotten the idea?" But still in my denial habit, I didn't take this information seriously. My bulldog psyche was still hanging on to the hope that eventually Phil would return and we'd all be happy again.

Recreational drugs were beginning to appear on the Bay Area scene, including the psychedelic drug LSD. Ray Nelson brought some for Phil to take. The two of them sat together in Phil's house for eight hours while Phil had a terrible hallucination, sweating, feeling completely alone, reexperiencing a spear thrust through his body, and speaking Latin, as he relived a life as a Roman gladiator. He had such a bad trip that he never tried LSD again.

On Christmas Day 1964, I was pleased when Phil called and asked if he could come out to see us. He brought an armload of Christmas gifts, several packages for each of us, all of them nicely gift wrapped. But then he stayed only a little while and suddenly left angrily. Not knowing that he was coming, I had invited some other guests. Perhaps it was this that offended him, or was it because I asked him to mash the potatoes? It was impossible to know.

Kirsten told me, "At this time Phil thought that everyone was out to get him. He was hyper, running around doing bizarre things. At other times, he was charming and funny. I remember him gulping down pill cocktails. I couldn't believe the conglomerations of pills that he took. He wanted to commit everybody, Grania, Francine, a friend of Nancy's sister. He thought Nancy should take Thorazine and many of his other acquaintances should go to Langley Porter."

In early 1965, Phil was still phoning about once a month and coming to see me and the girls. He came one beautiful spring day and told me that he was "Nancy's consort." My heart sank. He even looked different, as if he had dissolved into a feckless nineteen-year-old. I knew *my* Phil was in that person somewhere, but where? I had been reading Martin Buber's *I and Thou* and wanted to discuss it with him. He was dancing, showing the girls how he could do the frug. So I gave up on Martin Buber and said, "I'll do the frug with you." His face changed, he looked very strange, stopped dancing, and suddenly left. I felt like an old discarded shoe.

After this, I was so miserable that I could hardly function. I could only find comfort lying in the sun at the beach or going back to bed in the morning— something I had never done in my life before. I waited anxiously for the phone to ring.

When I saw Dr. J, she told me that Phil only liked the house, not me or the girls. She said his loving side wasn't real. I insisted that I had seen a wonderful person in Phil. She told me this person was buried so deep that for all practical purposes *my* Phil was gone, and besides, now he had a commitment to Nancy. I couldn't believe *my* Phil was irrevocably gone.

How could he have made a commitment to Nancy when he'd made a commitment to me? Brooding at home, I had a terrible sense of evil. Not about Phil, not about any actual person, but about something I couldn't get into mental focus.

I would try to get my mind going in a positive direction and forget about Phil, but then he would call me and say, "Why don't you come over and see me in Oakland anymore?" He wrote more strange letters, giving me the impression of an almost depraved lifestyle. One time he called and told me that his house had been vandalized and all the literary novels that he had written had been totally destroyed. Another time he called and said in a pitiful tone of voice, "I'm in such bad shape I can't work on my own any more. The only way I can write is to work with someone else." He was writing *Deus Irae* with Roger Zelazny.

In the early summer of 1965, I taught jewelry making to a group of people from the Synanon drug-rehabilitation facility, which was located only a few miles north of where I lived. Six or seven people came down to my house once a week. One of the men in the group, a handsome, tall blond fellow whose family owned ranches in Nevada, became interested in me, and I dated him briefly. I thought perhaps I could make Phil jealous if I told him that someone else was interested in me. Perhaps it would make some change in the situation between us. Well it did all right, but not the way I'd hoped. After I told him, Phil became very cold in his tone of voice and didn't speak to me for several weeks. It seemed to me that the last thread in our relationship snapped at this time.

Phil's attorney, William Wolfson, was suing me for half of the house on Phil's behalf. Under the new no-fault divorce law, he very likely would succeed. I worried: "Where will I raise my girls?" My attorney, Anne Diamond, called a meeting with Phil and Wolfson in her San Rafael offices. She suggested that Phil consider the money he had put into our house as rent. Both he and his attorney were insulted. "Why?" I thought. "It seems so logical." On Phil's behalf, Wolfson refused the offers that my attorney had made. Phil sat there without saying anything, but managed to give the impression that he didn't like what had happened but had no power to do anything about it.

My clever attorney prepared legal papers for me to keep at my house in case Phil came out to Point Reyes again and, on September 29 he did. I asked him to sign the papers that would give the house back to me, and we went to a notary and he did. He seemed happy about this. When we returned to the house, I tried to hug him. He looked at me strangely and rushed out of the house.

The divorce was final on October 21, 1965. I went to court in the morning with my friend Inez Storer as my witness. Anne Diamond suggested that I not pick up the final papers, but I didn't understand her idea. She saw how much I loved Phil and felt that we might still get back together, that not taking the final step in the divorce action might keep the relationship alive. But I didn't "get it" and went ahead and finalized the legal action. Almost as soon as I had returned home, Phil called up and wanted me to tell him all about the divorce. He didn't sound sad or depressed, just cheerfully interested in hearing what went on in court that day.

About a month after the divorce, the girls and I met Phil once again at Jack London Square on the Oakland waterfront. I gave him a beautiful handmade beaded, fringed deerskin Indian jacket that had belonged to Richard. Phil put it on. Years later, a few months before his death in 1982, as we were talking on the phone long distance, he reminded me of that day. He said it was the last time he had seen all of the girls together. He sounded as if he were almost crying.

I didn't cry, not for eighteen more years, but I obsessively thought about my relationship with Phil sixteen hours a day, trying to understand what had happened. I worked on myself to change or remove traits that Phil had criticized. In the midst of my misery, I started seeing how beautiful ordinary people are. How almost everything we have, the thoughts in our minds, the words in our mouths, even the way we see the landscape, comes as a gift from other human beings. Sometimes a beautiful, numinous light seemed to be behind the hills and the line of eucalyptus trees at the edge of the field.

Lynne, Phil's stepsister, who had become a psychiatric social worker, told me that Phil had become much more ill and neurotic after he left Point Reyes. She said that there was no way that Phil could have returned.

Six
NANCY

...always agreeable, always willing to look up to him—he was, after all, so much older than she—as an authority. That perpetually pleased him. And it seemed to please her, too.
—Philip K. Dick, *Counter-Clock World*

I NEVER ENVISIONED having any relationship with Nancy. I hadn't seen her since she was a nineteen-year-old visitor in my house in the early 1960s, but amazingly, a friendship developed at the time of Phil's final illness, when I phoned her to give her news from the hospital in Los Angeles. I talked with Kleo at that time, too. Many barriers dropped when Phil was dying.

In 1982, when I met with her, Nancy was a fragile, feminine woman, evoking strong protective and compassionate feelings from those who came to know her. Although she said she didn't remember much about the past, she agreed to meet me for several interviews. We met for lunch at the Marin Mental Health Clinic, where she managed the medical-records system at the hospital she had gone to at one time for treatment. I also visited her in her pleasant Novato apartment where she lived with her two daughters, Isa and Tina. Isa was there one time I visited, and I remember she and Nancy laughed and giggled a lot. Both were beautiful women, delightful to be around. Nancy had a humble, almost childlike, manner, but she was direct and intelligent in her speech, although there seemed to be a note of mournfulness in the tone of her voice. She said frankly, "I made a mess of my early life." She was pleased that she had now lived in one place for ten years, maintained relationships that went back ten years, and created a life for herself and her children. She didn't want me to tape the interview, so I took notes by hand.

Nancy is a very religious person and after she left Phil she almost joined Jim Jones's community in northern California—before Jones moved it to Guyana. She shudders at her narrow escape. I keep in touch with Nancy every few years. My daughter and her daughter Isa have become close friends and manage the PKD estate together.

Nancy was the third child of three in an upper-middle-class family. She attended public schools until high school and was brought up in the Episcopal Church. She told me that her family had a strain of hereditary mental illness in it. Her adolescence was difficult. Her mother went into a coma caused by a brain tumor when Nancy was twelve and died when Nancy was eighteen. As is common in families where there is a lack of parenting, the brother and two sisters drew close together. After her father's second marriage broke up she went to boarding school, after persuading her grandmother to finance this. Maren Hackett was Nancy's second mother-in-law and gave Nancy the mothering that she had missed. The two became close.

Nancy was sent to a psychoanalyst for a full Freudian analysis when she was only a teenager. In retrospect, she thought this was very odd. She had an illness that was characterized by a period of overactivity and sleeplessness, followed by a long period of depression. These attacks were so terrible that Nancy told me that she had "looked forward to dying." In her adolescence this illness was believed to be psychogenic. This medical view put an impossible burden on her to "get well." Recently this illness, now called bipolar illness, is known to be due to a chemical imbalance in the brain and, like diabetes, can be controlled by medication. After years of suffering, Nancy found that she could enjoy life and work and function well.

After Phil evicted Jack from his house, he invited both Nancy and her sister, Anne, to live in his new cottage. He told Kirsten Nelson that he was in love with Anne. But Anne didn't return his interest. When Phil kept talking about the cat box being bugged, it frightened her. She was afraid that he really did think this. Phil switched his affections to Nancy, drawn to her by her fragility. Phil told Kirsten, "I am in the Christ sweepstakes. If I don't save Nancy, no one else will." Kirsten thought that Phil wanted to play doctor and take care of Nancy but didn't think Phil and Nancy were good for each other. "Neither of them was stable at that time," she told me.

Nancy had just returned from Spain, where she had been briefly hospitalized. She was depressed and taking strong medication. Philip took her to her appointments with her psychiatrist.

Phil wrote Maren Hackett on December 20, 1964:

I wanted to add a couple of things I didn't get a chance to say to you tonight.... First: it may seem to you that my attitude toward Nancy is irresponsible. If so, then what would be a responsible attitude toward her? Loving her surely isn't irresponsible.... [Y]ou yourself have made your own agreement on this matter—at least in the abstract—clear in past times. Treating her like an adult; that is, assuming that she is capable enough to know what she is doing? Well, here we have the "first stone" problem; none of us are utterly capable; none of us are totally without some sense.... Let's spell it out. I fell in love with Nancy.... I'm thirty-six years old, or some such absurdly huge figure.... I've seen a number of sorrows come and pass in my life.... I trust that having passed through that, and survived, I can probably deal with rather difficult and even brutally heartbreaking human relationships; I can take a hell of a lot and still grin and get by—without retaliating, or becoming bitter, or wanting to hurt someone back. Is Nancy's life none of my business? Idiotic; of course it's my business.... I'm glad to declare my aims as regards Nancy.... I have nothing to be ashamed of; what's your story? I love her and I want to be with her—all the time, if possible. Is this destroying her? Lord. Oh ye of little faith, Maren. Were I to want that of you, would you decline it as an act of destruction toward you? I rather doubt it.

Counter-Clock World came from this period. There's a nice portrait of Nancy in it as Lotta. Phil's old Berkeley friend, Maury Guy, came back from Canada where he'd been living. He stopped by to see Phil's parents, Dorothy and Joe Hudner. He was looking for a place to stay for a few days and called Phil from the Hudners' place. Phil was cordial. Maury said, "It was just like old times, Phil was so glad to hear my voice." Phil invited Maury and his new wife to stay with him in Oakland, but Maury began feeling uneasy. He said, "The drug ambience was so strong—I had been into amphetamines myself. I wasn't going to go near that scene. Phil told me he was going to marry this young girl whom he had just repatriated from a Spanish mental hospital. It was too much for me."

Maury expressed a concern for what was happening in Phil's life to Dorothy, and she replied sadly, "Phil has become a hopeless amphetamine addict."

Phil was the conservative one in the relationship with Nancy. The summer of love was approaching and drugs were "in." Nancy and Phil came out to West Marin to see his old friends and to look for a house in the area. After he visited various people they stopped speaking to me; he was still telling "monster" tales about me, and convincingly, too—but he wanted to move back near me and the children. The rents in West Marin were too much for Phil and Nancy's budget and instead they rented an apartment in San Rafael. Then they found a rental house in Santa Venetia, a lower-priced but attractive section of San Rafael near the Frank Lloyd Wright Civic Center, a quarter mile from an arm of San Francisco bay.

Alys Graveson remembered, "The house was charming, near the water, but it was too small for a writer, especially after the baby was born. There was no place for Phil to write."

"Baby paraphernalia was everywhere," Nancy said. "When Philip was married to me, he never wrote except when he needed money. Then he would write a novel in six days by using amphetamines."

In mid-June of 1966, my friend Sue Baty phoned me to warn me that Phil had called her husband, Judge David Baty, and had made an appointment to be married to Nancy in a civil ceremony at the Batys' house, which was where the judge performed marriages. Sue was disturbed by this and told me she didn't plan to be home.

The marriage was July 6. That same afternoon my daughter Tandy and I were singing in the chorus of the Inverness Music Festival's production of Haydn's *The Creation*.

Sue told me that Phil, Nancy, her sister and brother, Anne and Michael, Maren Hackett, and a gentleman dressed in a gray suit and a strange purplish-red shirt, whom no one introduced to the judge, made up the wedding party. After the civil ceremony, this gentleman stepped forward and blessed the marriage, Phil's fourth. This mysterious person turned out to be Bishop James A. Pike, the controversial Episcopal bishop of northern California and Maren Hackett's current paramour.

It was strange that Pike would bless this marriage, since the laws of the Episcopal Church at that time were similar to Roman Catholic laws, and Phil's marriage to me had not been annulled even though there had been a legal divorce. But then Pike never did play by the rules of the church that had entrusted him with the office of bishop. In fact, he used his power in the church to promote his own idiosyncratic brand of "theology."

When Father Read at St. Columba's Church heard about this wedding, he wrote in the church records that Phil had excommunicated himself. Fr. Read, a student of church law, disliked Pike intensely, and felt this was the thing to do, but I am not sure his action was legal, either, since a subsequent vicar told me that the current bishop would have had to approve this action, and Pike never would have. What a day. At the same time in the afternoon, the beautiful white borzoi, Ollie, that I loved so, dropped dead at the veterinarian's. The office was located a block from the Baty house. The dog hadn't been sick.

Years later, I asked Nancy why she and Phil had come out to Point Reyes to my friend's house to get married. Innocently, she replied, "That was the only place where Phil could go. He was in such a nervous state he couldn't go to a stranger's."

Kirsten Nelson's relationship with Phil changed after he married Nancy. She said, "Phil stopped writing to me—in some ways, he was a proper and conventional person and he would've thought it was the wrong thing to continue his intimate relationship with me via mail. He had to go by the book."

In all the time he was married to Nancy, Phil never came to Point Reyes Station to see me or the girls; he continued to phone, although at longer and longer intervals.

For the next few years, the girls and I were very poor. We lived on about half the income we'd had. It was our "vegetable soup period." We made vats of soup with nine-cents-a-pound lamb shanks and ate it with powerful whole-wheat bread made from an Adelle Davis recipe. I lost my fear of being poor; we *were* poor and it turned out that it was fun to meet the challenge. We even entertained frequently, serving the excellent soup and bread. Even though I continued to feel depressed at times I kept active in various community activities. My youngest daughters, Tandy and Laura, and I sang in the chorus of a number of operas produced by the Inverness Music Festival. I became a member of the board. Tandy and I scraped up a down payment, bought two nice horses on the installment plan, and did some trail riding. Luckily, the horses could live on the grass growing in our field. At that time I slipped into the demanding sport of dressage and spent the rest of my riding life trying to do it right. Meanwhile, my friends, concerned for our little family, got together and redecorated my house. I had managed to turn the jewelry business into a means of support with no business experience and no capital. The girls did all the housework, laundry, cooking, and shopping, and babysat to earn the money for their clothes in order for me to have the time to make and sell handcrafted jewelry. My next-door neighbor, Henryetta Russell, came over to help me, became a dear friend, and remained with Anne Dick Jewelry for the next forty years. As we worked together in my tiny studio, she sympathetically listened to my tales of woe. She was there polishing jewelry that last time Phil came home.

Periodically, Phil would call up and say he was coming to visit, and the girls would look forward eagerly to his arrival, but then he would call again, halfway to our house, and say, "The dog got sick in the car, so I have to go back," or, "I had a flat tire; I can't make it." This happened six or seven times. Santa Venetia was only twenty miles away from Point Reyes Station, but it might as well have been a million light-years. Next, Phil started calling to say he was on his way to visit us but never came and didn't even phone to give an excuse. He did this four or five times and the girls finally gave up on him. But I wasn't able to turn my back on Phil or the relationship that we'd had. How can you turn your back on love? I couldn't understand the present situation, it didn't make sense. I decided that I had to leave the door to my (ex?) relationship with Phil open a crack but get on with my life. I became terrified of running into Phil and wouldn't even drive anywhere near Santa Venetia.

On March 17, 1967, a baby girl was born to Phil and Nancy. Phil sent me a photograph of the new baby. He named her Isolde but he and Nancy called her Isa. She grew into a lovely young woman whom I am very fond of. Back then it was another turning point. I still remained emotionally attached to Phil—but less so.

Nancy and Phil frequently visited Bishop James Pike and Maren Hackett, Nancy's stepmother, at the older couple's San Francisco apartment. Then Pike's older son committed suicide and Pike turned to spiritual mediums in his grief. Because Pike was an Episcopal bishop, this made headlines all over the country. Nancy and Phil took part in some of these séances. Many years later, Phil wrote about these events in his last novel, *The Transmigration of Timothy Archer*.

After James Pike was forced to resign as bishop under the threat of a heresy trial, he took an appointment at the Institute for Democratic Studies, a think tank at Santa Barbara. In June 1967, Phil and Nancy went to visit Pike and Maren Hackett. Nancy recalled that Philip and Pike joked about Pike's near ex-communication. Pike openly and frankly denied the doctrines of the virgin birth, the trinity, and the deity of Christ and told Philip and Nancy that he had a lot of support for his positions from various organizations both in and out of the church.

But wasn't he smart enough to realize that if you can't believe in these ancient events literally you can still believe in them as metaphors?

Nancy never saw Maren again after that last visit. Maren committed suicide a few weeks later. She had a recurrence of a cancer that she had suffered many years earlier and, in addition, her relationship with Pike was threatened by his interest in other women. Bishop Pike partially destroyed her suicide note. That story was on the front page of San Francisco newspapers, too.

Two years later, in 1969, Pike died in the Judean desert when he turned off a road, without extra water or gas, in an area where surface temperatures can rise to 140°F. He had gone to Israel with his new wife to prove that Jesus really wasn't an important part of the Christian tradition. At that same time, my oldest daughter, Hatte, was in Jerusalem studying for a Ph.D. in Arabic and linguistics and coincidentally was a friend of Scott, Pike's new young brother-in-law, who was also in Israel. They had met at the University of California at Santa Cruz.

When Phil and Nancy were living in Santa Venetia, Lynne Hudner became very good friends with Nancy. Lynne, who had become a psychiatric social worker, observed, "Phil and Nancy's relationship was not a marriage between two adults. Phil did not take any typical male role. There was little involvement and little fulfillment in that marriage. Phil was preoccupied with Nancy's symptoms and her illness. He played the role of 'all-knowing psychiatrist' with her, analyzing her actions, dreams, and speech in terms of her illness—confirming her illness. It wasn't comfortable for Nancy. She didn't like it."

Nancy described her marriage: "There was only a short happy period at the beginning. It wasn't really like a marriage; it was more like a couple of people rooming together."

Although Phil never made it out to Point Reyes to visit the children, he continued to phone me about every other month. He talked about REM sleep, which he had become very interested in. He told me about his problems with the IRS. He talked about his writing. He never mentioned his home life. Were those the phone calls portrayed in *Ubik* when Glen Runciter has a fading communication with his dead wife, Ella? I think they were.

Then, suddenly, Phil accused me of not letting the children visit him, although he had never invited them to visit. He wrote me an unbelievably hateful letter. Up until this time we had been conversing in a civilized way. There had been no change in our relationship that could explain this sudden change of mood.

I picked up a copy of *Counter-Clock World* at a book stand in 1967 and read it halfway through. I wondered if Phil had wanted time to go backward when he wrote that book. As I read, I realized that I didn't want to learn about Phil's new life and his relationship with Nancy and Anne. I threw the novel into the wastebasket and never read another novel of Phil's until after his death.

Alys Graveson came to my home in Point Reyes Station for an interview. She still lived in Inverness on the other side of Tomales Bay.

Alys, whom Phil had portrayed so well in *Martian Time-Slip*, visited him in Santa Venetia. She told me Phil "took pills to wake up and he took pills to go to sleep; he took Dexedrine, Benzedrine, and antidepressants. He had three doctors prescribing for him and went to six drugstores to fill the prescriptions. One of the doctors, a prominent ear-nose-and-throat doctor in San Rafael, was later tried and convicted for misusing his license to supply drugs to addicts."

Nancy said, "Philip took Stelazine, muscle relaxants, stomach relaxants, Valium, tranquilizers, and stimulants. He went to three doctors and six pharmacies. He took seventy pills a day. He was so personable and knew what symptoms to describe to get doctors to prescribe the pills he wanted. One of his doctors went to jail. When Philip left the area, he left huge unpaid pharmacy and doctor bills."

Phil bought some contaminated amphetamines from a street dealer and was seriously poisoned. He went to Marin General Hospital with acute pancreatitis. He remained severely ill and in acute pain for a long period of time and could eat only cottage cheese and fruit.

In 1968, Joe and Dorothy Hudner put a down payment on a house on Hacienda Way in Santa Venetia for Phil and Nancy. The house was registered in Dorothy and Joe's name. It was a well-kept small house with a nice lawn and garden. The interior was in beautiful condition. The house cost $19,000. Phil would make the $167 a month payment.

When Kirsten and Ray Nelson visited Phil and Nancy, Ray thought everything was lovely and everyone was in love with everyone else as he walked along the water of the bay with Nancy, wearing his muumuu (later he wore a propeller beanie). He would have liked to have an "intellectual romance" with Nancy as Phil had with Kirsten.

Phil told Kirsten that Irmgard and Pris, two of the android females in *Do Androids Dream of Electric Sheep?* were based on her, and the android, Roy, was based on Ray.

"In fact," Ray told me in 1983, smoothing his hair, "the actor playing the part of Roy...in Blade Runner *looked just like me."*

Kirsten told Phil about a dog attacking her rabbit and he put this episode in

Flow My Tears, the Policeman Said. He told Kirsten she was Emily, the lady in the bar and the owner of the rabbit.

Phil was having the same up-and-down mood swings that he had had earlier in Oakland. He fought with Nancy. At times he said he wanted to have all the young people hanging around committed. He often called the police.

Phil wrote to his old friend Carol Carr, wife of science fiction editor Terry Carr, on July 7, 1967:

I have many apologies to make to both you and Terry for some of the things I've said in recent letters. What has happened is that I (finally) have had a nervous breakdown....
I was mildly paranoid and hostile for several weeks...and then on Wednesday...my "borderline psychotic symptoms" became the real thing. The actual period of the full break lasted only half a day, because I took a good big dose of phenothiazines and made it over to see the Dr. It was an amazing experience. I came out of it feeling active and vigorous and even elated—because, I reasoned, I had met it head-on and licked it.... Want to hear about it? Good...I'll quote my notes made during the period:

"Saw the baby as a horrid vegetable—pulpy, like a mushroom growing up and then sinking back, again and again. Vivid horrible tastes and pain of a tri-geminal sort. Inability to spell words or to type. Loss of memory—found snuff tin mysteriously in kitchen cupboard. Lost important IRS documents which I had previously carefully assembled (they still haven't turned up). Had Nancy hide my gun. Bees in head. Helplessness. I couldn't cross the room; it was at this point much as if I had gotten thoroughly drunk... which is an acutely alarming experience if you haven't drunk anything.

I thoroughly enjoyed a dish of ice cream. My prolepsis factor (time sense) went out completely. Had no idea how long I had been doing something (this also like LSD).

Delusion that an alien outside force was controlling my mind and directing me to commit suicide. Hence I was not motivated to do so; in fact I was motivated to resist any suicidal urge...which may be nuttier than my previous suicidal depressions, but possibly from a pragmatic standpoint could be considered an improvement.

Couldn't tell from which direction sounds were coming, or how loud they were. Also like LSD. Acute terror while feeding the baby. Fluctuations throughout the day of terror, anger, and (deep) sexual yearning. The interesting thing, now that I look back on that day, is the amount I got done. At 9 a.m. a T-man [i.e., a cop from the Treasury Department] showed up and demanded the back taxes I owe. I reached a settlement with him. Later on, Sears Roebuck delivered our new air conditioner. In company with Nancy's brother, I uncrated it and installed it. I wrote to Bishop Pike. I visited the Dr. I got manic; I could read a whole newspaper article in one or two seconds. I managed to stay cheerful, for the most part, even though I felt demoralized at becoming overtly psychotic—without any idea how long it would last or how much worse it could get. The Dr. thought it was remarkable that in such a state I could deal with the T-man, since I fear them above all other life forms, Terran or otherwise...."

When Phil described these severe mental symptoms, was he kidding? Were they real? Or both? Later that year Phil threatened to sue Terry Carr for $75,000 because of a letter that Carr had printed in his fanzine, *Lighthouse*, that Phil thought was defamatory.

Lynne Hudner noted that Phil was depressed most of the time. Although, initially, Phil had taken care of Nancy, now she had come out of her withdrawal and depression and was taking care of him. Nancy called him "Fuzzy." It was like a mother-child relationship.

Old friends from Point Reyes visited Phil in Santa Venetia. Jerry Kresy went once; he could get no feeling of Nancy's personality. Pete Stevens said sadly, "It wasn't our Phil anymore," and never went again.

Phil continued seeing Dr. A during his marriage. Nancy remembered, "Dr. A was always telling Philip that there was nothing the matter with him."

Over the phone, Phil told me about a group-therapy session arranged by Dr. A that he had gone to. He had tried to express his hostility and anger at this session. After he got started he couldn't stop and went on and on for forty-five minutes. When he was through there was dead silence. No one said anything. Phil thought that everyone was too horrified by his hostility to be able to speak. He got up and left the room and never went back. Alys Graveson, who was also a member of this group, said, "No one ever said anything—it was a boring group."

One day Phil suddenly phoned and said that I had been vindictive and cruel toward him when I didn't give him the Baldwin Acrosonic spinet when we divorced.

"But you never asked for it," I said, matter-of-factly. I listened to him carry on about how I had deprived him of the spinet until finally when I could get a word in edgewise I said, "Give me your address and I'll send it over." He was astonished and quickly backed down. "No, no," he said.

Nancy told me, "He never stopped talking about you and the children. He really loved those children. I always thought that Philip and you would get together again some day. One day I told him angrily, 'Why don't you and Anne get back together?'" It became obvious to Nancy that I wanted Phil to come and see the children, although he would say I wouldn't allow him to. "But he was too emotionally ill to leave the house," she reflected.

Phil's depression, added to her own problems, created a burden of guilt and concern too great for Nancy to bear. Phil wouldn't leave the house and would feel incredibly anxious if she did. If she wanted to go to her sister, Anne's, for dinner she would feel she had to call him as soon as she got there and ask, "Fuzzy, are you all right?" He would say, "No," and she'd have to rush back home. She wanted to get a job at the post office but Phil couldn't bear to be alone during the day either.

Nancy had a nervous breakdown in 1969. She knew that she needed to go to the hospital. She kept asking Phil to take her but he waited and waited, "until it was almost too late." In the hospital she didn't want Phil to come and see her. She had a feeling of evil, not that Phil was evil, but that there was evil somewhere in the situation.

All this time I still had hopes that Phil would someday come back. I still thought about him and kept trying to figure out what had happened. I didn't know much about his way of life. I didn't realize that he had changed so much. But I finally realized that I couldn't go on like this. Although I was a typical church-going agnostic, I started calling on the name of God every time I started running the script about Phil through my mind again. When I tried to sleep at night and, instead, started thinking about Phil, I said, "God-God-God-God-God"—on and on and on. I didn't realize it at the time but I had created a mantra for myself. I did this for three months. Suddenly God answered. It was awesome. More real than anything I had ever experienced. Everything in my personal universe shifted. My whole life changed. Although my love for Phil didn't end, it went into some back compartment of my psyche. It was no longer an anguishing burden for me, no longer a part of my daily life. The next time Phil called me I told him, of course, all about it. He made fun of this experience of mine in one of his novels.

It wasn't much later, in the early fall of 1970, when Phil called me up and said, "Nancy's run off with the black guy who lives across the street."

"Oh?" I said. If he'd called me a few weeks earlier, I probably would have said something that would have started an exchange between us about resuming our relationship. As it was, I left the initiative up to him.

At any rate, Phil's fourth wife had left him and he began a new and even worse life.

Seven
THE SCANNER DARKLY YEARS

...and let me know how you like my new book, *A Scanner Darkly*. It is an autobiographical novel, and so I thought you might want to read it, since it describes a bad and sad time in your father's life...but it sure is one hell of a novel.

—Philip K. Dick, letter to our daughter, Laura, 1977

As I LEARNED about this period of Phil's life, I seriously contemplated abandoning my whole project. But then Phil had already written about it in his novel about the drug world from within, *A Scanner Darkly*, supposedly fiction. The names of the real participants in Phil's *Scanner* world have been changed in this chapter. After writing this book, I would see Cindy occasionally at her husband's convenience food store in Petaluma; then they divorced and I lost track of her. Sheila came down to Point Reyes Station to visit me once with her new baby and her pleasant husband. I was happy to see she had made a good life for herself.

In *A Scanner Darkly*, policeman Bob Arctor poses as a hard-core drug junkie. In the course of his undercover police investigations, he lives in a house with a bunch of junkies. At times he is back at the police station, observing the house through a police scanner, which is attached to the house. He observes his own gradual absorption into the drug world and his total deterioration from the large amounts of heavy drugs he is taking. Finally, his brain totally burned out, he becomes a vegetable, and is committed to New-Path, a rehabilitation center for ex-cons and junkies.

When Phil lived in Santa Venetia after Nancy left him, there was no longer any order in his household. He didn't take care of his mental or physical health and had only a panicky last-minute concern for financial matters. He couldn't stand to be alone and invited anyone who would to move in with him. Some pretty rough people, heavily involved with drugs, came. Phil phoned his stepsister Lynne to come over and shop and cook for him. He told her, "I can't go out, the CIA is after me."

For a while Lynne brought food and cooked for Phil, "But, as much as I wanted to help him, the scene there was just too much for me. I just couldn't go anymore, no matter how much he needed me. Phil was not himself. He was bizarre. He hit rock bottom at this time. I wasn't sure what was real and what wasn't. He wrote some nasty letters to Mom. The letters were so bad that Dorothy and Joe changed their wills and cut Phil out."

Kirsten and Ray Nelson didn't see much of Phil at this time either. Kirsten felt uncomfortable around the "motorcycle types" who were hanging around: "In the disturbed period of 1964–65, the people were science fiction people, they were groupies and did ridiculous things, but these people projected, 'I'd just as soon not know you.' One group of Phil's friends who lived nearby dealt in stolen goods: motorcycles, TV sets, and radios. If the hangers-around were there when Ray and I came to visit, we would leave."

Kirsten remembered that Phil called the police "three times a day." Phil told Kirsten melodramatic things about the people hanging around his place. Kirsten had no idea if what he said was true or not. Phil would call the Nelsons and Ray would drive over to Santa Venetia, pick Phil up, and bring him over to the Nelsons' house in Albany and then later take him back to Santa Venetia. Ray believed that the drugs Phil took didn't affect him much, that Phil was always on top of his drug situation.

Phil was still phoning me in Point Reyes, but he painted a picture of his life nothing like what the Nelsons were observing. I remember one phone call especially. While I was having a party at Christmas time, Phil called, and neglecting my guests, I talked with him for almost an hour. The conversation was warm and friendly. It never occurred to me to invite him over. I thought that if he wanted to see me he would let me know. Phil describes a conversation at Christmas time with a disagreeable ex-wife, Kathy, in *Galactic Pot-Healer*. His protagonist was very resentful that Kathy didn't invite him over on Christmas Day.

Grania Davis, formerly Grania Davidson, was in touch with Phil after Nancy left him. Grania had married a doctor, Steve Davis, and lived nearby in Sausalito. Grania remembered, "Phil liked Steve; Steve's a doctor, Phil's a hypochondriac."

Phil often called or came by at odd hours with an emergency, an anxiety attack, or a horrible personal or medical problem. But he told about them in

Philip K. Dick, sitting on patio bench, 1963.

Anne R. Dick, sitting on fench, back yard,
Point Reyes Station, 1959.

Hatte, Jayne, and Tandy Rubenstein
reading pop-up book, 1960.

Tandy and Hatte Rubenstein, patio,
Point Reyes Station, 1961.

Phil and Jayne, 1959.

Laura, 1963.

Phil with sheep, 1960.

Phil with cat, 1961.

a hilariously funny way—funny, but not cheerful. "He looked terrible, puffy, bleary-eyed."

Grania and Steve remained supportive when Phil started hanging around "with all those leather-jacketed hoodlum types in their late teens." But the Davises didn't want to go over to Phil's house in Santa Venetia. What disturbed Grania most was that all those "creepy-looking people were sitting around doing nothing. They weren't even having a party. They were just there in separate rooms." Phil told Grania that his hi-fi had been stolen, all his belongings rifled through. His Omega watch was taken. He told her that he thought the CIA was ripping him off.

After searching for a year I finally located Cindy D. (not her real name). She was warm and cordial over the telephone and took great interest in my project. We made an appointment to meet. On a peaceful, sunny afternoon, in a pleasant new subdivision in Petaluma, I walked by a Trans Am parked in the driveway and azaleas blooming along the walkway, and as I rang the bell, I noticed that the mailbox had been hand-painted in a floral design.

A robust, tall woman with long black curly hair answered the door. Cindy, now thirty-one years old, wore tight jeans, had a rich, bold voice, and was an animated talker. She wasn't afraid of saying anything. She introduced me to her Latino husband, George, and her seven-year-old boy. Cindy and George owned the 7-Eleven store a mile away from their house and Cindy also worked nights at Safeway to supplement the family income. Cindy told me her story and helped me get in touch with some of the other "kids" (now young adults) who were part of Phil's Scanner Darkly *world.*

Cindy and George, Sheila, Craig, Don, and I met one night at Cindy's house and sat drinking vodka and orange juice until 2 a.m. Each of them told me his or her story. Phil's novel, A Scanner Darkly *gave a picture of their world back then, they all agreed, except things were much worse than the novel described. The story that follows is not an exact account of what they told me. I made it less complicated and less disturbing.*

CINDY'S STORY

In 1970, Cindy, a seventeen-year-old high school girl, rode to Phil's house on the back of her boyfriend's motorcycle. John, a member of the Hell's Angels, was Phil's methedrine supplier. Cindy showed me a picture of her boyfriend on his Harley. He had on a black leather vest that showed his huge naked shoulders; there was a biceps cuff around his muscled upper arm. He had a large bushy beard and wore jeans and motorcycle boots. Cindy became friendly with Phil and came over to visit him more and more frequently. When she felt misunderstood by her parents, Phil listened with paternal sympathy. When she had an abortion in her junior year of high school, Phil drove her to the abortionist. She said that she, herself, never took money from Phil but she noticed that the other people who were hanging around his house were "ripping him off" all the time. Cindy worked at a local fish-and-chips restaurant. Someone living at Phil's house stole her key, entered the restaurant late at night, and stole all the money in the cash register. When Cindy met Phil, he was just finishing *Flow My Tears, the Policeman Said.*

Phil describes Cindy as a heroin addict in his letters but she told me that she "only smoked a little pot." Cindy and Sheila—who stayed at Phil's house later on—became the models for two female characters in *A Scanner Darkly.* One day, Cindy stole several cases of Coca-Cola from the back of a delivery truck and later on turned in the empty bottles for the deposit. Phil was intrigued and put this event in his novel.

Cindy told me, "He was taking a lot of speed. He would take a hundred 'beans' and then another hundred 'beans' an hour later. He would take a thousand 'beans' a week and write. Then he would crash and sleep for a week. He was grouchy, depressed, and irritable when he wasn't high. His doctor prescribed amphetamines for him when he couldn't buy them. Phil wouldn't touch pot, he hated it. He liked how he felt on speed—powerful—he could do anything. One time when Phil saw a police car drive by outside, he flushed a thousand 'beans' down the toilet. I was stunned, since they cost $100 a jar." Cindy remembered Phil hiding his "stash" under the plants outside the house because he thought the police might come. Later, when he'd decided they weren't going to, he would have to tear up the half the yard to find where he had buried it.

The Santa Venetia house was a "sort of paradise" for the unhappy, runaway kids that hung around there. There was "lots of pot, free drugs, beer, wine, imported Player's cigarettes, aqua filters, and little cans of different flavored snuff all over the house." The house was filled with rock music: Janis Joplin, the Sons of Champlin, the Quicksilver Messenger Service, Grace Slick, Hank Williams, and the Beatles, as well as Phil's classical music, which he played at such high volume that the walls shook. Phil bought a potter's wheel and made some pottery. Cindy and fifteen-year-old Craig worked on the wheel, too. There were several dogs and cats. Phil would fix Mr. Sims, a Yorkie that Nancy had owned, Alpo with chocolate sauce over it. There was a black Lab, and Mary Lou's black and white puppy. One day Phil gave one of the cats a "bean" and the cat cried for hours under the coffee table.

Phil had a couple of girlfriends who came over occasionally and spent the night. One was Carla, who had met Phil when he gave a lecture at the College of Marin. James, a relative, lived with Phil for a while. Once he almost died of a drug reaction like Jerry in *A Scanner Darkly*. After James moved out, Clint and Sean, who had just been released from the state mental hospital, moved in. Both are dead now. Each lived in the Santa Venetia house with a girlfriend. Clint's first girlfriend was Karen, whom he later replaced with Sheila.

A musician named Jim played the bass guitar and sang while living in Phil's house with his girlfriend, Mary Lou, who went to San Rafael High. Jim rode a motorcycle and shot heroin. At times, he and Mary Lou had violent fights. Both Jim and Phil had guns and were always playing around with them; once Phil shot a hole in the window. Several times Phil became angry with Mary Lou and threw her bodily out the door and her things after her. The next day, he would phone, begging her to return.

A few years later Phil told his Los Angeles friends about a girl of Japanese origin suddenly pulling out a jackknife, leaping on a man who was lying on the couch, and knifing him in the chest. The knife went all the way in to the hilt, but didn't hit anything vital.

Other hangers-on included eleven-year-old Sam (Ratty), Craig's brother; another Clint, a drug addict, ex-thief, and Jesus freak; Shirley and Jimmy, who lived in a parked car in front of the house; and Vic, a guy from the Haight-Ashbury, with wild, blond curly hair and no shoes, who, at times, slept on one of the beaches. He did acid or whatever was around and told the other kids that he had seen God.

DON

It was well after midnight and we had almost finished all the potato chips and the vodka when Don made his entrance. He was a nice-looking, blond man of about thirty. His eyes glittered. He told me he was a carpenter now. Not long after we were introduced he pulled up his shirt and showed me a beautifully done eagle tattoo that covered most of his upper back. Like Sheila, an attractive blonde woman of about the same age, he had the aura of a survivor of some long-ago cataclysm.

In 1971, Don was known as "the kid." He was a fifteen-year-old runaway with long, long hair, who had just come out of juvenile hall. "I felt like a little ragamuffin and hid when Phil's science fiction and literary friends came over with their ties on."

Phil told Don, "The more company I have, the safer I feel." The most amazing thing to Don was how Phil would change when his science fiction friends came by: "He acted totally straight."

Don remembered long, heavy political discussions, Phil telling the kids that he didn't like most of what went on in the country: "He put things into words so that we young kids could understand. Then sometimes he would speak in other languages. When the book *Helter Skelter* came out, we all had a big discussion about Manson and his 'family.' Phil wanted this sort of relationship but without the crime."

When Don first moved into the house, Phil's office was immaculate. Phil would lock himself in to write. Later Don saw Phil flying into fits of rage, taking books off the shelves, and throwing them, picking up plants, and knocking over the speakers. Don hid behind the couch or a chair. He couldn't understand what Phil was saying, Phil was talking so fast. In the middle of one topic, he would switch to another. Don thought that Phil would let his emotions build up and then they would explode.

Don liked and admired Clint. Clint was handsome, with blue-black hair and dark eyes and skin. He was an excellent mechanic and repaired Phil's car for him. But he began to tinker and "do weird things" with the car. He fixed the brakes before a trip to Mount Tam. The brakes failed and the whole crowd almost got killed as they came down the mountain. Clint was a genius at electronics. He played the guitar, the harmonica, drums, and "did vocals." He took a lot of speed, so much that he thought spiders were crawling on him and asked Don to spray Raid on him. At times, Clint picked imaginary bugs off the carpet. He thought a shoe box in the hall closet was full of bugs. Phil and Clint were close. But one day Phil put sand in the rug and sprayed Clint with hair spray. The sand stuck to the hair spray and Clint freaked out about the bugs crawling on him. Don couldn't understand why Phil had done this, because Phil knew that Clint was terrified of insects. Once Clint took a hundred hits, and, barefooted and shirtless, drove his car down the freeway. His lips began to crack and bleed from the drug overdose. Phil and Clint were both "doing so much methedrine they were hallucinating."

Don noticed that some days Phil was normal; some days he was in a dream; some days he was flipped out. Don bought one hundred methedrine pills from Phil. "How much should I pay you?" he asked. Phil told Don, "$2." Don gave him $4. The next day Phil burned the money. Clint went back home to live with his parents. A few days later Richard, his brother, found him in the bathroom with his wrists slashed, lying in a pool of blood but still alive. He had become involved in an unhappy love affair with a girl named Laura May, who had been sent to a drug-rehabilitation home. After this terrible event, Clint still hung around Phil's house but didn't live there anymore. Don read in the papers a few years later that Clint had killed himself in the Civic Center parking lot, running a hose from the exhaust pipe into his car at 3 a.m. one morning.

SEAN

Sean had scary, wild eyes, an aquiline nose, was about five feet nine inches tall and very thin. He was a speed freak, too. Sean shot invisible bugs at Clint and Clint put them in a box. Cindy thought that Sean was crazy but not violent. His parents had kicked him out of their house when he began taking drugs. Sean was in his mid-thirties and had never been married. He fidgeted a lot. Phil would send him away for a couple of days and then allow him to come back. His parents owned a large amount of land in Ignacio, and, after visiting them he'd come back with wads of money.

When Sean moved in, he brought fifteen rifles, all loaded and cocked, and hid them under his bed. Secretly, Phil and Don took all the ammunition out of the guns. Sean bought more, so Phil and Don took out the firing pins. Sean and Phil were in agreement that the FBI and the CIA were observing the house.

SHEILA

Sheila was the last person to tell her story that evening. She had run away from home and at San Rafael High another student had told her, "Oh, you can live at Phil's house." At that time Clint was just breaking up with Karen. Sheila fell in love with Clint and soon was sharing his room. Sheila noted that everyone at that house was moody. Often Phil and Clint would be angry and in a "leave me alone" mood.

Sheila watched Phil consult the *I Ching* every morning. Phil went on and on about how he hated the IRS because it had attached his bank account: "Phil did a lot of talking—sometimes incoherent talking—a lot of the time I didn't listen." One day, a science fiction writer from Finland came to see Phil, and Phil pulled himself together and had an intelligent conversation with this fellow.

Phil worried all the time about money. He would wait and wait for a check from his agent, and then, when it came, splurge and spend it all in a week. He would give money away and then be worried sick about making the house payments. Then he would get angry at his roommates, call the cops, and send them away. At other times, he bought food and clothes for everyone. He bought Cindy, Sam, and Clint leather jackets. He bought Sheila and Mary Lou clothes in Northgate, a nice Marin County shopping area. Phil himself had hardly any clothes. He wore a paisley Nehru tunic most of the time. One day while he was driving along Fourth Street in San Rafael, he saw a powder-blue Pontiac Catalina ragtop in beautiful condition at a used car lot. He stopped and bought it, paying cash.

Sheila noticed that Phil was afraid of his roommates. He thought someone was going to steal his Hugo Award and took it off the wall, where it had been prominently displayed, and hid it.

One Friday Nancy brought Isa to visit for the weekend. The next day over the phone, Nancy and Phil had a fight, and Nancy came and picked up Isa early. Phil cried after they left. Phil told Sheila that he was still in love with Nancy and hoped that she would return. Phil worried about Isa. Would she forget him? Then Phil told Nancy he was going to sue for custody of Isa. After he had threatened to do this, he became afraid that Nancy's boyfriend was going to kill him. Phil called three guys who he claimed were contract killers. They came over to the house with shotguns and sat in the house ready to shoot anything that moved.

Sheila got a black Labrador puppy from the pound while the contract killers sat in Phil's house with their guns ready. Sheila and Phil didn't sleep for the next three days. Then, exhausted, Sheila slept for eighteen hours. Phil was still up and tried to wake Sheila up so she could feed the dog. She was difficult to awaken. Then Phil told Sheila that he was going to kill the dog with a hatchet.

She began crying and carrying on. She became so upset that Phil took her to see his psychiatrist. After she had told the psychiatrist her story, he said, "I've known Phil for a long time. You should get out of there as soon as possible." But she had no place to go.

Neil Hudner, Phil's stepbrother, visited Phil, who showed Neil the plaster dust that was all that remained of one of Joe Hudner's sculptures. Neil loved his father and was proud of his work. The sculpture had been wedged in the door, Phil told Neil, when his house had been raided by pushers who wanted money for drugs they had sold to Phil and his roommates. Shots were fired through the windows. Phil showed Neil a bullet hole. Phil and his roommates barricaded the door with Joe's plaster sculpture and called the police. When the police arrived they pretended that the problem was in the house and broke down the door, destroying the sculpture. Phil told Neil that he had to talk fast to the police to keep himself out of jail. His friends were taken to jail because drugs were found in the house. Before Neil left, Phil showed him a letter he had received from the Pentagon, thanking him for an idea for an automated battlefield. From the way Neil told me all this I gathered that he believed this entire story.

Sheila stayed after Clint moved out. She had no money, nowhere to go, and it was out of the question for her to return to her parents. Phil told her that he wanted to marry her, live happily ever after, and have babies with her, but Sheila wasn't interested. Phil was old enough to be her father. She arranged to be rescued by a fellow she knew, but Phil prevented her from taking her clothes and she ended up coming back to the Santa Venetia house.

When he was at home, Phil generally ate chocolate, cookies, and junk food, but frequently he and Sheila went out to eat at a nice restaurant close by, Le Chalet Basque. They also often went to Lyons, a chain restaurant on the freeway, for breakfast. One night after going to Chalet Basque for dinner, Sheila, Phil, and another young man, Rick, brought a bottle of Beaujolais back to the house. During the evening, Rick asked Sheila to come away with him. Phil threw the bottle, the remains of the Beaujolais, two glasses, and the coffee table against the wall and then picked up a metal chair and threatened Sheila.

In the summer of 1971, Phil suddenly arrived at my house one afternoon accompanied by a teenage girl whom he introduced as Sheila. (That evening my second daughter, Jayne, told me that the girl was a classmate of hers at San Rafael High.) I hadn't seen Phil for five years. Both he and this girl looked terrible. His skin was sallow and sagging; his clothes looked as if they hadn't been washed for weeks. They were both shabby. I assumed the girl was Phil's girlfriend and was disturbed to see him with such a young girl. Phil's manner was as pleasant as ever. I made a pot of tea and gave them each a cup and we sat and chatted for a while—they didn't stay long. I formed an even worse impression of Phil's life than earlier but still didn't really get the picture. I still had in my mind the image of the man I had loved. It was confusing but by then I wasn't as involved with Phil and so I didn't dwell on all this very long. I was very busy with all my activities, including a new one, a dressage group that came to my house for three days every month to take lessons with a famous dressage maestro.

Strange things began happening at Phil's house. Someone cut all the wires in the Bogen amplifier. Everyone wondered who it was? Was it Clint? Was it Phil himself? Phil told everyone the postman had done it. Clint put the amplifier back together. Next all the doorknobs were stolen. These events made Sheila very nervous; she thought, "Boy, I better get out of here."

In August 1971, Phil went to see Dr. A, who saw that Phil was in terrible shape. Phil told Dr. A that he believed that the FBI and the CIA were tapping his phone, breaking into his house, and stealing his papers. He told Dr. A he wanted to go to the hospital for protection. Dr. A told Phil he should get rid of all the young unstable people hanging around his house. Phil told him, "I know I should, but they need me."

Dr. A arranged for Phil to enter the Marin Mental Health Clinic. Although Phil kept telling Dr. A he was a drug addict, Dr. A believed Phil was just being hypochondriacal. He observed Phil in the hospital and noted that Phil had no withdrawal symptoms. This verified his conclusion. When I told Cindy this she said emphatically, "Phil carried his 'beans' with him wherever he went."

Phil charmed the staff, advised them how they should run the facility and tried to help the other patients. William Wolfson, Phil's old friend and lawyer, visited him in the hospital and held his hand. He saw that Phil's manner was tremendously rational and cogent, but at the same time Phil told stories about people who were trying to kill him. Phil acquired a new lady friend, a nice-looking blonde lady who was a patient, too. She lived in Ross, an expensive part of Marin County, and had a swimming pool painted the color of Lake Tahoe. After they both got out of the hospital she came over to Phil's house every day. Sheila thought she was in love with Phil but she was also very nervous.

A short time after Phil got home he answered the phone, but there was only silence and a click. Sean had recently moved out, and Phil told Sheila, "Sean is going to kill me tonight." He got out a hatchet and hammer and told her, "Sean is going to kill you, too." Both of them hid in the back bedroom, terrified at hearing noises, and ate "beans" to keep their spirits up. Phil said, "I've got to get help," and called two black guys, Luke and Matthew, members of a paramilitary organization, and who lived in the neighborhood, to protect them. Luke and Matthew wanted $600 a day. Phil asked his lady friend to help him. She came over to Phil's house with a "bunch" of gold coins and gave them to Phil. Phil gave Sheila one of the coins. When later she cashed it she found it was worth $20. Phil gave the rest of the gold coins to Luke and Matthew. They took them and went back to their own house, telling Phil, "Call us if you have any trouble."

Sheila continued to resist Phil's overtures. Once, Phil threw a chair. Sheila told him, "Go ahead and kill me." Phil went in his room and cried. Then Phil began telling Sheila that she was addicted to heroin. "Yes," Sheila replied, "I am addicted to heroin. I'm going to go and get treatment." She went to Marin Open House, a treatment facility, and said that she was a heroin addict so that she could be admitted.

Phil phoned William Wolfson and asked him to come over. When he got there, William didn't want to go in the house: "The shades were drawn, the grass was mostly mud, the house smelled musty. I felt uncomfortable there." Phil gave Bill the manuscript of *Flow My Tears, the Policeman Said* to keep for him. He was afraid it would be stolen or destroyed.

When Grania and Steve Davis came over to see Phil, he took them on a tour of his house. He told them, "This is my dead lawn. Do you want to see my garden?" He took them across the lawn and said, "This is my dead tree." He took them to another spot in the yard "This is my dead bush. I'm afraid pretty soon the unwelcome wagon is coming for me."

Phil didn't make the payments on the house, and the Co-Op Credit Union called Joe Hudner and told him that they were foreclosing on the loan. Joe had a heart attack and died. The family felt that Phil had killed Joe. Dorothy prevented Neil from saying anything to Phil. She felt that such an accusation would finish Phil off, he was at such a low point.

Phil went to a clinic south of San Francisco for treatment for drug addiction. When he was released he was able to cut down significantly on the amount of methedrine he took.

That fall, Phil came to visit us in Point Reyes Station. As soon as he walked in the door, he went into my workshop to see if the workbench he had made for me was still there. He seemed relieved that it was. I assumed that he had come to see Laura, but Laura only stayed around for a few minutes, and then ran outside to play with a friend. Phil sat on the couch and burst into tears, and as usual I didn't know what to say. I stood in the doorway between the kitchen and the living room and said, "I'm terribly sorry that you're so upset."

Phil replied, "The fact that you care means more to me than anything in the world." I continued standing there. Nothing more came to me to say or do than to say again, "I'm terribly sorry that you feel so upset." At that point, Phil smiled, wiped his eyes, got up, and walked out of the house. I watched out the window as he got in his car and drove off.

I still loved him, but I didn't know how to say, "Look, Phil, I wish you'd get your life together and who knows...." I was afraid, too—afraid to have him around the children, afraid of his lifestyle, afraid of his tendency to act in bizarre and unexpected ways.

In January, Phil received a letter inviting him to Vancouver, Canada, to be the keynote speaker at the V-Con, the science fiction convention held there in February 1972. He asked Cindy to go with him and bought her an airplane ticket. A few weeks before Cindy and Phil were to leave, Cindy came by to visit and found that "the whole study was torn apart, all the papers were out of the file cabinet and strewn all over the floor. Phil was striding around with a loaded shotgun as though someone else had done it. The window was broken; there was a hole in the wall." Cindy said, "Clint told me, 'Phil did it.' But Clint could have done it, too."

Ray Nelson had a strong belief that the safe had been bombed by drug dealers that Phil owed a great deal of money to. *Rolling Stone* later published a famous story about this incident.

Professor Willis McNelly, a science fiction scholar and head of the English Department at California State University at Fullerton, came by to visit Phil a week later. Nothing had been cleaned up or repaired. Windows were broken and paper litter and bits of towel were everywhere. Phil told Professor McNelly that the house had been bombed. He said that a wet towel had been wrapped around his files to dull the effect of the plastic bomb. Phil believed that the FBI had done this because he had inadvertently written about a secret weapon in one of his novels. He had picked up the information telepathically.

Cindy's parents were upset at the idea of Cindy leaving town with a man old enough to be her father. She decided that she didn't want to go, turned in her ticket, and bought some clothes with the money. She told Phil, "Someday, I'm going to move north to Oregon and live in the snow. I'm going to shovel snow off the front walk every morning and have a little house and a garden with vegetables. Mr. Right will come along and get it for me."

After Phil left for Canada, the house in Santa Venetia went into foreclosure. Phil's mother came and packed up all the papers and what was left of Phil's personal possessions and stored them for him.

Eight
THE VANCOUVER SCIENCE FICTION
CONVENTION

Suddenly I looked up and saw, through the glass side of the house, a horse coming at me, head on, driven by a rider; it was virtually on me, about to shatter the glass. I've never seen or dreamed such an animal before: its thin body, elongated, pumping legs, goggling eyes—like a racehorse, swift and furious and silent it came at me, and then it leaped up to hurdle the house.

—Philip K. Dick, letter to Dorothy Hudner, 1972

PHIL WENT OFF to Vancouver alone. Two days before the V-Con in February 1972, Phil gave a speech at the University of British Columbia. It was received with cheers and a standing ovation. Phil told his new friend Mike Bailey that the reception he received from this appreciative audience helped his mental state a great deal. He decided to stay in British Columbia.

It was hard to find anyone who had known Phil during his stay in Vancouver, January to March 1972. Phil's letters to me from there were friendly and upbeat letters giving the impression that things were going well in his life, and to my chagrin, mentioning various new girlfriends. I didn't answer. I knew nothing about his attempted suicide or his stay at X-Kalay, a rehab facility in Vancouver similar to Synanon.

It took a lot of phoning before I could find anyone who had known Phil during the two months he was there. Professor Willis McNelly of the California State University at Fullerton had given me a Xerox of a letter Phil had written him from X-Kalay. I called Vancouver information to see if I could find any of the people listed on the letterhead. Not a single one was in the phone company's records and X-Kalay no longer existed. It seemed as if the people who had been involved in it had also vanished into thin air. I called science fiction writer Poul Anderson for a lead, knowing that he went to many sci-fi conventions. He gave me the name of a fan in Seattle who "may have gone to V-Con II." I called F. M. Busby and, although he hadn't gone to that particular convention, he thought he knew someone who had, a fan named Francine. Although Francine hadn't gone to V-Con II either, she had heard the legendary stories about Phil's visit and knew that a Mike Bailey, a newsman in Vancouver, had shown him around the town. I finally found Mike through information. We had a great talk. He gave me the name and phone number of Michael and Susan Walsh. The Walshes were a gold mine.

Mike observed that "Phil was very quick to answer people, and he turned a lot of people off, but he handled himself well, considering he was taking menthol nose drops with amphetamines in them." Phil told Mike, "I'm going to die." He was forty-four years old at this time. Mike was concerned about a girl named Jamis, who was "hanging on Phil and bleeding him" and had another boyfriend. Mike and other new friends of Phil's "got rid of her"—they thought.

Phil wrote his mother about his "mad love" for Jamis, this:

…little dark-haired hippy girl…who eats nothing but peanut butter sandwiches and wants to leave her body and fly to Mars…. She rapped to me for hours about Philosophy and God and flying saucers and the esoteric wisdom of the ancient Egyptians…. [Up in Vancouver] I was happy at first, as you know, and then I've gotten progressively more and more unhappy…. Everything everyone has done…didn't fill in the void…. I decided to give up and go back to the States. I missed Cindy too much; it constellated around her…. It's been a day-to-day struggle to keep from succumbing psychologically. But now, all at once, Jamis…is back…. I was just looking for a place to take her where we could sit and talk…. The image I have followed has been all my life the image of Jamis…. [O]n Friday night a beautiful dream came into existence; Jamis and I flashed on each other, and for the first time in my life I got it all together. But it is a beautiful dream that I wish would pass…. Despite the fact that, after I got home here Friday night after leaving Jamis off at her place, I knew I'd for the first time finally found what Faust found: that which he did not want to see pass in favor of something else. But God, what a tragedy. My pain ended. The void inside me, the ache, was gone. But—at what a price? Because it is going to kill little Jamis. It is all wrong for her.

That night, Friday night, about 5 a.m., I had a dream not like any other I'd ever had. I was back in West Marin, in the big glass-walled living room, with friends and animals and children. Suddenly I looked up and saw, through the glass side of the house, a horse coming at me, head on, driven by a rider; it was virtually on me, about to shatter the glass. I've never seen or dreamed such an animal before: its thin body, elongated, pumping legs, goggling eyes—like a racehorse, swift and furious and silent it came at me, and then it leaped up to hurdle the house. I ducked. Too late to escape; I crouch down, waiting for it to crash onto the roof above me and collapse the house. Impossible for it to clear. But it did. No crash. No collapse. The horse had cleared. I ran out front, knowing it must have hit dirt cataclysmically. There it was, thrashing in the mud and foliage, broken and mutilated, horrible…it would have to be destroyed…. I was okay. Intact. Safe. It, the great soaring, pulsing life-force, had expended itself in one mighty last effort, and perished in chaos and ruin and thrashing debris…. It was like the dream said this: the moment of Truth you have waited for all your life, the great ultimate contest or test or day of revelation, came just now; you got by, you survived. Everything else perished, though…. True, the horse did not try to vault the house in order to spare me; it did not even notice me. I just happened to be there. The house, not me—that was what the horse tried to—and succeeded in—leaping…. I am that broken horse.

Phil was the giant destructive horse about to run into the glass-walled house and also the man inside. The horse jumped over the house instead of crashing into it, saving the house but destroying itself.

While staying at the Biltmore Hotel where V-Con II was being held, Phil met Michael and Susan Walsh. They invited him to stay with them at their apartment. Susan "couldn't help but immediately notice the massive mood shifts that Phil exhibited—hideous troughs of feeling—he told me that his body manufactured drugs that affected his mind the same way as amphetamines."

Michael, Susan's husband, thought that Phil was playing for effect, that Phil wanted to test out how gullible people were. Michael, a phlegmatic person, "valued personal privacy and intended to give others a great deal of it. I didn't pry into Phil's affairs. I didn't even ask further when Phil said that he had been in fear of his life in San Rafael." Phil couldn't needle Michael, either. Michael saw that there was a lot of testing behavior going on. Phil was afraid of revealing too much of himself—Phil saw conspiracy all around him.

Susan found Phil to be intense, needing to be the center of everything. He was exhausting: "I recall him as a bearlike presence hunched into a ratty trench coat, sort of like Sam Spade. He took menthol snuff continually. I couldn't tell when he was telling the truth—even when I knew it was truth, it had so much else mixed in with it. Often his conversation seemed to be based on finding the other person's weak spot. He could have a person in a screaming rage within ten minutes. He would save up information on a person's weak spots to needle him with later on. A friend of ours, Mary, got into a van that Phil happened to be riding in. Out of the blue, Phil started telling her bad things about us. Later, Mary asked me about the matters Phil had told her about. Nothing like what he'd described had happened at all. His version of events was often quite different from those of other participants."

Susan remembered Jamis, all right. Phil gave Jamis Susan's copy of *The Three Stigmata of Palmer Eldritch*. Susan began laughing as she told a story about Phil and a Kirby vacuum-cleaner demonstrator who had made an appointment to come to her apartment. "You're not having a demonstration by one of those high-pressure salesman," Phil said. "Yes," Susan said, "it will be a three-hour demonstration." "Okay," Phil told the Walshes, "let's have some fun. Michael, I'm your brother-in-law, a writer who is sponging off you and Susan. You, Michael, are Mickey, a husband too cheap to buy the vacuum cleaner. That's the scenario. I'll try to draw you into a family argument, because I think you should buy my sister this vacuum cleaner. We'll get the salesman into the argument."

The vacuum-cleaner salesman, whose name was Frank Noseworthy, proceeded to demonstrate the vacuum cleaner. Phil chatted with Frank, "South Pasadena is my favorite city," while Frank dumped little papers of dust throughout the apartment and proceeded to vacuum them up. Phil chatted on, "I wanted my other brother, Bill, who drives a bus, to drive me out from Chicago, but those city buses can't make the trip." Picking up the sweeper and examining it, he remarked, "My ex-wife used to have one of these. She insisted that she get it in the divorce settlement."

By this time the Walshes were smothering apoplectic laughter and couldn't even stay in the room. Meanwhile, Frank Noseworthy was vacuuming the mattress, exhibiting the vacuum cleaner with a bench grinder and polisher attachment, and polishing Susan's wedding ring.

"How much is this vacuum cleaner?" Phil asked. "$800," Frank Noseworthy replied. Phil couldn't get Frank into a family argument, although he kept needling Michael about buying this vacuum for "Sis." Then he said, "Isn't it wonderful to think that in hundreds of years we'll all be dust, but that this Kirby will still be in working condition?" Then he said something about vacuuming up a can of eight-legged bugs.

Frank Noseworthy became more and more disaffected. Finally, when

Michael said that he would not buy the vacuum cleaner, Frank huffily packed up all of his equipment and left, saying, "Well, if you want to continue living in these conditions...."

Michael had a record of Marshall McLuhan's, *The Medium Is the Message*, with multiple sound channels. On it McLuhan presents his material with illustrations: music, sex, little girl's voices, etc. It's a James Joycean sort of thing, an incoherent cacophony of sound. When Michael played it for Phil, Phil clapped his hands over his ears and screamed, "Turn it off. Turn it off. It sounds like the inside of my head when I go mad and have to go to the hospital."

After Phil had stayed with the Walshes for two weeks, he started picking on Michael in an area where Michael was sensitive. He told Michael that he was a bad husband and that he, Phil, was going to take Susan away and make her happy. After listening to this for a couple of days, Michael became angry and kicked Phil out of the apartment.

Phil found another place to live. Then he phoned Susan and said, "I'm going to turn out the lights." Susan couldn't imagine what Phil was talking about and soon hung up on him. But Phil *had* taken a lethal dose of some kind of pill and actually was on his way out. However, he had written the number of the suicide prevention squad on a small piece of paper and put it in front of the phone in case he changed his mind. He did change his mind and called them, and they came and took him to the hospital and saved his life. When Michael and Susan Walsh came to see him, he told them, "I was committing suicide, you didn't care, you didn't come over, you didn't do anything about it."

Phil signed himself into X-Kalay, a self-help organization inspired by Synanon and inhabited by ex-convicts and ex-drug addicts. Michael Walsh later wondered cynically, "Was the suicide attempt only to get into X-Kalay for material to write a novel?"

Susan and Michael visited Phil in X-Kalay. Phil was wearing a ski jacket and looked strange to them, after his trench-coat persona. The doors were locked and some X-Kalay people stayed in the room during the entire visit. Phil, still of the opinion that the Walshes had failed him, was cold.

Michael Walsh found the ex-head of X-Kalay, Dave Berner, for me. Dave had a talk program on Station CJOR across the street from the Province, *the newspaper where Michael Walsh worked. I interviewed Dave Berner by telephone. In exchange he interviewed me, live, the next day for his program.*

David Berner told me, "X-Kalay means 'the unknown path.' Phil came out of nowhere and went back to nowhere. When I first saw him, he looked like a burnt-out middle-age drunk. He shook, he was thin, his skin was blotchy. He told me that he was a writer. 'You're not a writer,' I told him. 'Whatever you did before to get yourself in here, you're not going to do again. You're going to wash dishes and mop floors.' Phil's imagination was wild. In the games, he was bugged and haunted by monsters he'd made a long time ago. After he had been with us thirty days, he came to me again and said, 'I really am a writer,' and volunteered to write for X-Kalay. Altogether, he stayed at X-Kalay for three months. Later, I saw his novels at a bookstand. 'Is that that nut burger?' I thought."

During the entire time Phil was staying in Vancouver he wrote me friendly, upbeat letters, giving me the impression that he was having a good life in Canada, and, to my chagrin, mentioning various new girlfriends. I didn't answer. He told me nothing about his attempted suicide or his stay at X-Kalay.

In March 1972, Phil wrote Professor McNelly in Fullerton:

Well, it happened. I flipped out. Grief, loneliness, despair, the alienation of being in a strange country in an unfamiliar city, knowing virtually no one and at the same time…being so dependent on those few people I met here…. [A]nyhow, the X-Kalay people stepped in and have begun putting the pieces back together. Into something else, they tell me. Something that has a better chance of survival. Without them I wouldn't be alive now. It's hard to get into X-Kalay and easy to get out. I don't really know what happened. It started back in San Rafael several months ago at least, possibly longer. With effort I can sort of remember. But perhaps it's better if I don't; remembering serves no useful purpose. "Our pasts have been written and cannot be erased," the X-Kalay Philosophy says. "Therefore we must work for today with a vision of tomorrow." That's what I'm doing.

And in a later letter to McNelly:

I want to go back [to San Rafael], even though, really I can't. My house is gone, and, god forbid, all my stuff has been shipped off, without my knowledge or permission, and stored. All I have is what I brought with me to Vancouver in one small suitcase, just a few clothes. My books, MSS, typewriter—everything either thrown away by the realtor, or stored some-where. In my absence my senile old mother gave the realtor permission…. It was all done without my knowledge, as soon as I informed my mother I was remaining in Canada. Mothers should be towed out to sea and sunk. As a health hazard, like lead in the atmosphere.

What is it about s-f writers that so turns off the establishment, and also the criminals of the gutter? We are universally distrusted. As Cindy told me once, "It's because they can't figure you out; you're an unusual person." I asked her what she personally thought of me. "You're a great man," she said. "And you're kind. Hey, can you lend me two bucks for a bottle of vodka so I can take it to the drive-in movie and turn on while we watch *The Planet of the Apes*?" .... Without Cindy, the death that I feared, the death she has shielded me from, seems to be coming. But I worry about her. It's Cindy who matters, as far as I'm concerned.

Phil wrote Cindy back in San Rafael: "I'm afraid I won't ever see you again, Cindy. Have a happy life. I'll never forget you, Cindy. You were the best, the dearest, the prettiest."

Phil must have been in contact with the girl Jamis while he was in X-Kalay, because he writes in a letter to an unknown person:

Jamis is the rational one and I'm the dingbat.... Maybe the gulf I sense between us is because I'm so spaced. "You really get down over nothing," she said to me last night. Right on.... Somehow, Jamis embodies all I've lost, the whole past that's over, and in clinging to her—and constantly feeling myself losing her—I'm clinging onto something that is gone, ought to be gone, which I just can't let go of. I can't really lock myself into the present as long as I'm involved with her. She's not here, with me, now; she's gone, in the past, there, not with me, lost forever, never to be found or seen again. She's the rock, drug, hippy, kid, California culture I've got to cut loose from and let die and leave me. The unresolved conflicts, issues, feelings, and involvements of the past are still being thrashed out within the context of my relationship with her. It should just end, everybody thinks, but maybe it's got to be worked through and out, not ended; otherwise it'll just resume with someone else.

This enormous hostility that I feel is probably the primary hostility that underlay my depression which in turn led to my suicide attempt. I am mad at everyone and everything. So the X-Kalay game is working. Their analysis is that I'm possessive, that I want a chick to be MY chick and not independent. This is not true.

From X-Kalay on April 4, 1972, Phil wrote Willis McNelly's wife, Sue:

I'm doing a lot better now. The ache inside me has virtually dimmed-out. Due mainly to the people I've been living with, here at X-Kalay. The furies are no longer driving me....

[I]n some ways the lessons in toughness that I'm learning here are perhaps not such a good thing. I don't suffer, because I am ceasing to care. It's easier on me, but is this really the solution? I feel like they're burning out a part of my brain, the part that listens to the heartbeat of my brothers.

"Wait'll I get you in a game," one woman said to me. "I'll reveal your real nature. I'll show everyone what you're really like, under the lies." There is an assumption, possibly false, certainly metaphysical, that there is a "real" hidden, authentic personality hidden within and behind the false fronts of each of us....

"Lizard-eyed and liver-lipped" is the way I describe the faces here; cold and amused, mocking, detached, efficient.

And in a later letter to an unknown person:

I am leaving X-Kalay on Thursday.... Gradually, over the last week, person after person has left, and in a few days I will be going. There are many negative elements here that cause me to want to go, but basically I'm leaving because there is something better—I think—that I'll be going to. If I'm wrong, I'll come back. Really, though, if I were to pinpoint the elements here that have driven me off, I'd say that the enthusiasm, the energy, the excitement, the plans I had about doing things with X-Kalay have been killed off by X-Kalay itself.... I think my two basic plans were good: the point is that for over a year I have had no plans, no goals, and now, with X-Kalay's help, I got myself together and did look forward, did have ideas I wanted to put into action—and at that point X-Kalay said, in effect, "No, you are not here for that. We are not doing that. Mind your own business; take orders and be quiet." Initiative and inventiveness are discouraged, but not merely in the usual bureaucratic sense; what I bitterly resent is the use of the game, the encounter therapy sessions, brought into play as a method—THE method—by which actions on my part and on the part of others that do not conform to the group's standards and views are zapped out of existence, zapped out before they can take place, by the effective technique of wiping out the individual's faith in those proposed actions and ultimately in himself as the inventor of the actions.... But I have a viable alternative elsewhere that I'm going to, and I hope, when I get there I'll feel a return of the energy and goal-oriented activity that I had here. Meanwhile, I feel fine. I am looking forward to productive, creative work elsewhere with other people along the same lines as here.

Phil left Vancouver in April 1972, "disappearing into the wilds of southern California," Mike Bailey said, "to begin a whole new life."

Nine
MORE DARK-HAIRED GIRLS: LINDA, TESSA

Phil was smiling that wonderful smile but looking unsure of himself. He carried a battered, old suitcase with an electric cord tied around it.

—Tim Powers, 1982 interview

IN LATE 1982, I drove alone the five hundred miles to Los Angeles. Once there, ensconced at my cousin David's apartment in Arcadia, I drove many miles daily on the scary Los Angeles freeways to Fullerton in Orange County where some of Phil's close friends and the Fullerton State University Library were located. The Philip Dick his Orange County friends talked about didn't seem to be the same Phil that I had known. When he and I had talked occasionally over the phone in the months and years before his death, he had sounded pretty much like the same Phil. Tim Powers told me, "When you talk about [Phil] it doesn't sound like anyone we knew."

One of my main goals was to research the library archives at Fullerton, where Phil's papers and manuscripts were located. Professor McNelly showed me how to use the library and gave me letters, papers, and fruitful leads. McNelly, a Jungian, told me, "Phil had a powerful shadow." I was taken aback when he asked, "Was Phil a good lover?" He told me that he was worried about his wife in regard to Phil: "Phil was just too damn charismatic."

I read as much in the library as I could during the two days I was there. I was shocked by an incredibly poisonous letter that Phil wrote to Carol Carr in 1964 about his insane ex-wife—me. Later, a friend wrote me from Washington, D.C., that there was a letter in the Washington Post protesting the publication of letters of Philip K. Dick, some of which were scurrilous about an ex-wife. I finally decided that anything negative that Phil or his fans said about me wasn't my problem. When very occasionally someone says something negative to me, I tell them jokingly, "Sorry, you can't insult me; I've been insulted by a world-famous expert."

One day I drove to Santa Ana and spent a morning with Phil's best southern California friend, young sci-fi writer Tim Powers, and his wife, Serena, a very pleasant couple. Tim had written a daily journal in the early seventies and made it available to me.

I spent Sunday afternoon in North Hollywood with K. W. Jeter, Phil's other "best friend," and his wife, Jeri. They were a handsome couple and lived in a handsome apartment. Both were dressed as if they were on their way to work in an expensive law firm (or for the FBI). K. W. had on a well-tailored, well-pressed three-piece suit. Not what one expects in La La Land.

I talked several times on the phone with Linda Levy, another great lost love of Phil's. Later, she moved to the San Francisco Bay Area, and we had lunch together. Mary Wilson, Phil's super girlfriend-secretary, and I talked on the phone when Phil was dying in the hospital, and again later. Jim Blaylock was a gracious phone interviewee who had enjoyed his relationship with Phil a great deal. Tessa Busby, Phil's young, fifth ex-wife, declined to be interviewed. Her stepmother, Nita Busby, who had known Phil in Professor McNelly's class, gave me a brief telephone interview.

Gwen Lee had a wonderful taped interview of Phil's ideas for his next novel, The Owl in Daylight, *an interview he had done only a few months before his death. She read the whole thing to me over the phone. I was again impressed and awed by Phil's imagination. I wondered if Phil had in mind the owl we saw taking a shower bath in the first rains of winter in the cypress trees in our front yard so many years ago.*

Tim Powers, Joanne McMahon, Sue Hoglind, and Linda Levy met Phil at the Orange County airport in April 1972. Phil had been allowed to leave X-Kalay only after finding someone who would sponsor him. He had written an emotional letter to Professor Willis McNelly at California State University, Fullerton, asking for help. McNelly had agreed to sponsor Phil and read the letter to his science fiction English class.

"Can anybody here help Philip K. Dick?" he asked his class.

Two girls, science fiction fans, Sue Hoglind and Joanne McMahon, raised their hands: "We can put him up." Phil moved in with Joanne and Sue and slept on their living room couch—but the living situation was uncomfortable, and the three of them didn't get along particularly well. While giving a talk to Professor McNelly's class, Phil joked about his awkward living situation. Another student, Joel Stein, raised his hand and told Phil, "I've just split up with my wife and have an extra bedroom in my apartment." Phil accepted

Joel's offer and continued with his talk.

Joel Stein was thirty-five years old then, and aspiring to be a writer. In 1983 when I reached him by long-distance telephone, he was a pit boss for Harrah's Club in Reno.

"With Phil," Joel said, "there was never a dull moment. Phil was a catalyst. There was never any peace and quiet while Phil was around.... Phil ranged between the agony and the ecstasy." Joel would come home from work and find Phil sitting in a chair in a deep depression because four police cars had just gone by. The next night Phil would be bouncing off the walls with joy. It was a financially hard time for both men. They took turns buying food. Phil stayed with Joel almost six months.

Phil and Tim Powers soon became good friends. Phil told Tim that he was afraid of returning to Marin County, so many people there were "out to get him"; the police were down on him, and a paramilitary group in the area was hostile to him. He told Tim that this group had stolen disorientation-drug weapons from an Air Force warehouse and was selling them on the street as recreational dope. Phil described knifings that occurred at his house. Phil was off drugs and wouldn't allow any drugs around the apartment at all. He told Joel Stein, "The cops will come and break down the doors."

Joel and Phil got along well, although there were times when Phil was morose and would only grunt when Joel tried to talk to him. Joel felt sorry for Phil because of his age and the topsy-turviness of his universe, and because he had only a bunch of kids to rely on. Phil didn't seem be strong at all. "He had coughing fits, his shoulder kept coming out of its socket, and was in a sling, and here he was, trying to keep up with nineteen- and twenty-year-old kids."

Although Phil engaged in many strange, flaky conversations, Joel noted that he was businesslike about his writing and publishing. He was just finishing *A Scanner Darkly*. Later, Phil thought Joel was trying to kill him. Joel noted that Phil seemed to think that anyone he was getting close to was trying to kill him. Phil told a story, too, that Tim had menaced him with a knife.

LINDA LEVY

Joel told me, "I remember Phil was primarily concerned with chasing young dark-haired girls around—desperately. He felt his life was slipping away, and he was trying to get as much out of it as he could. He was terribly romantic about women to the point of unreality. He would describe a girl he'd just met as a goddess with an effervescent personality and long, flowing hair. I would get all excited, and then I would meet the girl and find her quite drab. However, Linda Levy was intelligent and attractive. A heck of a girl, sharp, witty, strong-willed."

Linda had written Phil a letter while he was at X-Kalay, in response to the letter from Phil that Professor Willis McNelly had read to his class. Shortly afterward, Linda was summoned to Professor McNelly's office and told that Phil would be arriving at LAX and wanted her to pick him up. She went with Tim Powers and Phil's two roommates-to-be, Sue and Joanne. "My first impression was of a man with a long, gray beard, wearing a trench coat, carrying in one hand a box wrapped in brown paper…and a Bible in the other. He reminded me of a derelict rabbi. When he saw me, he stopped suddenly, eyes fixed on me. He never took his eyes off me the whole evening."

Within two weeks Phil was intensely, mystically in love with Linda. He wrote her:

> Linda, for God's sake be eternal. Can you manage that? For all of us? Because I have this strange feeling that you can; that the decision, the choice, lies up to you…. If something happened to you intrinsically it would be a world disaster…. I would look up into the sky at night and see the stars flickering off one by one, and I'd be…indifferent. I'd walk through the side of a building and it'd collapse into dust. Wheels would fall off cars, like in an old W. C. Fields movie. Finally my foot would sink through the sidewalk…. All I ever want to do is hug you again and again, just wrap you up in my arms and hug you and hold you close to me forever and ever without letting loose, without change, and then after that we can pack a lunch, take a boiled egg and a thermos of warm purple, and go to the seashore. And there we're going to have a real ball, Linda…. [W]e're going to run along the beach with the seagulls hurrying to keep up with us so they don't miss their handout…the sun over the water with a bright star at its tip going gazanggg…. We'll come across a gigantic driftwood thing that resembles every conceivable imaginable good thing we ever saw or thought of, and we'll sit there just being happy…. P.S. Linda, I am much, deeply in love with you. So this is what I'd like to ask you: will you marry me?

Linda recalled with astonishment, "Phil proposed in a letter after he had known me only two weeks. It made me uncomfortable, because I didn't know how to respond. He later said it was a joke."

She continued, "Phil's intense attention could be unnerving to experience, and I saw him undergo personality changes that were frightening. Others in the group didn't have the same experiences that I did. They saw him as a completely different person, and that made me uncomfortable also. I began to question my own sanity, since my experiences were so vastly different. I felt consumed by him, possessed, trapped. Phil's flattery fed my ego, but the price I had to pay was too high. I was afraid of Phil, and his mood swings."

Phil wrote to a friend back in Vancouver about Linda:

> I've become involved with a black-haired groovy spaced-out foxy chick (as we say here), a wild, self-destructive, beautiful girl named Linda whom I love much, but who is hurting me and whom, I'm afraid, I'm hurting, too.... There is a sort of perpetual misunderstanding between us.... Destiny in a miniskirt...Durability...permanency, is what I want most of all.... That, I think, I do have with Linda; it appears to be a durable relationship.
>
> I think, for me, knowing Linda and being with her, puts out of my mind a certain despair that comes when your attention wanders from the present and back to former times. I always have the feeling that things used to be better.

One evening, Linda and Phil went out together to have dinner and to see the movie *Fiddler on the Roof*. On the way home, Linda stopped for gas, remembering only belatedly that the gas station attendant was someone whom she had dated. Knowing how intensely jealous Phil was and wanting to avoid a confrontation, she got out of the car to talk to the attendant because:

> I didn't want him sticking his head in the window and saying something that would make Phil angry. He was angry anyway because I got out of the car to talk to this guy and after I drove out of the gas station and back on the road, Phil suddenly reached over and grabbed the wheel of my car and steered it into the path of the oncoming traffic. I was terrified and fought with him for control of the car; at the last possible second I was able to pull it back to the right side of the road. We were near Phil's apartment. I pulled up in front and, heart pounding, ordered him out of the car. He had a sling on his arm from having dislocated his shoulder a few weeks before. He grabbed my windpipe with his slinged hand and began punching me in the face with his free hand. We struggled again and I finally broke free and ordered him out of my car. I determined at that point that I wasn't safe and wanted to have nothing further to do with him, at least not until there was someone else in his life on whom he could focus that terrible intensity.

Phil wrote to Linda afterward:

> I have so much regretted the trouble between us, Linda, that caused the breakdown of our relationship. You are a dear, good, wild, funny, terrific person....

But later Phil told some of his acquaintances that the reason he and Linda broke up was that she attacked him. Phil's account of the breakup to Tim was different still. He told Tim that Linda had led him on, and then when he proposed to her, she was angry because he'd "ruined" the nice relationship they'd had. He told Tim he'd struck her once in hurt and anger.

Phil's collection of letters to Linda forms part of a manuscript of a book of his letters titled *The Dark-Haired Girl*. Following the letters to Linda, Phil records a dream: "TERRIBLE—a child, a naked baby in a frying pan, suffering. The child is on fire; flames surround it and it burns shiny red. It leaps into the ring of fire beneath the frying pan to escape; but it has made a mistake. It is now down below, in hell, in the flames themselves, from which it was trying to escape."

Phil, Joel, and Tim met the women in the next apartment, Mary Lou Malone, Mary Wilson, and Cindy Stanlow. The night they met they went out on a date to see *A Clockwork Orange*. They became close friends.

Another new friend was K. W. Jeter, a young science fiction writer who had studied Phil's works and revered Phil before he had even met him. But Phil's fear of the FBI and CIA continued to haunt him. After an initial friendly period, Phil suddenly stopped speaking to K. W. Several years later when they had become friendly again, Phil told K. W. that he had dropped him because he believed that K. W. was an FBI informer.

TESSA BUSBY DICK

Linda was not the last of the dark-haired women whom Phil fell instantly in love with. In July, Phil started dating tall, slim twenty-seven-year-old Ginger Smith, whom he had met at the Westercon in Long Beach. Everyone was asked to wear a name tag, so Phil wore the name of an early obscure *Amazing Stories* writer. A month later Ginger planned a beach party, but the several groups who were planning to drive to the beach decided to go to someone's house instead. Ginger had invited seventeen-year-old Tessa Busby. She knew Tessa because Tessa had been on the high-school bus Ginger drove.

Everyone was drinking Jack Daniel's and Coke. Tim Powers was having a good time at the party when, "The next thing I noticed was that Phil was huddled with Tess on the couch and they were whispering and muttering to each other. I thought, 'Wow. That's quick. What happened here? I only just turned around and went for a beer.'"

Ginger wasn't at all mad. Tim said that it almost seemed like a setup. Later, there were mysterious interpretations of exactly what happened that evening. That night Tessa moved in with Phil at Joel Stein's apartment. Within a week the new couple had rented their own place across the hall from Joel's place.

Phil, deliriously happy, was hopeful that a whole new life was starting for him. The first thing he did was go on a diet and put a big sign on the refrigerator saying, "He whom the Gods would destroy, they first make fat." He was intensely involved with Tessa. Tim noted, "Phil and Tess were almost physically inseparable, even always leaning against each other." Phil continually told all his friends how brilliant Tessa was. He made her his executive secretary. Soon after Phil had moved in with Tessa, he largely withdrew from his group of young friends.

Phil wrote, in an undated letter to Tessa: "Dark hair, fair skin, small bare feet, unaware, this girl, that he had gone off for a moment: she was oblivious to such minor matters…how much he needed her, how much she meant to him. She filled the empty spaces that had, for most of his life, surrounded him…. With her nearby, his world perpetuated itself by its own strength and intrinsic reality. He knew that if he shut his eyes or turned his back it would still go on…."

Needy himself, Phil equally needed to be needed and seemed quite proud when he told Tim, "Tess has epilepsy. She had a psychomotor seizure last night. She has to take Dilantin and phenobarbitol. I have to take her to several doctors." And another time, he said to Tim, "pleased as Punch," "See that chip in the kitchen wall, Tim? Tess threw a knife in my direction."

Phil wrote to a friend in Vancouver:

I've been happy here in Fullerton…. Tess is a little black-haired chick, exactly like I'm not supposed to get involved with (according to X-Kalay), eighteen, who writes (she's sold an article already), pretty and bright. Tomboyish but sexy, small, talks weird, sort of straight, politically uncommitted, rides horses, has never traveled, wants to see Canada…. I love her with all my heart…. She's the most emphatic person I've ever encountered: wise and gentle, but independent. And tactful.... I'm just now, with Tess, beginning to get my head back together.

Phil wrote his mother, Dorothy, about Tessa:

I have meant for some time to write you a good accurate letter about Tessa, whom I love so much and hope to spend the rest of my life with. But it is hard to describe her; she changes so much from day to day: she is warm but so elusive...as if I've imagined her out of my own head. You see, I wrote all three letters, the two supposedly from her and the one from me mentioning our activities.... Tessa is the girl I've searched for always and never found, never will find. On the other hand, perhaps Tessa is real...and it's just my mental problems that cause me to believe I made her up....

There is some basic, overwhelming mystery about Tessa that I cannot get at.... Again and again I've come up with a theory to account for the strangeness about her, and each time she has, reluctantly, admitted that I'm right, that she has been lying to me and now I've found the truth. Again I come up with a theory, a better one.... A day later I figure out that that theory is false, too, and, under duress, she admits it.... We are living in a Philip K. Dick novel.... We are persons who have tried to think our way through life and now are falling back on feeling, on rage and love and grief and humor....

In 1975, Phil came up to Marin County for his divorce from Nancy. He brought Tessa with him to testify to his poor financial status. Phil's old friend Kirsten Nelson met the couple at the airport. She said, "Tessa was a tough little girl. I was surprised that she couldn't go to a bar, she was too young. Phil was in seventh heaven. Tessa was flattered that an older man, a famous writer, was paying her all this attention. I liked Tessa and thought she might be good for Phil, since she wasn't timid or frightened and Phil seemed so much better."

The only time Nancy ever saw Tessa was in court the day she got divorced from Philip. Tess had on a voluminous red coat and a strange hat. Nancy was so relieved that Philip was going to marry Tessa because she wouldn't have to feel responsible for him anymore. She had felt very guilty about leaving him. Nancy greeted Philip in a friendly fashion, calling him by her old pet name for him, "Fuzzy." Phil was affronted by this "inappropriate familiarity." The court awarded Nancy $75 a month child support.

Tessa and Phil returned to Orange County. Tim was there "one of the times" Phil proposed to Tessa. A group had gone to Disneyland and planned to meet at five o'clock at the Carnation Cafe on Main Street. Tim's account:

> We were sitting at an outside table, Phil and Tess on that side of the table and me at the other, just finishing up some sandwiches we'd had and looking and wondering where the others were. Phil leaned over and said "Tess, will you marry me?" And I thought, "Oh God, I wish I wasn't here.... let me back off." So I sort of withdrew and as I did, I reached over and grabbed a pickle off Phil's plate so I could munch on it and seem to be devoting my attention elsewhere. But, before Tess could answer, Phil says, "Powers, what are you doing with that pickle?" I said, "Well, you were done." And he said, "No, I wasn't done. I was saving it." I said, "Oh sorry, here, have it." And he said, "I don't want it now, you've been chewing on it." And I said, "Look, the waitress'll give you another pickle." He said, "I don't want to bother the waitress about it, I just want to let you know that before you take somebody's pickle off their plate, you ought to have the decency to ask." By this time, the rest of the group had wandered up and Tessa, who had been hanging on the edge of her chair, never got a chance to answer. Evidently, he asked her another time when I wasn't there to interfere.

Phil and Tessa rented an older three-bedroom house on Santa Isabel in Fullerton, a nice house, although not fancy, with a beamed living room, the glass wall of which looked out on an overgrown small backyard. Isa began coming down from Marin County to visit every three months. She played baseball with Phil and Tessa and their friends and had lots of fun. Tessa was nice to Isa and the two of them got along well.

Meanwhile, Phil was paid small sums for lecturing to Willis McNelly's class at Cal State, Fullerton. He talked about his writing and about his life. Among his topics was the cruelty of one of his ex-wives who wouldn't allow him to visit his child and his beloved stepchildren. While at the university, Phil met many young science fiction fans, aspiring young writers, and published writers and invited many of them over to his place.

Doris Sauter came over to Phil and Tessa's house with her boyfriend, science fiction writer Norman Spinrad. She noted how quiet Tessa was: "Tessa sat and read and didn't participate in the conversation."

Writer Jim Blaylock met Phil the day Ray Bradbury spoke in Professor McNelly's class. Jim was also invited over to the Fullerton house: "Somehow Phil had come into possession of a rifle but he was in such fear of it that he pitched it under the bed like it was a snake."

I hadn't been in touch with Phil since he went to Vancouver. The news about Phil's marriage came to me in Point Reyes from an unexpected source. That summer, I had been surprised when I heard via the Point Reyes grapevine that Dorothy and her twin stepchildren Lynne and Neil had bought a house in Inverness just a few miles from where I lived. After wrestling with my feelings, I was prepared, when Dorothy phoned me, to forget the past. After this, Dorothy, Laura, and I saw each other on a regular basis. I was happy Laura was getting to know her grandmother, and Dorothy and I rediscovered a pleasant relationship. It was from Dorothy and Lynne that I learned that Phil had remarried a young girl. Disgustedly, I gathered all Phil's letters, put them in the fireplace, and burned them. Then I gave all my copies of his novels away.

Dorothy only lived in Inverness for two years and then moved to a retirement home, the Redwoods, in Mill Valley, still fairly close. After being there a year she moved to Santa Rosa to be near Lynne, and we were no longer able to socialize with her because of the distance, but we kept in touch by phone.

It wasn't long after Phil's marriage that Laura and I began getting a whole new batch of letters. On July 9, he wrote Laura:

> You might tell your mother that *The Man in the High Castle* is supposed to be republished here in the United States again, and it's dedicated to her, although she didn't like the dedication. I guess I could change it when the novel comes out again…. You might ask her if she wants me to. Love, Daddy

But he never spoke to me directly about this and I didn't pay attention. Of course he wouldn't change the dedication. Later my third daughter, Tandy, picked up a copy of *The Man in the High Castle* at a bookstore in order to show a friend Phil's dedication to her mother. She was shocked to see that the novel was now dedicated to Tessa. I felt bad and, as usual, couldn't believe that Phil would do such a thing, but perhaps he'd thought he'd asked me if I still wanted the dedication—and I hadn't bothered to answer.

Phil was quite ill that summer. He had a bout of extreme hypertension and was hospitalized. Soon after this illness, Christopher Kenneth Dick was born on July 25, 1973. Phil was pleased; he had always wanted a boy.

That fall I ran into Nancy Hackett at the Oakland Coliseum at a huge church rally that we had both attended. We exchanged greetings and, perhaps because we were both in a special kind of environment, the conversation immediately moved into deeper matters. Nancy asked me to forgive her for getting involved with my husband and I told her, "I do forgive you, Nancy." She lit up like a Christmas tree.

Phil hadn't called me for a couple of years, but the next day he called me and said, "I understand you've forgiven Nancy," and he paused hopefully. Yes, I had forgiven Nancy but I hadn't forgiven him. Nevertheless, we had a long, friendly conversation. I gave him the news of our family. Hatte was in Israel doing graduate work in Arabic linguistics. I had visited her in June soon after my house had burnt halfway down. Tandy was hitchhiking through Europe. She would spend the winter skiing in Switzerland and working in a Swiss restaurant. Jayne had married, moved to Point Reyes, and was working with me in the jewelry business. She was pregnant and expecting twins. I had been elected the first woman warden of St. Columba's mission church and was also president of the local West Marin planning group.

Long-term employees were running my jewelry business so that I could coach a team, including second daughter Jayne and fourth daughter Laura, in a new-to-the-United States sport, vaulting—a gymnastic dance of eight teenagers jumping on and off a cantering horse, better than anything at that time in the circus. Phil was delighted to hear all my news. Then the girls came to the phone and talked with Phil. Later we compared notes and they told me that Phil talked only jive talk to them. While talking to me he had been dignified and serious and brought a lot of religion into the conversation. From this time on Phil wrote or phoned about once a month. He also got in touch with Kleo and communicated with her regularly. When Norman Mini died, he sent Kleo money for funeral expenses.

In December 1973, Phil wrote me:

It was so nice to get a letter from you, and so gracious of you to write. And all the news is appreciated.... [Y]ou certainly seem to be doing wonderfully in your jewelry business, and if I talk in superlatives it is both because I mean what I say—which is fine—and because I now live, as you know, in the L.A. area. It does things to you; or as they say here, it does a number on your head. I'll try to talk as real people do; if I fail, it's due to a bad environment. Okay?

...[T]he air pollution has...done me dreadful harm, but don't please worry, since we intend to leave and anyhow I was not nearly as sick this year as I was last; last year I almost died.... In fact, I saw Mr. Death standing in the corner of the bedroom. He wore a modern polyester suit and carried an attaché case, which he opened in order to show me a psychological test. I took the test, I had a temperature of 102, which is high, but I couldn't breathe and was asphyxiating night after night. He informed me that, according to the results, I was completely insane and he would take me to a fine mental hospital, high in the wooded hills. I was delighted and agreed, with enthusiasm, to go with him. I felt completely relieved but fortunately someone came into the bedroom and Mr. Death vanished....

You certainly do sound well, Anne, and full of life, creative and spiritual life—all kinds of life. Great, and again, thank you for writing and thank you for all the news. Incredible, Jayne grown up and married and about to have—what, two or three babies, possibly? You must let me know. And Tandy in Switzerland...incredible. I have trouble getting up to Trader Joe's, our local store.... Remember Disneyland when we visited it?...Love, Phil.

I must have written him once but I felt more comfortable talking on the phone. Besides, I didn't want to get letters with those "we's" in them.

In March 1974, Phil had a mystical experience, which he describes in his novel *VALIS*. He called it his "pink light experience." This epiphany was so important to him that he began writing a meditation about it late at night, much of it in longhand. The manuscript grew to be a million words by the time of his death and occupied two full-size file drawers. He called it *The Exegesis*. He also began writing a novel based on this experience and on his theological ideas, titled *Valisystem A*. A short time later he was hospitalized again for extreme high blood pressure, which, he told Tim Powers, he connected with his mystical experience.

In April 1974, Phil wrote Laura:

I'm still screwed up although...it was one of the better ecstatic delights of my life to talk to you on the phone.... But I owe the IRS thousands. So money is a problem (... [t]hey may seize my assets).... I wear a crucifix always now—I feel God (or whatever His name is) saved me, although my blood pressure is still up a little.

In July, in a different mood, he wrote her:

I did not manage to force the Polish Government to pay me the royalty money they owe me, although they still intend to publish my novel *Ubik* this year.... I did not manage to force my agent who I've been with for 22 years to come through with the written assurances regarding the back royalties due me from Ace Books, so I fired him.... For months—almost three months—I've been having the same dream over and over again. Things in writing, important, are held up for me to read, but I can't discern what is written. Within the last month it's become this great huge thick book, which contains all the wisdom of the ages. Each night I keep trying to see what it is, to catch a glimpse of the title. Each night it becomes more clear. Finally I see what it is. It is a huge blue hardbound book just under 700 pages of tiny type called *The Shadow of Blooming Grove*. It is a biography of Warren G. Harding.

Phil wrote and phoned my oldest daughter, Hatte, who was living in Austin, Texas, with her Israeli husband. Both of them were taking advanced degrees at the University of Texas. They spoke at great length. It was the first time they had communicated since Phil had left Point Reyes. Phil told Hatte he wanted to bring Tessa and come to Texas to visit her, but Hatte didn't feel comfortable about this and said that she didn't have any extra room in her house. Phil sent Hatte a German-language edition of one of his novels and inscribed it to her in German.

Phil described the beginning of some problems in his new marriage in a hilarious letter to Tessa:

Well, here I am in sunny Cleveland, having won first prize in the Fullerton Stink Bug look-alike contest (first prize, which I won, is a week in Cleveland; second prize is two weeks in Cleveland).... Wow, but it's nice here. Tall buildings, big potholes, fat cops. Tawdry old bags in place of women.... It hurts when the one you love goes away. But you wouldn't understand, cruel-hearted Tess with the lovely black hair and firm, high breasts—you, Tess, who has (have?) hurt, even wounded, men such as I again and again. Specifically, YOU HAVE WOUNDED MY HEART BY YOUR CRUELTY AND INDIFFERENCE (sp?) AND YOUR HAUGHTY MANNER, FOR INSTANCE YOUR READING ALL DAY AND NOT DOING THE DISHES. More about this later.

That last moment when we were together, before parting, at the 30-minute zone of the parking lot at Fullerton International, you asked me candidly why I had accepted the prize in the Fullerton Stink Bug look-alike contest (a week in Cleveland), leaving you behind and going away forever (a week in Cleveland is forever). I didn't have the fortitude to lay it on you then, with you standing there close enough to hit me, why I was taking advantage of this once-in-a-lifetime opportunity to get away from you for what has proved to be forever...squirming out of the grip that your love has fastened hammerlock-wise around my neck.... I was limping as I ran for the Fullerton plane as it took off (you may have noticed, too, that I caught it). This pronounced limping is because, Tess, in point of fact I am as I was when you first encountered me still: a sick and wounded animal injured by the hate and violence of modern American life in this culture which we have all around us (except in Cleveland). I recall, back at that party Ginger had, that you noticed the sorrow and grief in my eye (actually, both eyes). And, to assuage that grief and sorrow, you cleverly crept up on my lap and I cleverly put my arms around you and so on.... Anyhow, I am still that limping beast of the field that Christ wrote about in his memoirs that neither spins nor reaps or however it goes. Meaning, your warm firm breasts and arms enfolding me may have banished my suffering AT THE TIME (say, for six months), but only really actually on the surface.... My heart, while living with you day by day, Tessa, was like that pot of warm glue bubbling and boiling and suffering with pain on the stove of your furnace-hot intensity.... You have again and again so wounded my suffering bubbling heart that, Tess...you have lost me.... Right now I know how really mad you are, Tess. But you can't get me because all Cleveland loves me and you'll never find me here...even with all the influence and power and money you've achieved writing those funky one-liners for the septic tank people. Cleveland will surround me like a protecting shroud, veiling my comings and goings.... I intend to take out citizenship, here, Tess, permanent Cleveland citizenship. I feel safe. I shake the fist of wrath and defiance at you in the face here from sunny Cleveland, where neither you nor your rat Seymour (may he have a coronary running around his wheel) can get me.

Now, about your not doing the dishes. Or emptying the garbage. Or vacuuming. Or shopping. Or fixing dinner. Or anything. Your just sitting drinking coffee in that incredible, prolonged, insipid way you have, day after day, month after month, just glancing up now and then when I dusted you off. While I earned the money, cleaned up after you, dusted things, made your coffee, and so on....

I'm starting a new life, Tess, free of the fear of being suspended for an eternal terror-stricken instant over the void that is the garbage disposal in the middle of the night when I haven't done anything to no man. Especially not to you.... Actually, in my own way I did a lot for you, Tess. I bought you a $6.50 electric can opener and a $4.00 cute little matching skirt and blouse. And a patty melt several times at Fiddler's Three (total cost to me: $1.68) where you said as usual that the service was lousy and the food worse, especially compared to Alfie's. And after a few kicks and blows from you I ceased conversing with the pretty waitresses, a big sacrifice on my part for your sake. That was honor and loyalty and a great deal more you wouldn't understand. My heart was bound to yours out of cords of silent love and tenderness and devotion and fright. But that's over now. Starting with the fright and working backwards to silent love. What I have, instead, is loud hate. Can you hear it? My hate shouting at you across the miles, dinning the inner ear of your being? It's my hate talking to your laziness, Tess. But you're probably too indolent to listen to my hate, just as you were too indolent to listen, when it existed, to my love. That's the trouble with silent love anyhow; nobody hears it....

You are a good little lady, Tessa, and filled with love, but love does not in itself keep a creature alive.... Anyhow, I am not really in Cleveland, as you may have guessed; I am seated in the kitchen, our own kitchen, at our own mutual typing machine, simulating being in Cleveland, writing to you what I can't verbally say (I know "verbally" is technically wrong, but "orally" always suggests a thermometer or worse, so the hell with it)....

When Phil went over to Tessa's father and stepmother's house, he wouldn't sit down. He wouldn't come to family holiday gatherings, but had a plate of food brought to him at his apartment. When Nita Busby, Tessa's stepmother, whom he also knew from Willis McNelly's class, said something to him that he didn't like, he told her, "If you say anything like that again, I'll put you in my next novel as a plain mud road." Phil seemed to her to be morose and unhappy, impatient and irritable.

Tim Powers said, "In the fall of 1975, Phil gave a big house party. It seemed that he and Tess were no longer a going thing. Phil was earnestly pursuing another lady throughout the evening, trying to monopolize her attention." During 1974 and 1975, Phil told friends that Tessa had left him three times, taking the checkbook, giving a retainer to a divorce lawyer, and renting an apartment. Each time, she came back. There were great debates at Cal State about the relationship between Phil and Tess and who, if anyone, was the villain.

Despite domestic problems, Phil's career and reputation continued to climb. In late 1975, Phil sent me a copy of *Science Fiction Studies*, an academic journal that had devoted one whole issue to his work. I was impressed and told him so over the phone the next time he called. He said to me, "You'll notice that they say all my best novels were written in the early sixties when I was married to you."

Early in 1976, Phil and Tessa split up for the final time. In February 1976, Phil and Tim Powers were sitting at a table in Phil's house in Fullerton, drinking wine that Tim had brought. While they were sitting together, Tessa and her brother came to move out Tessa's share of the furniture. Phil said, "Well, Tim," as he took a drink of wine, "never oversee what the ex-wives take. It's much better to let them have what they want and then later inventory what you've got left."

At that point, Tessa's brother came over to them and said, "Say, would you mind picking your glasses up off that table?" and took the table.

Tim told me,

Phil was in good spirits right then, but the next evening he tried to commit suicide. Tim visited Phil in the hospital the next afternoon. He told me, "It was raining like a barrage.... He was in the intensive care unit, sitting up in a bed with monitoring screens over him.... They had shaved his arm where he had cut his wrist...and he was plugged in eight million ways to this machine. There was an old lady in the bed next to him, an incredibly old lady, and she had one of those "beep, beep, beeps" going. As we were sitting there talking, it went "beeeep, beeeep." And a bunch of doctors ran over and pulled the curtain and after a while turned the machine off. Phil said, "Oh, this is a terrible place, Powers."

Phil was amiable, though, and told me what had happened. He had become intensely depressed over the loss of [his son] Christopher and took forty-nine Lenoxin tablets [digitalis]. Then he took eight Libriums to calm his nerves and laid down in bed to wait for the cardiac arrest. After an hour, it hadn't happened, so he went to the bathroom and cut his left wrist. He got an arterial spurt that sent blood to the ceiling, but after a while the blood coagulated and the cut stopped bleeding.... He went into the garage and started the Fiat in an attempt to kill himself by carbon monoxide poisoning...the car kept stalling. So he went inside and went to bed.

In the morning he felt terrible—the digitalis had destroyed all the potassium in his blood, and he was weak. When the mail arrived in the middle of the morning, though, he managed to walk outside and bring it in. He also put down a pan of water for the cats. He called his analyst then, having...changed his mind about wanting to die. The analyst told him, "That was a silly thing to do. Call the paramedics." He did and they arrived in time; another hour would have given the digitalis enough time to poison him off.... He had even tied a bandage on his wrist.... As absurd as this attempt was, Phil meant to die. Phil describes all this pretty accurately in *VALIS*.

I called the hospital for him Friday. I was relayed to the psychiatric ward; they gave me a run-around, asking me if I was a member of the family...and, finally, they had him call me. He sounded worried and even scared. He said they were keeping him indefinitely and they were right to do it, because he was crazy. The last time I'd seen him he told me that Tess had, when called by a medic about it, claimed to be too busy to come. "I hope she rots in hell for twelve eons," he told me.

Tessa did come to the psychiatric ward where Phil had been transferred, finally, and brought a few clothes. Tim brought a Bible and several tins of Dean Swift snuff.

Phil was discharged in mid-February and went home to find that Tess had returned. Tim said, "He's apparently letting her stay. I can't understand it, but I guess I don't have to. I thought Phil was crazy to let Tessa stay. But she didn't stay for long."

At that time, Phil began calling me more often, maybe every other week. He didn't say anything about having tried to commit suicide. He told me that he had been in the hospital with a severe, life-threatening potassium deficiency. He said he was taking the Bach flower remedies. Later I found out there really was such a thing. I could hear in the tone of his voice that he was depressed. I must have found the right words to say to him, because each time he phoned, by the time we'd hang up he was sounding better. Phil turned to Tim for comfort, too, at this time, and he was also able to cheer Phil up.

Good memories of the past returned to me when, late in 1975, my oldest daughter, Hatte, called me to tell me that *Confessions of a Crap Artist* had been published. She had just read it. "Mother, you mustn't read it, you'll be too upset," she said. I laughed and told her, "Hatte, I already read it when he wrote it—when Phil and I were first married." I was glad that one of Phil's literary novels was finally being published, although I didn't reread it until after Phil's death. It's not my favorite novel of Phil's. I don't like the whole tone of it. It's taken me a long time, blinded by my romantic feelings for Phil, to see how outrageous it was, what an ambivalent and negative depiction of me. But I called Phil up to congratulate him, and feeling sentimental, I told him, "*Confessions of a Crap Artist* reminds me of the old days, when we were so happy. I want to tell you, Phil, I don't regret anything." He deftly moved the conversation to another topic.

When I reread *Confessions* after Phil's death I was struck by a letter of Phil's quoted in the introduction to the Entwhistle Press edition. Phil went on and on about what a fine fellow Jack Isidore (that rat fink) was, and never even mentioned Fay Hume. And in the dedication, he wrote, "To Tessa, the dark-haired girl who cared about me when it mattered the most, that is, all the time...."

Ten
DORIS AND JOAN

It had been Fat's delusion for years that he could help people. His psychiatrist once told
him that to get well he would have to do two things: get off dope (which he hadn't done)
and to stop trying to help people (he still tried to help people).

—Philip K. Dick, *VALIS*

PHIL DIDN'T REMAIN without female companionship for long. Soon he was calling
me and telling me that he was taking care of an Episcopal nun who had cancer.
I didn't believe him, although I didn't say so, but, indeed, Doris Sauter had been
a lay sister in an Episcopal order and had been diagnosed with cancer in 1975. At
the time Phil called me, her cancer was in remission from chemotherapy.

*In Los Angeles, I had obtained a lead to Doris Sauter in Yuba City, where she was
the assistant to an Episcopal priest. We talked at great length on the phone, and
later she came to Point Reyes to spend a weekend with me. We had a picnic on
top of Mt. Vision and she recorded three tapes about her life with Phil. Doris, a
stocky young woman with short dark hair, had lost her mother as a teenager. She
went through some hard times growing up—times, she said, that toughened and
matured her rather than leaving psychological scars. She wrote poetry and science
fiction and was interested in psychology, philosophy, and astronomy. At the time she
met Phil, she was planning to study for the Episcopal priesthood and eventually did
become an ordained minister in a different Protestant denomination.*

Phil had asked Doris to marry him while he and Tessa were still living together
but Doris turned him down. She told me, "When Tessa and Phil split the
last time, it was pretty much because of indifference on both their parts, and,
anyway, they had lost the lease on their house. Phil moved into an apartment
in Santa Ana, where there really wasn't any room for Tessa and Christopher. I

moved in with him for three weeks. For Phil, it was a romance, but for me, it was a convenient situation. I loved Phil, but I wasn't in love with him. Phil and I lived together for health reasons. Phil was worried about his heart and I had a history of seizures."

Doris was from a conventional background and felt uncomfortable when her aunt called once from New York at 8 a.m. and Phil sleepily answered the phone. Her aunt asked her, "What's that man doing there in your apartment?"

Doris said, "I came from a family situation where you didn't live with people unless you were married to them. I felt a lack of privacy, too. Phil never let me alone; he wanted to talk to me about theological topics or his latest novel, or the latest news event...all the time. I needed time to be alone and I wasn't getting any." Doris told Phil that she was going to move next door. Phil was upset, but she showed him her front door, which was only five feet from his front door. "Look, Phil, I'm almost as close as I was. We'll have dinner together every night and visit back and forth during the day." Doris and Phil lived in side-by-side apartments for several years until the apartment went condo and Doris had to move because she couldn't come up with a down payment.

Doris felt her relationship was with the person, not the writer, and was careful to keep it on a personal level. However, she did read *VALIS*. "I was Sherry in *VALIS*, and the theological conversation about that fish was exactly the way it happened. We had endless theological arguments. The conversation about whether Jesus communicated in a secret code was not complete. Phil found a section in the New Testament which seemed to support his position, but I brought in some irrefutable arguments to support my position. Phil left those out when he incorporated our discussion in *VALIS*."

Right after this argument with Doris, Phil joined a group that maintained the New Testament was written in code. He became involved with one religious cult after another, like a kid who's onto something, is keen on it, then finds a flaw and goes off on something else. Finally, Phil's religious goings-on began to sound like a bunch of hooey to Doris, but she listened and didn't argue with him.

She told me, "Phil would sometimes put on a scatterbrain act. But it was just an act. If he was talking business, he would just cut out all that crap and get right down to work. Sometimes he would go to bed at 4 a.m. and Russ Galen, his agent, would call him at 9 a.m. New York time, which would be 6 a.m. Santa Ana time, but Phil would be right there. He was pretty astute when he wanted to be."

During this period, Phil led a quiet life except for his Thursday nights out when he had a few drinks with the boys at Tim Powers's apartment. Doris believed he was off all drugs and didn't take any amphetamines at all. "He did a little grass, a little coke; that was all." Tessa would visit once a week, bringing Christopher.

Phil was a night owl. He went to bed at 4 a.m. and got up at 12 or 1. He would eat a little breakfast and then go to the post office and the bank. He was just waking up when Doris would arrive at his apartment at 5 p.m. with take-out dinner from the Chinese restaurant around the corner. Phil's apartment had no table to eat on, so he and Doris ate in the living room with their plates on their laps. After dinner, Phil and Doris would watch a movie, or Phil would work: "He worked steadily on his *Exegesis* or on research every evening. When he worked on a novel, he would write eighteen hours a day for a three-week period and then be exhausted."

Women who visited Phil's place noted that it was rundown and seedy. The carpet, a hideous green shag, was cheap and soiled. There were papers all over, and the garbage needed taking out. The color TV only got shades of green. The furniture was from a secondhand store. Men friends termed Phil's place "a typical bachelor pad."

Doris told me, "Phil wasn't really into housekeeping, but then, I didn't notice, because I was also a terrible housekeeper." Phil chronicled Doris's terrible housekeeping in *The Divine Invasion*. Rybys, the mother of God in *The Divine Invasion*, lived in an igloo filled with litter. Rybys was perhaps a combination of Doris and Phil's later girlfriend, Joan Simpson.

Phil had two cats at this period, Harvey Wallbanger and Mrs. Tubbs. He had Harvey blessed by proxy at the local Episcopal church where Doris worked. One time when there was a fire drill at the apartment house, Doris grabbed some possessions from her apartment, and Phil grabbed some from his place, and they hurried down the apartment stairs. Then Phil realized he had forgotten the cats. "He felt so bad," Doris said.

Doris remembered, "Phil was kind to me; he bought me a bed, gave me a car. However, when I had men friends over, Phil became jealous and angry. I didn't consider it dating, though. Later on, he seemed to adjust."

In the fall of 1976, Doris lost her remission from cancer. Phil seemed happy for the first time in years. His blood pressure was down. He felt really needed.

Phil wrote me on December 12, 1976, wanting to bring Doris to our place for Christmas: "[Laura] invited me up...but as I told her there is this woman living in the apartment next to me who has inoperable cancer...whom I've been shopping for.... She has no family she can be with at Christmas. Laura suggested I bring her up. I wonder, though, if that is a good idea. I'd like your thoughts about it...."

I didn't answer. In the next month or so, Phil called and told me delightedly, "I'm writing an autobiography about both of my personalities.... I'm calling it *VALIS*." *VALIS* was a completely new version of *Valisystem A*. His editors had rejected the former; it was too autobiographical.

All during 1977, Doris was in chemotherapy. She told me, "Phil helped take care of me. I remember how kind he was and how good he was in emergencies. Once I had to go to the hospital because of a bad reaction to the anti-cancer drugs. Phil was level-headed and knew just what to do."

Meanwhile, Phil's novels had become an enormous success in Europe and suddenly he was rolling in money; he had a six-figure income but he was uncomfortable with all this money. He seemed to feel better if he could get rid of it and he began giving it away. He sponsored three children through the Christian Children's Fund and wrote to them for two years. He was terrified, though, that he'd end up poor again.

Some of this money even came our way. I had no idea that Phil was now a big financial success. He didn't tell me about this. Our daughter, Laura, had passed the high school proficiency test and needed transportation to junior college courses during her last year of high school. When she wrote Phil about this he offered to send her money for a car. Phil made out the check to me and wrote me: "Enclosed is my check to you for $1,400. I told Laura on the phone I'd reconcile my checkbook and see just how much I had, and, if possible, send more than the thousand I promised. It really gives me enormous pleasure to send this to you. I hope she can get a car with it, and one she likes." We took the money for the car, and with half of it we bought an old clunker and with the other half made a down payment on a lovely thoroughbred mare.

On February 18, 1977, Phil wrote Laura:

It was sure neat talking to you on the phone last night, and to your mother. As I told you, my friend [Doris] and I are out of money right now, and so we have to postpone our trip up there.... I am alone in my apartment, with my cats, Harvey and Mrs. Tubbs, eating frozen TV dinners and watching tacky TV situation comedy programs. That's about all I do, except to get together with my buddies every day or so. I really am enjoying the car I bought, the '73 Capri, except that it needs work. How is your car doing?

I told everybody down here about your prowess…in [horse] vaulting, and they are indeed impressed. As they should be…. You can see from this letter that about all I have going for me right now is my professional-intellectual-creative life, but it is a life, except that I get lonely. The other morning, forgetting how I now live, I asked Mrs. Tubbs (seriously) if she wanted a cup of coffee. Oh well.

During the period when Doris was living in the apartment next door, K. W. Jeter and Phil reestablished a relationship and became close friends. K. W. told me, "Phil couldn't stand to be alone, he had to create some sort of family situation. He asked Tim to share the apartment after Doris had moved out. Tim told him that he liked the place where he was; then Phil turned to me and said, 'How about you?'"

K. W. was working on the night shift at juvenile hall. Phil would phone him and the two of them would talk all night long. Both men, recently divorced, felt they had a lot in common. Sometimes, on his days off, K. W. would drop in at Phil's to listen to the six o'clock news. They'd have dinner together and talk until 4 or 5 a.m. the next morning. K. W. told me, "Wonderful conversations, I wish I had tapes of them. One week Phil would say, 'I'm a Buddhist.' A week later he'd have a different idea—he'd be a Taoist. Phil had to test everything from the inside. He'd adopt a religion like an experiment, like he did his marriages. Phil and I spent the whole night taking the universe apart. We were glad that we could put it back together before people woke up." K. W. noticed huge piles of paper for *The Exegesis* accumulating in boxes in Phil's apartment.

Phil told K. W. that Tessa and Linda were the worst things that ever happened to him. He told K. W. that he tried to get custody of Christopher, but, because of his suicide attempt, his attorney said that there was no hope of this. Phil told K. W. that all his female friends were trying to get money from him all the time.

Jim Blaylock became friendlier with Phil at this time, and the two got together for conversations also. Sometimes Tim Powers was there. Jim said:

I would rather spend an evening with Phil Dick than anyone else. Phil always saw the humor behind what he was…. He lamented about having been married to a number of women and not being able to make any of the marriages work. In spite of this, he told me and Tim, he was monogamous…. He didn't speak well of his mother…. Regardless of how many friends he had, he always struck me as being solitary. He went out on a limb for his friends. He was in ill health to a degree; he recognized that he'd ruined his health in the sixties and early seventies. He took a lot of prescription drugs.

We talked about everything from spirituality to world affairs. Phil would peer at matters from every conceivable angle. He had the power to convince anybody in the world of anything. One night he convinced Powers and me that gravity was diminishing. Another time, he told us that he had come into the possession of two-thousand-year-old information, the knowledge of which had led to the disappearance of many famous people throughout history. He told us that we three, sitting in that room in Santa Ana late that night, were within an ace of being murdered. The KGB was outside, and as he said, "And do you know what this information is?" Tim leaped out of his chair and yelled, "No. No. Don't tell us." Was Phil pulling our leg? Was it true? Was he crazy? Or all three?

JOAN

Joan Simpson, a lively, intelligent person, was very enjoyable to spend time with. We visited back and forth between Point Reyes and her new, owner-designed home in Sonoma County. She was enthusiastic and helpful with my project. I thought we were going to be friends, that we were friends, but suddenly she dropped me. I never knew why. I felt a little like Phil must have felt. Years have passed and just recently we have been e-mailing and talking about getting together for lunch, but she has become ill, and I don't think it will happen.

In the middle of his relationship with Doris Sauter, Phil had his last serious romance, his swan song, he called it, with Joan Simpson. Joan, a small attractive brunette in her mid-thirties, had worked as a psychiatric social worker at the state hospital for the mentally ill at Napa. At the time she met Phil, in 1977, she was a client's rights advocate for the retarded patients at Sonoma State Hospital.

Joan had read Phil's novels in college. She had loved *Confessions of a Crap Artist*. She told me, "It blew my socks away. Then I read *Ubik*. I looked for everything Philip K. Dick had written. I read everything he'd published two or three times over. I thought he was the closest thing to a genius writer in the USA. He stretched your mind and delighted you. A philosopher, a poet, just tremendous."

An old flame of Joan's, Ray Torrence, also a science fiction writer, said to Joan one day in late spring 1977, "Who would you most like to meet in the world? Bill Graham, the rock music promoter, or Philip K. Dick?"

"Philip K. Dick," she responded. Ray told her, "I'm going to make that happen." And he wrote Phil, told him about Joan, and gave him Joan's phone number. About a week later, the phone rang at Joan's place. A voice said, "Hello, Joan, this is Philip K. Dick."

Joan said sarcastically, "Oh, sure."

But it was Philip K. Dick. He invited her to come down to Santa Ana and see him. She had a vacation coming, and two weeks later, she drove down to Santa Ana in her Honda Civic.

As Joan approached the huge white stucco apartment complex locked away by its wrought-iron gate, she thought of *The Man in the High Castle* and *Martian Time-Slip*. She was awed. She felt as if she were walking into a Philip K. Dick novel.

She rang the bell, and, as she walked up the stairs a bearded face peeked over the railing. "Hello," it said, and disappeared. Joan continued walking up to the open doorway. She saw a big, bearded man with a pot belly, built like a bull, jumping from one foot to another like a little kid.

"You're a fox, you're a fox. Come in, come in," he said as he grabbed her by the wrist. "I have to call up Jeter." He called up Jeter: "She's a fox."

Joan was flattered, but thought it was unusually adolescent behavior for a grown man. They sat down to talk. She was nervous, but Phil's humble manner soon put her at ease. Phil invited Joan to stay in the extra bedroom and she accepted, staying three weeks. She gave Doris, who was living in the adjacent apartment, some of her chemotherapy shots. She met Tessa, who was often there with little Christopher. Phil played on the floor with Christopher like another child. Joan noticed that Tessa was tolerant of Phil and kidded him a lot. She met Phil's friends, an adoring young crowd. She was the oldest person there. All Phil's friends told her that she was the best thing that had ever happened to Phil.

"Phil talked to me for hours and hours," Joan told me, "about life, ideas, novels, writing, *The Exegesis*, acid trips, Nancy, Anne, Kleo. He was open about everything. He told me about his entire past, his books—that certain anti-heroines were Anne, certain anti-heroines were Nancy. Those books were real."

Phil was magnanimous with Joan. "I'll take care of everything," he said. "Let's get married." But Joan refused:

We talked, we hugged, we kissed a little, but mostly I seemed to do a lot of mothering. Phil was so tentative, it's as if I would have to stand him on his head and do the dance of the seven veils around him. What would it take to get this guy to perk up sexually? He would hug me, but it was more like a child. He didn't seem to know that he was a sexual being.

At that point in time, Phil was really and truly kissing it all good-bye—he was checking out on life. He was extremely smart, amazing—but if I had met him at Napa State Hospital, I wouldn't have been surprised. He was nuts, paranoid, tremendously suspicious, afraid to have people in. He had great difficulty in leaving the apartment, great difficulty in dealing with money. He was taken care of by his agent, his banker. Tessa and Doris were there telling him, "Don't take too many drugs," and going to the grocery store for him. I felt he was damaged, that he had given up on certain areas of his life that had been too difficult. Things were going physiologically wrong. He would get excited and run around for three hours and then collapse with physical and mental exhaustion. At other times, he would get into a state of almost catatonia. He would say, "I have the flu."

He wasn't taking recreational drugs, but he had many prescriptions and several doctors prescribing for him; by this time the drugs had, of necessity, all become prescribed. He could afford to have people take care of him legally, financially, psychologically. He stayed home and petted the cat, talked to me, and listened to the record player.

Joan's feeling was that Phil had never been a healthy person.

Joan had to go home. Her vacation time was up. She invited Phil to come up to her place. She thought it was amazing that he came. While she had been in Santa Ana, it had been a major project for him to get the car out of the garage and go to the store. "Okay, it's time for me to go north," he said, and got in Joan's Honda. After they had been in Sonoma two weeks, he told Joan he wanted to go over to Point Reyes and see Anne, Laura, and Jayne, although, he told Joan, he was frightened of Anne. She had used and abused him and treated him like a servant.

When Joan and Phil came to Point Reyes on a pleasant summer afternoon, the visit wasn't all that meaningful to me, even though I hadn't seen Phil for seven years. I never enjoyed hearing about Phil's girlfriends, much less meeting one. But I politely gave them tea. I thought Joan was Phil's Episcopal nun friend who had cancer. Laura and Jayne and I were readying our horse-vaulting team to go to the national meet (where we would win the "B" Team

Championship of the United States), and my energy was focused on this imminent competition.

Laura, now a tall platinum blonde beauty of seventeen years, vaulted over the car for Phil and showed him her horse. Phil was amazed. He had expected to see a little girl—the ten-year-old he had seen last—not a grown young woman.

Joan said that Phil had been very apprehensive about coming to see me that day, but afterward it was as if a great weight had been lifted from him: "The horror image of you, Anne, had been dispelled." But Phil told Joan that he was terribly disappointed that he hadn't found the skinny young blonde mother of little girls that he'd expected to find. Anne didn't "emote" the way he'd remembered. But, Joan said, "A kind of peace seemed to settle on him after this visit."

Then he told Joan that, of the older girls, he'd always loved Jayne the best. It was Jayne that he should've married, not Hatte. When Joan told me this in 1983, we both looked at each other in a kind of amazed horror. We agreed that it was a bizarre utterance.

Phil told Joan that he was too afraid of Nancy to visit her—Nancy, the most fragile and nonthreatening person I have ever met.

After Phil had been in Sonoma a few weeks, he asked Joan to come back to Santa Ana with him. She decided to quit her job and go. After the couple returned to Santa Ana, they started planning a permanent relationship. "We decided to set up house together in Sonoma. In July, Phil bought furniture for the apartment we found and we shared the cost of a washer and dryer."

In September 1977, Phil had been invited to Metz, France for the Festival International de la Science-Fiction. He would be the Guest of Honor, provide the keynote speech, and accept the Grand Prix du Festival (the Graoully d'Or), for *A Scanner Darkly*. He invited Joan to go with him. Phil was excited to be going to the country that appreciated his work so much. When he arrived there, he found beautiful hardcover editions of his novels in every bookstore. He had been nominated for the Nobel Prize by some of his French followers.

But for Joan, "The trip was horrible. The main thing I did was take care of Phil, wash his undies, make him eat, put him to bed, and tell him, 'Don't worry, Phil, I am here, and I will protect you from the dark powers of the universe.' Phil was brave to go to France."

During the stay in Metz, Joan was sick in bed, off and on, for two weeks, although she also went out with Phil between bouts of flu. But Phil told acquaintances that Joan had had a nervous breakdown, that's why she was staying in bed. He described her rocking back and forth, refusing to go out because her hairdresser hadn't done her hair right. He continued to tell this story after he returned to Santa Ana. To this day, Phil's friends in southern California believe that Joan had a nervous breakdown on that trip.

"When we returned," Joan told me, "the relationship had started to fall apart and I was ready to come home to Sonoma. I said, in effect, to Phil, 'The house is ready. Come on up.' Phil would say, 'I'll be there tomorrow, I'll be there next week.' I had made it clear that I needed to continue to lead my own life and could not run down to Santa Ana with him all the time. But he wasn't going to move up to Sonoma and I wasn't going to move down to Santa Ana. He was involved with Doris and her cancer before, during, and after his relationship with me."

Phil told all his friends that Joan had dumped him after he bought furniture for her and that there was another man involved with her at the same time she was offering to share her apartment with him. Every friend of Phil's knew about the stove and refrigerator that Joan, faithlessly, let Phil buy for her. Phil told Tim that Joan had assigned him a windowless room in their house, that he had paid more than his fair share, that when they split up, she wouldn't let him take the hi-fi speakers, that he felt stifled by Joan, and that they were at odds over the decor of the house.

Joan's views were quite different: "I would've had to sustain me and Phil both. I would've tried this if I had been younger and dumber. I loved Phil, but was not in love with him. I viewed him as an Einstein-like person, who was so lost in his own brilliance that he couldn't tie his own shoelaces. I didn't want to be the one to do it for him, as much as I admired his genius."

Joan reflected:

God had not returned to him after his revelation that gave him the wonderful peace-providing, elevating experience of his life. He kept looking for this to happen again. Doris was getting well, Tessa was going to school, Phil couldn't write, no one was there to make it okay. Everyone let him die. He could've lived longer but no one could take on that tremendous responsibility.

He had such a fear in him, probably from when he was a tiny baby and his sister was dying; it sprouted all these different roots. One was the agoraphobia, one was

The Search for Philip K. Dick

physiological, one was the money thing. He did a thousand and one things that equaled: "I cannot take care of myself, you must take care of me, but you have to make me feel that you're not, and you have to do it exactly the way I want you to." He blamed all his problems on a woman, whoever she was at the moment. He felt totally helpless and dependent. But also, he was powerful and could be destructive.

When he was good, he was very good. He was funny, smart, a genius, and a kind man. A dear, brilliant, driven, guilt-burdened man, a caring man, but too far gone. He had great magnetism and charm, tremendous language skills. He had fought the good fight as best he could in an extraordinarily bizarre world. There was a demonic power possessing him. After all those fifty years, it finally got him. The power of light was having a hard time. But if you asked Phil, "Whose side are you on?" he would say, "Light, Light, Light."

He was so naive, like a child. He sacrificed himself. He gave himself up to it, that dark force. And it would make it better, not fighting it any more. This was a victory in itself. And he said with his life, "Here I am, love me, love me, love me.... I don't know anything else to do. Because this thing we are born into, gets you. Have we done anything evil? No. Then why does it get you?.... There's this dark force, and by virtue of the fact that you are innocent and good, you get done to."

I could love and respect him, admire the hell out of him, and help him as much as I could, but if that meant giving up my own life, no, no.

Joan's Phil was certainly different from my Phil. I did sense a despair in him in those last years, but I wondered, too, if the helpless role that Phil played with Joan, ombudsperson to the severely mentally retarded people at Sonoma State Hospital, was completely real.

Eleven
DEATH OF A SCIENCE FICTION WRITER

Boldness is no virtue
If it causes the surprised organism
To fall a thousand years,
Wondering as he plunges
Where he went wrong,
Where error lay....
There was no road back, even had he lived.
—Philip K. Dick, poem in a letter to Anne Dick, 1977

TRYING TO PUT his relationship with Joan together one last time, Phil got his car out of the garage and, amazingly, drove alone from Santa Ana to Sonoma to visit Joan.

I was surprised when in Point Reyes on a beautiful, sunny afternoon the phone rang and I heard Phil's voice say, "I just happened to be driving through town and thought I might stop by, if it's convenient."

As if this were an everyday occurrence, I said, "Yes, do come right up." Luckily, Laura was home from school. When Phil drove in the driveway, I walked out to meet him in order to greet him and put him at ease. I hadn't seen him since 1971 when he came out to visit with Sheila. Phil had a well-trimmed beard and a good haircut. He was a little heavier than I remembered him, but overall he looked well and attractive. He was dressed neatly in a good-quality plaid wool rancher's jacket and jeans, a nice flannel shirt, and new shoes.

As we walked back to the house I started talking, Phil started talking, and the same wonderful conversation that we had had all through our marriage began again. We sat down out on the patio. I assumed that Phil was there to visit Laura but he directed all his attention to me. We talked and talked as if the conversation that we'd been having fourteen years ago had never ended, as if no time had passed. No shadow of old problems appeared. It was as if none had ever existed.

It was "instant family" that afternoon and evening. Later, Phil talked to his friend Kirsten about an intention to move back to Point Reyes.

After a while, we went to "downtown" Point Reyes Station to see Jayne, her husband, and their three-year-old twin boys. Jayne lived in a white frame cottage much like the one Phil had owned when he moved to Point Reyes Station. Phil took her a bouquet of flowers. For a split second, when he met Jayne's twin boys, Christopher and Aaron, his face twisted with some expression that I couldn't quite read. It almost seemed to be anger. Then Phil, Laura, and I went to the Palace Market, just as we had all those years ago, and shopped for dinner. When we came home, we unpacked the groceries, and all of us hung out in the kitchen, cooking and talking. Phil set the table and opened the wine. We sat down, ate a marvelous dinner together, and never stopping talking. Afterward, Laura and Phil made a lemon meringue pie. At nine o'clock, Phil said he had to go. As I walked with him out to his car, we were still conversing. It had been a wonderful visit. I thought, "This was such a happy meeting, I'm sure I'll be seeing Phil now occasionally, and who knows...."

I was never to see him again.

Goodbye, Phil.

In November, Phil phoned Kirsten Nelson and told her he was coming to northern California to the Santa Rosa Science Fiction Convention. He planned to stay with the Nelsons. Phil told Kirsten that he had some unfinished business to take care of in Point Reyes. "I wondered," she said, "reading between the lines, if there might be some sort of reconciliation with you, Anne, going to happen."

Phil called later and told Kirsten that his son had an ear infection, and he couldn't come.

He wrote a letter addressed to both Laura and me, on December 24, 1977:

I am enclosing a poem I recently wrote. When I was last up at Sonoma I had a friend feed my two cats, and he phoned me to say that Harvey, my big black part-Siamese tom, had fallen over the railing of my third-floor apartment patio, and evidently had been killed. I did not return to Santa Ana for five more days, and when I drove into the underground parking area of our building I heard him calling me. He had not only survived the fall, but had been smart enough to go down into the basement to wait for my return. His faith that I would eventually return deeply moved me; hence this poem.

On a Cat Which Fell Three Stories and Survived

Boldness is no virtue
If it causes the surprised organism
To fall a thousand years,
Wondering as he plunges
Where he went wrong,
Where error lay.
Little bodies coast on wind:
Spiders, for example, sail on strands
And cats (they say) align themselves according to the tides.
But humans and their like drop as iron would drop:
Crushing and crushed, amazed and smashed.
God seems to harbor an inverse ratio to size.
There was no road back, even had he lived. And yet he found it, crouched in basement darkness,
Terrified by cars and groaning noise.
First one day, then a next, then other days,
On and on: infinitudes of time within a little mind,
But mind devoted to remembered safeness:
Once a spot to eat and lie,
Once human friends,
Once peace;
Now torn away and only roarings left
And knowledge of the doom of living things.

When I read this letter years ago, I regarded it as a self-pitying ploy from Phil to draw me back into his web, and from past experience I believed that as soon as I did he would pull the emotional rug out from under me. It was a nice poem, but the tone of self-pity put me off, and maybe it was just about his cat anyway. Pity is a degrading emotion to have toward someone. Self-pity is even worse and never to be encouraged.

Be Spartan, I had been taught by my big brothers. I expected Phil to be Spartan, too. But the main problem was that he hadn't honestly informed me about his life over the years, I knew very little about what had been happening to him since he had left me, and he had given me no basis to understand the message of this poem—that he really had been suffering for a long, long time. Now this poem makes me sad for him— twenty-seven years after his death, I understand a lot more.

When Phil wrote the next letter to Laura on December 28, 1977, she was no longer living at home and sharing her letters with me:

> I'm glad to hear you say that my letters brighten up your life; one of the main reasons I haven't written to you is that I haven't wanted to depress you. If I were to tell you what's going on in my life…I'd have to cop out to a basically bummer situation…. I think being lonely is the pits, the absolute pits. That's what I'm facing without Joan. However, my best friend, who is also a science fiction writer, is going to be moving into this building in a couple of days. We spend a lot of time together shooting the breeze. We're engaged in a long study of a number of religions of the Greco-Roman-Celtic period. The research is basically for my novel-in-progress, *VALIS*, and we have uncovered some extraordinary things that few people know, even scholars. In fact we are discerning the outlines of a vast, buried, suppressed religion….

Another letter to Laura came on the same day:

> I am really lonely, Laura, and I am reaching out to you, but at the same time trying not to be a bummer burden by laying my troubles on you. Christmas is not a good time to be alone, eating a frozen TV Mexican dinner. I'm glad I have my black cat, Harvey, back, though. Ever since his fall he's been so subdued and thoughtful…. I guess he learned a lot. I wonder what his theory of the universe is now.

About this same time Phil finished *VALIS*—his autobiography, he said, of both his personalities. Horselover Fat, one of Phil's personas, had also taken a trip to Sonoma. After he (they) comes (come) back to Santa Ana, unchronicled forces have healed the psychological split in him caused by Gloria's suicide and allowed his two personalities to be healed and reunited. Fat/Phil no longer feels terrible guilt for not preventing Gloria's death, but Fat/Phil now realizes he will never be able to restore Gloria to this world as he had longed to do. When she read this book, Nancy was puzzled by Phil's intense feelings about Gloria's suicide—she said that Gloria was a young woman whom they hardly knew.

Phil wrote Laura on January 3, 1978:

> It's been raining down here at last. I'm sitting around doing research for my new novel, as usual.... We've now gotten into research on Soviet microwave boosting of what are called "psychotronic" signals, which are actually telepathic signals. These psychotronic signals are amplified electronically and then beamed by the Russians to a satellite, whereupon the satellite emits them downward to United States cities, screwing up radio and TV reception (usually late at night when United States radio and TV transmitters cut their power down). The result is that the Soviets are able to include a lot of subliminal information (fired off at nano second intervals and received by peoples' right brain hemispheres but not the left) in what we are consciously seeing or hearing. There is no international law prohibiting this (there was an article in the *L.A. Times* about it). We are probably doing the same thing to the Soviets, although the United States is far behind them in work with ESP. The Soviets got interested in telepathy as a medium of communication to reach distant satellites and spaceships because there is no time-lag with telepathic signals as there is with radio signals. They've done some enormously radical work in the U.S.S.R. that we know little about; for instance, there is a lab in Siberia run by the KGB (the Soviet secret police) which is off-limits to even Soviet scientists. What they are doing no one seems to know, except that a defector from it said that the work includes the influencing of minds by ESP, and that they've been successful. It's all scary, but interesting.

In January, Phil, talking to Kirsten Nelson, again told her that he was thinking of moving back to Point Reyes. Laura was now the focus of his hopes for someone to love, someone to love him. Writing her in this same month he talks about a move to Sonoma: "An important matter to me is whether you're going to be in the Bay Area during the next couple of years, since I am seriously thinking of taking over the house in Sonoma which Joan and I rented together and which she is living in. She'd move out, I'd move in, and then I could see you from time to time—IF you were still in the Bay Area. It's an idea; as we say down here, 'It's a plan.'"

In the spring of 1978, Laura applied for admittance to Stanford University. I had told her, "It's almost impossible to get in. If you do get in, where will you get the money to go to this incredibly expensive school?"

She told me, "That's where I'm going." And she was admitted, winning several scholarships. Phil was ecstatic. (As was I.) He told us over the phone he would send money to help with her expenses, money for clothes, and money for a hi-fi.

Shortly after this conversation, I discovered that my office manager, a young woman whom I had thought of as almost another daughter, had embezzled $20,000 from my jewelry business, totally stripping it of working capital and leaving me in horrendous debt for payroll taxes, etc. I missed out on a free trip with the vaulting team to Europe to the International Vaulting Competition in San Moritz, Switzerland. I had to stay home and pursue a court case against her in the hopes of recovering the money (which I did). When I told Phil about this, he was very sympathetic. He said, "Maybe I should send the money that I'm going to send to Laura for college to you instead." I thanked him but didn't accept Laura's college money. My vaulting team had a great European trip and did very well in the individual events.

Later that year, Laura invited Phil to come to Point Reyes to see her graduate from high school. Over the phone I also urged Phil to come and told him he could stay with us in one of our spare bedrooms. He was astonished. He said, "You mean you'd let me stay in your house?" We really thought he was going to come, but at the last minute he wrote Laura a long, sad letter saying that he couldn't come—that all he had in his life was his writing.

Phil's mother was quite ill all this year, and Phil talked for long periods on the phone to her. Lynne, Phil's stepsister, said, "Phil was really tuned in to Mom's illness." The two of them resolved a lot of the problems that had existed between them over the years. Dorothy died in late summer. By happenstance, I talked with her on the phone the night before she died. She was to have an operation that might help her but was risky. She told me that she was totally unafraid. Phil was in touch with his second wife, Kleo, too, and talked with her about Dorothy's death.

When he talked to me, he didn't seem the least bit grieved. But Kleo was indignant that Phil was "so lugubrious" about his mother's death after having had such a bad relationship with Dorothy his entire life. It seemed to me that there was a change for the better in Phil after his mother's death. He seemed freer, happier.

Phil's role playing, which almost amounted to putting on a different identity, was quite remarkable in other situations. Kleo and I both noticed that when

Phil had been interviewed by such diverse publications as *Vortex Magazine*, *The New Yorker*, and *Rolling Stone*, etc. Phil played to and played with each interviewer, assuming a different persona for each one.

As well as having a versatile personality, Phil was generous with his praise and even with his writing. In a correspondence with a young science fiction writer, Daniel Gilbert, he heaped praise on Daniel's efforts and gave him a free bit of manuscript to add to a story. In September 1978, he wrote: "Dear Daniel...I like the 7 pages of "Confessions of a Troublemaker," which you sent me, and as regards these 7 pages you have my permission to make use of me in them by name as a character.... You'll find enclosed a freebee little 2 pages that I tacked on to your 7 pages; you can use it all or any part.... [I]t's a present to you."

The text that Phil sent Daniel:

In the back of the bus an old wino in tattered clothing sat hunched over, holding a wine bottle ill-concealed in a brown paper bag. He seemed to be staring at me—in a listless and depressed sort of way—and I found myself returning his stare.

"Don't you recognize me?" the old wino said suddenly. "No," I answered, hoping his limited span of attention would wander away from me. But the old wino lurched to his feet, shambled over and seated himself beside me. "I'm Phil Dick," he said hoarsely. "At the end of my life. Changed, haven't I?" He chuckled, but without mirth.

"This is how a giant of the field winds up?" I said, amazed, distress filling me. "My life was an unending failure," Phil said, and I saw now that it was, indeed, Phil Dick; I recognized the eyes, the sorrow-drenched but still proud glare of a person who had known torment but had not bowed to it. "Marriage after marriage down the rathole... money gone...my children and friends deserting me...all my hopes for a family and stability shot." He took a covert swig from the bottle; it was, I saw, Ripple. "I may have been a success as a writer," he continued, "but what does that matter really? Living alone year after year in a rented room, paying off the IRS and my endless child support, waiting vainly for the right girl, the girl who, when she finally showed up, merely laughed at me." Tears filled his eyes. "Being a giant of science fiction is not all that much," he rasped. "It's like Goethe said: the peasant with his hearth and wife and children is happier than the greatest philosopher."

From behind us a sharp laugh sounded. "I'm doing fine," a needlelike voice penetrated at the two of us. Turning, I saw that it was Harlan Ellison, wearing a snappy suit, his face dancing with satisfaction. "Tough luck, Phil, but we get what we deserve. There's a logic to the universe."

"Okay, Harlan," Phil murmured, clutching his wine bottle. "Lay off."

"You may have wound up in the gutter," Harlan continued, unabashed, "but I have my big house in Sherman Oaks; I have my library of all my thousands of—"

"I knew you when you were a twerp fan," Phil broke in. "Back in 1954. I gave you a story for your fanzine."

"And a crummy story it was," Harlan said, with a smirk.

Falteringly, Phil murmured, "But you said you liked it."

"I liked the name of the main character," Harlan corrected. "Waldo. I remember exactly what I said; I said, 'I always admire people named Waldo.' I threw the story away."

Slumped over in misery, Phil said nothing. The bus continued on; and, as I scrutinized the gloating, amused face of Harlan Ellison and the unhappy, defeated figure beside me I wondered what it was all about, what it was all for. Which of the two of them did I feel the most pity for? Gloating cruelty and triumph, or wretched despair? It was hard to say.

Phil's letter to Daniel continued:

Meanwhile, due to all the money I'm making I'm experiencing a vast depression, mirrored by a decay in the reality around me. (1) The refrigerator makes odd noises. (2) There is CB interference on my TV. (3) The rear-end of my car is leaking oil. See? *Ubik* revisited. However, my girlfriend who has had cancer has been pronounced cured. I guess that's good (boy, I AM depressed).

In a later letter to Daniel, Phil writes:

You're off to a terrific start. You really are. The two stories are full of life and vigor and wit, and the endings in both are superb. I foresee a career for you. Yes, you're right; it's like when "Roog" [Phil's first published short story] came out…and I feel it, too; I share your excitement (which seems out of line to me, because after all they are your stories, not mine; but, nonetheless, I feel a deep pride in them and a sense of the new beginnings of creativity. It's as if time has rolled back to 1952 for me).

On her own, while she was going to Stanford University, Laura visited Phil in early 1979. Phil was out of his mind with joy that his beautiful grown-up daughter was visiting him. He took her out, bought her clothes, and gave her money. After this first visit, Laura went down to Santa Ana several times.

Phil wrote to Laura right after that visit, on February 19, 1979: "Generally I have tended to think of my success or failure in terms of my writing, but I realized tonight that for me having you as my daughter, and being so close to you—I really have felt incredibly close to you these last days—means more to me."

On March 12, 1979, he wrote her:

You know, your visit here with me has had a strange effect on me. I go into a peculiar state or mood which is a mixture of absolute joy and bitter pain. The joy is easily understood, but the pain has puzzled me. I've decided it's simply because I miss you. That's easy to understand. Anyhow, the joy is winning out.

Keep in touch. I really intend to make major changes in my life; I feel new tides and new waves flowing in me and over me, the winds of something I have never done before, never been before, a new start, the end of the old. It's as if an old fossilized part of me has perished, and should perish, and, like my jade plant, I am thrusting out new leaves. Wow. It's painful, like birth, but good. I feel like I could go anywhere and do anything.

But by April 2, 1979, his mood had changed:

I woke up this morning—all freaked out—it has to do with the Three Mile Island reactor, I think, because I stayed up until 4 a.m. to get the final news over my rock station, and I was so sleepy I couldn't understand what they were saying. I found this morning that I had the impression that a meltdown was taking place right now, but today's news was good, so I guess the only meltdown is in my own brain. You're right; it's amazing that so few people are upset by this. They just do not understand. I remember when I was a child on December 7, 1941, and there was the news on the radio about the Japanese bombing Pearl Harbor; I phoned my mother to tell her. "We're at war with Germany, Italy, and Japan." I yelled, to which she replied calmly, "No, I don't think so, Phil," and went back to her gardening. I was 12 years old and I was more in touch than a grown person. That made a big impression on me, my mother's failure to react; it was both an intellectual failure and an emotional one, if you ponder it.

This, maybe, is one reason I get along so well with people a lot younger than me; I think the older you get the dumber you get; I mean people in general. You start losing touch with reality by subtle, gradual degrees until you wind up puttering around with your flowers in the backyard while World War Three breaks out. This is how I imagine my father, assuming he's still alive: out in his back yard unaware of the world and, worse, wanting to be unaware of the world.

Phil didn't know that his long-estranged father was still alive. Laura had discovered that Edgar Dick, her grandfather, lived literally right over the fence of the Stanford campus. She climbed it, went over to his house, and introduced herself to her grandfather and his wife, Gertrude. She visited them frequently and did her homework lying on her stomach on their living room floor. I went down to Menlo Park to meet Edgar and Gertrude with Laura. Edgar was a spritely and intelligent man in his eighties, interested in politics, conservative. The next time I talked to Phil on the phone I told him, "Your father is okay, Phil." Phil called his father, and a telephone dialogue began between the two of them that continued until Phil's death. Phil sent his father autographed copies of some of his novels and copies of magazine interviews. His father was immensely proud of them.

Phil wrote Laura on May 27, 1979, complaining of deep fatigue:

Yesterday (Saturday) I was exhausted and unable to function. On Friday I completed my tax work and it left me drained. Yesterday I took a long nap and had a sort of dream, almost a delusional vision, in which I was meeting you at the airport and putting my arms around you and hugging you and giving you a kiss. I woke up and felt pain in my jaw from trying to kiss you. Never have I known such pain. I felt as if my jaw would break. I asked myself, "How has it come about that I screwed up so badly? What is wrong with me?" I sense something wrong with me, something profound. I can't discern its nature but it scares me. I ask myself, "Am I afraid of something? Afraid to love my own daughter? And if so, why? Is it because I have lost person after person that I loved, so that now I am damaged?" I feel damaged. I sense myself taking the line of least resistance, in every situation. I am conserving my psychological energy. But only an organism preparing to die does that. Am I withdrawing from life itself? Maybe that is it. I don't know.

Then I think…another thing that has drained me: my writing. Five years on my recent novel, *VALIS*, which I sent off last November. And I am working on a follow-up to it. Night after night I work until 4 or 5 a.m. During the day I am exhausted. But I have to do it; it's my job. This is that goddamn Protestant work-ethic. Can't I forget about my book? I can't. Twenty-eight years of writing—decades of writing—have cut into my brain so that in my brain there is this rut and I keep going around and around in the rut....

I have reached the point of exhaustion. They are turning this apartment building into condominiums and I have to deal with that. My life may change radically—I may move away from Orange County—and here I am exhausted from my professional work and my friendship with a sick girl. I am neglecting entire parts of my life such as my relationships with my children because of my worry and exhaustion. I have become a machine which thinks and does nothing else. It scares me. How did this come about? I posed myself a problem and I cannot forget the problem but I cannot answer the problem, so I am stuck in fly-paper. I can't get loose; it's like a self-imposed karma at work. Every day my world gets smaller. I work more, I live less. Whole systems and circuits in my brain, I believe, I sense, are shutting down. I am like a ship which people are preparing to abandon. The power is being shut off. And yet at the same time I have a clear idea of what I want; I want to be with my children. I want to be with Laura. Then why am I working on my goddamn book? Have I no power to stop? Right; I have no power to stop: I am obsessive. The epistemological/theological/philosophical problem which I posed to myself years ago runs me and has turned me into a servo-assist mechanism. Somewhere along the line, maybe years ago, I lost control of the idea so that it began to dominate me rather than I it. I have become a mechanical function of my own idea, the idea that something is wrong in the cosmos and I have to figure out what it is. No one ever has been able to do this but I am going to do this. I am like a rat trying to get aboard a rat-proof ship; there is simply no way that rat is going to get aboard the ship—no matter how long he tries to figure the situation out. He is on a rope leading to the ship but there is one of those rat guards that no rat can cross.

Meanwhile I wear myself out more each day; my energy level drops. Every now and then I imagine I've figured out some small clue in my epistemological search. But for every clue I figure out, ten more unexplained things pop up. The ratio between what I know and what I don't know worsens. This means that the longer I continue to try the worse it's going to get; all I know right now is that I do not know. A mystery confronts me. God is a mystery and the reason for God's silence is a mystery....

Phil was still giving away money to his friends and others. He paid $2,700 to the Church of the Messiah for the community services project from which Doris was drawing a salary. K. W. Jeter said that Phil was an easy touch for rent, groceries, and car money for Tessa and Doris. Phil offered to put up the down payment on a condominium for best friend, Tim Powers, and his new wife, Serena, but Tim wouldn't accept the money.

Jim Blaylock said, "Phil was the most generous person with money that I ever saw. If someone said to him, 'I need a thousand dollars by Friday,' Phil would reply, 'Okay, when can I get it to you?' The teller who had worked at the local bank asked Phil for a loan of a thousand dollars. Phil didn't loan it to her: he gave it to her."

Phil was generous with his praise when I sent him a sixteen-page color brochure that I had made to promote my handcrafted jewelry. By then I was selling to galleries, museum shops, and fine stores all over the United States and employed thirteen people. I was the largest employer in Point Reyes Station. Phil lavishly praised the designs, the graphics, and the logo, and showed the catalogue to everyone who came by his condominium. Tim said that Phil seemed to be more proud of it than he was of his own work.

By this time, Doris had moved to another apartment and saw Phil less. Although she dated others, she still brought meals over to Phil's place. Phil couldn't go out to eat at this time. His throat constricted when he was in a restaurant and he couldn't swallow.

Laura was to be married in August 1980. Throughout the year, Laura had been writing and talking with Phil about coming to Point Reyes and taking part in the wedding. I had seconded her invitation, and Phil sounded as if he would actually come. He asked Laura to make him a list of what his obligations were and sent money for much of the wedding expense. As the wedding came close, he called and told me, "I can't come. My doctor says that my tachycardia is too bad and that I might drop dead from the excitement of being in a strange situation."

I didn't feel I could urge him to come if he was liable to have a heart attack, but Laura and I were both disappointed. It wasn't six weeks later that Phil told me that he'd accepted an invitation to go to Metz. I didn't ask him about his tachycardia. But Phil told Doris and Tim that he didn't come to Laura's wedding, because "Anne didn't really want me to come."

Laura sent him the book of wedding pictures (at his request) showing a large group of family and friends smiling and having a wonderful time at the wedding at St. Columba's and the subsequent party on our patio. The next time Phil called, I asked him how he had liked the pictures. He was so short with me that he was almost rude and wouldn't comment on the pictures or wedding at all. He must have believed his own version of why he didn't come to Laura's wedding.

In the fall of 1980, Phil wrote a story, "Frozen Journey," for *Playboy* magazine, depicting a man who is burdened with terrible guilt and terrible fear, emotions that destroy all possibility for inner comfort. When an early wife, older now, appears to comfort him, he can't believe in her reality.

During the last year of his life, 1981, Phil continued in his night-owl routine in Santa Ana. He'd do his shopping at midnight, buying kitty litter and frozen chocolate pies at Ralph's grocery store, around the corner from his condominium. The people who worked at Ralph's loved Phil.

Doris and Tessa were still hanging around Phil's apartment, and sometimes Christopher came over to play. But when Doris moved away from Santa Ana in 1981, Phil felt deserted. The close friendship that these two had had disappeared. When Doris tried to talk to Phil by long distance, he was cold and unresponsive. Then Phil started dating Tessa and there was some talk between them of remarriage.

During this last period, Phil seemed to be on top of the world in some ways. He was continuing to make a lot of money. He was excited about his novel *Do Androids Dream of Electric Sheep?* being made into a 30 million dollar movie, *Blade Runner*, starring Harrison Ford. One day, the studio sent a limousine to pick Phil up and take him to the studio to see an early version of the movie.

His doctor had told him to lose some weight and he did so, quite rapidly, getting back his old slim figure and a lower blood pressure reading. He bought some fashionable clothes, had his beard and hair trimmed by a good barber, and looked quite elegant. He was dating several ladies and going out socially more than he ever had before. He told his friend Tim Powers how good he felt as he munched on his diet of Rice Krispies and chocolate cookies.

He was extremely pleased that, finally, a literary novel of his would be published. A major New York publisher, Simon and Schuster, would be publishing *The Transmigration of Timothy Archer* in May 1982. This novel summed up much of Phil's past. It dealt with Phil's experiences with Bishop James Pike but it was set in the Berkeley of Phil's youth. Phil told Laura that Angel Archer, the leading female character, was based on her. This powerful, blunt, direct young woman is the most sympathetic female character in all of Phil's forty novels, and *The Transmigration of Timothy Archer* is the only novel written from a female point of view.

In 1983, Pike's widow and younger son, Chris, lived in Inverness and also went to St. Columba's Church. At the coffee shop one day, Chris happened to be sitting next to me at the counter. We struck up a conversation, and after a while he asked me if the story about his late brother, Jim, in The Transmigration of Timothy Archer *was true. His mother had read it recently and was worried that Jim had really had an affair with Maren Hackett. "No," I said. "It was Philip's way in his writing to fictionalize real people and manipulate their actions whatever way he fancied that day." Chris was very relieved and said his mother would be, too.*

Phil was even having his biography written. He had invited Gregg Rickman, a librarian at the Los Angeles Public Library, to his apartment for a series of taped interviews, because Gregg had written an article in a fanzine about the empathy Phil had for "people, animals, and life." The first time Gregg came, Phil told him that he recently had lost a great deal of weight. He said that he hadn't been able to eat because of grief and his hyper-empathy.

Phil made Gregg his official biographer. On one tape that Gregg and Phil made, Phil talked about his mother. He said that when he was a small child, he believed his mother was trying to kill him.

Phil was still giving money away. He gave $10,000 to the Quakers for Cambodian relief. He gave Kleo $1,200 when her husband, Phil's old friend Norman Mini, died.

Phil phoned his friend Jim Blaylock one evening and said he was being paid $40,000 for *Blade Runner*. He asked Jim, "What will I do with the money?" He told Jim that he couldn't think of anything he wanted but a ham sandwich—so he went out and bought a ham sandwich.

Phil was still telling stories to Tim Powers about his wife, his house, his kids, and his animals back in Point Reyes Station. Tim told me, "Anne, I could draw a floor plan of your house. In 1981, Phil still told stories of how you had chased him with a gun for two years after the divorce, tried to run him down with a white Jaguar, and waved knives at him. He told these stories with great relish."

My own conversations with Phil had become more and more relaxed. He seemed so much less touchy that finally, after eighteen years, I got up the nerve to ask him a few things. I said, "I heard from Laura that you've helped Nancy and others with money, why haven't you ever helped me?" I was thinking of the back child support of $75 a month. I didn't really have any idea of how successful he'd become.

He replied bitterly, "You're too strong." I was so surprised I couldn't think of a response or my other questions. Later, in another phone conversation I asked him, "Phil, why did you leave Point Reyes? I really never knew." He answered so quickly and mechanically it was as if he had been waiting for me to ask him this question for years. As if by rote, he said, "I thought that we fought too much. It was bad for the children."

About two months before Phil's death I thought, "It's important to tell people how you feel about them while you can." I didn't have any premonition about Phil's impending death, at least not consciously, but I wanted to express to him in some nonthreatening way that I had loved him and that love was still there. The next time we talked I told him, "I always loved you." He didn't respond at all. It was as if he didn't even hear me. I was so nervous and timid about talking about love to him—maybe he didn't want to hear what I wanted to say—that I didn't know how to continue or even if I should continue. Still, I was glad I had put my feelings in words even though he may not have believed me or didn't like me telling him this. It may even have been a burden to him—more guilt to carry.

Tessa was serious about remarrying Phil, but Phil told his friend Tim that the prospect of remarrying Tessa terrified him more than anything in the world. He started going with Mary Wilson and invited her to go to the next Metz meeting with him. He told me over the phone, "She's a kind of super-secretary, not a girlfriend."

Mary said, "We had a relationship on so many levels, it was hard to describe. We were going to sign partnership papers. Phil was going to back my acting career. He liked to have me around to gauge people's reactions."

Phil was also dating a woman architect in her early thirties who lived by the beach and drove a turbo Porsche. It annoyed Phil when she talked about her great car.

Old friend and fellow sci-fi writer Ray Nelson came down from Berkeley and visited Phil in December. Phil was expecting one of his current girlfriends to visit and told Ray, "She'll be here any minute, and I'll introduce you to the girl I'm going to marry." Then he got an odd look on his face and said, "But I can't remember her name." He got out his address book, looked up the woman's name, and wrote it on the inside of his hand. "Now I won't have any problem," he told Ray, happily.

Ray wrote me in 1988:

I visited Phil in L.A. shortly before his death, and found him pleased with his newfound wealth and delighted with the movie version of *Do Androids Dream of Electric Sheep?* even though a series of screenwriters had made major changes in it. We talked about his various wives and girlfriends and he went out of his way to indicate to me that he didn't care about any of them, that he couldn't even remember their names.

Most of the time he put on a great show of happiness, yet whenever we left the world of literature and entered the world of personal relations, a great void of sadness seemed to open up behind his eyes.

Only once did he seem to be speaking to me as a real person and not a mask. We'd been talking about old friends when suddenly, seriously, he said, "How's Anne?"

Phil's days were busy and productive. He was active in the management of his condominium complex. The Perezes, his next-door neighbors who lived in Doris's old apartment, were extremely fond of him and invited him over for dinner two nights a week.

The last time I talked to Phil on the phone, three weeks before he died, he was carrying on about Mary Wilson, and I thought to myself, "There he goes again."

Phil had a stroke on February 18, on a Thursday. He called his doctor in the morning and described pre-stroke symptoms. His doctor urged him to go to the hospital, but evidently he either didn't go or couldn't. The Perezes found him on the floor of his apartment late that afternoon. Tim Powers rushed over to be with him while he was being taken to the intensive care unit of nearby Western Hospital.

Laura, back in Michigan, Phil's only adult relative, was notified and phoned me. The next morning I called the hospital, and the head nurse on the floor told me that Phil had had a mild stroke and there was every reason to believe that he would have a full recovery. But on Saturday morning, when I phoned again, he had had a much worse stroke. The nurse told me he had been resuscitated and was now in intensive care. Laura flew out from Michigan on the advice of the hospital staff. Phil recovered consciousness Saturday evening when Laura arrived and was extremely glad to see her. I was on the phone half the day with Laura, the hospital, and other relatives. My telephone bill was $1,000 that month, a great deal of money at that time.

I debated with myself about whether it was the right thing to do to go down to see Phil one last time, but Laura told me that I wouldn't have been admitted.

Many friends were trying to get in to see Phil, and science fiction fans were hanging around in the corridors—one even managed to get into the intensive care section. Reporters from *Newsweek* and *Time* magazines were phoning. Ex-wives and old girlfriends were coming out of the woodwork. There was a lot of intrigue. Finally, the hospital withdrew visitation privileges from everyone except the family: Laura, the only adult family member.

Phil sank rapidly on Sunday. On Monday, strongly against the wishes of Phil's current girlfriend, Laura brought in an Episcopal priest, who "laid on hands" and prayed for healing for Phil. But by Tuesday, Phil had sunk further, and the priest, who had come again, told Laura that they must read the last rites. Phil was anointed with unction, and, standing by his bed, Laura read the responses: "Have mercy upon him...have mercy upon him...grant him your peace." Laura thought that Phil squeezed her hand faintly at the end of this ritual. He fell into a deeper and deeper coma and suffered extreme tachychardia and many heart failures. Toward the end of the week, the nurses and doctors told Laura to go up to stay with Jayne and me in Point Reyes Station. She was emotionally exhausted, and there was nothing more she could do. Phil was gone. There was only a body being kept artificially alive. Doris Sauter was allowed to sit by Phil's bed and read the Episcopal litanies. There had been no brain activity for five days when on March 2, the head of the hospital's neurological division called Laura. We had all been sitting around the kitchen table at Jayne's house talking and waiting. The neurologist told Laura that if there were no objections from the family, he would order the life-support system turned off. He stated that it was cruel to keep it going. Laura hesitated. Perhaps some of her concern was that some of the women in Phil's life were in a state of denial and were sure he would somehow recover and, also, she was only twenty-two years old. Without thinking I said firmly, "I'll take the responsibility."

A memorial service was held in Santa Ana. I worked out a plan with Phil's father, who arranged for Phil's ashes to be flown back to Fort Morgan, Colorado, and buried beside his twin sister, Jane. Later, at Paul Williams's suggestion, I arranged another service in St. Columba's Church in Inverness for Phil's northern California friends and relatives.

Phil finally got into *Time* magazine. It printed a short obituary.

There was great shock and grief among Phil's friends and in the science fiction community when Phil died. One friend said, "He was one of those special people whose like will not be seen again...."

PART III: 1928-58

As I learned about Phil's life after Point Reyes, it seemed to me that the luminous spirit of the man I had known had been obscured. It was still there—but like a dim reflection in an old scratched mirror. I had wanted to understand what had happened between Phil and me, but what I found still didn't make an understandable pattern. I decided to learn everything I could about Phil's past—and there was my Phil again!

Twelve
EARLY YEARS

Phil was a Sunday's Child, high spirited, yelling, full of life from the minute he was born.

—Edgar Dick, 1983 interview

When her labor pains began more than a month early, on December 16, 1928, Dorothy Kindred Dick had no idea she was going to have twins. She and her husband, Edgar, were at home in their Chicago apartment, and the woman doctor whom Dorothy, an early feminist, had chosen had not yet arrived, much to Edgar's disgust. He didn't think his wife should have chosen a woman doctor. A tiny blond boy was born at 8 a.m. Over fifty years later, his father, long estranged from the family, still spoke of that child fondly and tenderly. Edgar wiped the mucus from the newborn baby's face. "I knew how because I had delivered a lot of calves," he told me at his home in Menlo Park when I interviewed him in 1983.

Much to the couple's and the doctor's surprise, labor pains started again. A tiny, quiet, dark-haired girl was born. Dorothy and Edgar named her Jane Charlotte.

Dorothy, always thin and frail, had no milk, and Edgar wanted the babies to be sent to the hospital, but the doctor disagreed. There were great discussions about what the babies should be fed. Edgar said that Dorothy "even consulted the janitor," who suggested goat's milk.

Dorothy's mother, Meemaw, was sent for, but Edgar said, "She didn't remember much about raising babies." She arrived in Chicago two weeks later, but very soon it was clear that the situation was too much for her. When the babies were three weeks old, two visiting nurses came to the house to check the children for an insurance policy Edgar had taken out on them. The nurses saw that the babies were dying and insisted on taking them immediately to the hospital. Meemaw grabbed Phil and ran into the bathroom and hid. She was afraid he would never come back. But the nurses prevailed and both children were taken to the hospital.

The two babies were diagnosed as being severely dehydrated. Jane died soon after. Phil was put in an incubator and improved enough in two weeks to be brought back home. A wet nurse was found, a big Polish woman, and baby Phil smiled his first smile at her.

The death of Jane had a profound affect on Phil's entire life. The separation from that incredible closeness that twins experience in the womb, the separation from his mother, the physical deprivation the tiny baby experienced—all left their mark. Dorothy talked mournfully about Jane's death throughout Phil's childhood. "I heard about Jane a lot," he said years later, "and it wasn't good for me. I felt guilty—somehow I got all the milk." As a child he imagined a playmate whom he called "Becky." He thought of her as his lost sister.

Jane's body was sent back to Colorado. Edgar's family held a graveside ceremony in a blinding snowstorm at the Fort Morgan cemetery. When Dorothy told about this terrible time, she repeatedly stated that Edgar had stayed at his club. He wasn't there to help her when things were really rough. Edgar's account made him sound like a good guy and portrayed Dorothy as having bad judgment and bad instincts.

When Phil was born, Edgar and Dorothy had already been married eight years. They had met in their home state of Colorado, when Edgar came back in 1918 from serving with the Fifth Marines in France, the most highly decorated infantry battalion in the history of the U.S. Marine Corps.

Edgar was second oldest of a farming family of ten boys and four girls. Dorothy told me that the family ate in two shifts. The dining room table wasn't big enough for them to all eat together. Edgar had been born in Johnstone, Pennsylvania, at the turn of the century. In a memoir that he wrote about his natal family, Edgar referred to his mother, Bessie Mack, as Irish, but another time he said she was Scotch-Irish, as was his father. Phil, as an adult, put great emphasis on the one-quarter German blood he claimed to inherit, but actually his mother was of English descent and his father's family was Scotch-Irish. Phil had no German blood in him at all—but he never mentioned any Irish ancestry.

Edgar adored his mother, and saw her as "protecting her children's lives and a wonderful cook." He spoke of his father as an excessively severe, although intelligent, man: "I can remember my father whipping us for trying to mimic him gargling." Edgar's father was frugal, organized, and hardworking and taught his son to be this way.

In the teens of the twentieth century, Edgar thought his father made a terrible mistake when he moved his family from the Pennsylvania farm to a desolate, water-deprived area near Cedarwood, Colorado. The family starved physically and mentally for more than three years on a homestead that was "ruled by dry, hot wind, tumbleweeds, jack rabbits, coyotes, rattlesnakes, and prairie dogs." Later they moved to Fort Morgan in northeastern Colorado and went into sugar beet farming. Brothers of Edgar's still own land and farm in this area.

In 1917, when the United States declared war on Germany, Edgar "wanted to go to defeat the Kaiser." Although he was only seventeen, he was six feet tall and a big, husky young man. He persuaded his father and mother to go with him, and one night they went by lantern light to the tiny post office in Fort Morgan and signed his enlistment papers for the Marines. "When I left Colorado on the train, I told my mother I'd wave to her as I went by the house. I remember her standing there on the front steps waving good-bye to me. I'll never forget. I can still see her standing there."

After training for six months in Pennsylvania, Edgar went to France. He was, he said, "a corporal, like Napoleon and Hitler," and became a runner taking messages from one company to another at the front, because he could spot German machine-gunners in the trees when no one else could. The Fifth Marines were shock troops that were brought to the front lines of battle in difficult military situations. Edgar fought in the battles of Belleau Wood, the Argonne, and Chateau Thierry. He loved the adventure of being a soldier and told me he was sad when the war was over and he had to go back home.

He met Dorothy Kindred from the Rocky Mountain town of Greeley, and they married September 29, 1920. In 1923, the young couple moved to Washington, D.C., to take advantage of a federal scholarship at Georgetown University that was granted to ex-servicemen. Pursuing agricultural studies, Edgar graduated in 1927 and became a scientific aide at an experimental live-stock farm near the capital.

Dorothy Grant Kindred, Phil's mother, was the middle child of three. Her father, Earl Grant Kindred, "a big handsome, brilliant man," as Edgar de-scribed him, was a self-taught lawyer, something that was still possible when he was a young man. Earl Kindred had married Edna Matilda Archer in 1892 in

Iowa. When Dorothy was born, the family lived on a ranch they owned near Greeley. According to Edgar, Earl made and lost fortunes. He had bad luck. After he went bankrupt and sold the family ranch, potash was found there and made the next owner a millionaire. Earl couldn't support his family most of the time. Dorothy told me that on two occasions her father, seeing bad times coming, shot all the children's pets because he felt there wouldn't be enough money to buy feed for them. This was traumatic for Dorothy, an animal lover. She had dearly loved her horse Brownie, which she owned as a young girl, and her love of cats was enormous. Phil used the story of Earl's killing the family's pets in *Confessions of a Crap Artist*.

Earl Kindred left the family home in Colorado on many occasions "seeking his fortune" and then, later, came back. While he was gone, the job of supporting the family fell on Dorothy's shoulders. Although only a teenager, she went to work to support Meemaw and her younger sister, Marion. Older brother Harold left home permanently when he was twelve. The family legend was that he was very angry, but Edgar didn't know what he was angry about.

Dorothy was furious when her father would come back from his wandering and Meemaw would take him in again. Perhaps the stress of this period contributed to her contracting typhoid fever at seventeen and then Bright's disease. The doctors gave her only a few years to live. She never recovered her health completely and was ill with kidney problems all her life.

Much of the information about Dorothy's early years with her natal family came from Lynne Hudner, Dorothy's stepdaughter. Lynne came down from Santa Rosa for an interview and spent the night at my house. We talked all afternoon and evening. It was the first time we'd had an opportunity to visit since those pleasant times in 1973 when Lynne and Dorothy lived in Inverness.

Lynne said that Dorothy, although sickly and frail all her life, as sickly people sometimes are, "went on to become a gifted and brilliant woman, intellectual, articulate, powerful—a person with definite ideas—but there was another side of Dorothy that came out of that difficult childhood and adolescence, a fearful and reclusive side, and guilt-ridden." She was ill with an unending series of kidney infections and other physical problems "and like some chronically ill persons she was hypochondriacal. She was overly concerned with Phil's health, and years later in her second family, with the health of [Lynne] and [her] twin brother, Neil. Illness was a way of life for Dorothy, and she used her illnesses to manipulate and control her family."

Lynne thought that Dorothy "had insight into her tendency to be reclusive. Paradoxically, she also liked people and fought her inclination to guard her psychological territory. But she had a view of life as intrinsically not good, a view of herself as not a good person, and a real worry that the world would be destroyed. She believed the parent was responsible for making the child into a good person. As a mother she was loving and intelligent but guilt provoking." Phil, earlier, and Lynne, in Dorothy's later family, both felt they'd be cut off from Dorothy's love if…???

Dorothy and Phil, when he was growing up, weren't part of any large family group and didn't belong to any community groups or church. Lynne thought Phil never learned to adjust to certain aspects of life.

Lynne, a psychiatric social worker looking back on her childhood, wondered if the ambivalent feelings of love and hate that both she and Phil had for Dorothy were due, in part, to a misunderstanding on the children's part of an undercurrent of suffering and limitation that created an atmosphere of heaviness and somberness in Dorothy's household. "Dorothy was a restrained person, relating outwardly mainly on an intellectual level, not given to expressions of affection—not open with her feelings." Lynne thought that Dorothy must have been "overpowering to Phil as a small child." Lynne herself had a father and a brother to insulate her.

"Dorothy, a pacifist, dedicated to nonviolence, would not allow any expression of anger—but she herself could show disapproval by a withering glance. Her household wasn't one of emotional self-expression; there was no give and take, and no yelling, ever. If Phil did something wrong, he wouldn't quite know what it was. Yet there was a tremendous, deep closeness between Phil and Dorothy. It mattered a great deal to Phil what Dorothy thought. But also he wanted to fight, to get away." Lynne felt that a part of herself, a part of Phil, and a part of her twin brother, Neil, always remained a child around Dorothy. Phil's hurt and his deep love for his mother were by far the most intense. Lynne said that Phil adopted a lot of Dorothy's patterns. He was frugal and orderly like his mother and became a writer because of his mother's admiration for this profession.

To compound the paradox and the complexity around Dorothy, Neil remembered Dorothy with a deep love that had no reservations. He told me,

"My mother, Dorothy, was a wonderful person. There were never any problems between me and her. All my friends liked her, too. But Dorothy had a love-hate relationship with Phil. Dorothy always loved Phil but he sometimes hated her." Dorothy maintained an excellent relationship with her second husband, Joe Hudner, for many years until his death.

Phil, as an adult, referring to Dorothy, called her "a rotten mother who didn't like kids at all." He thought that Dorothy was responsible for all his problems. Mothers of that generation were blamed for everything. But Dorothy was loyal to a fault to Phil. All during the Depression she worked hard, holding the same government job for years to support herself and Phil. Perhaps divorcing Edgar was a mistake, perhaps not. Despite our considerable social skills, Laura and I weren't able to sustain a relationship with him.

In 1929, Dorothy, Edgar, and baby Phil took a trip back to Colorado to visit their families. Dorothy decided to stay for a while. Edgar had to go back to Chicago to work. Little Phil was already talking at eight months old. Dorothy also had him wearing finger restraints to prevent thumb sucking, a common practice at this time.

Dorothy, an observant mother, wrote a detailed notebook about her baby:

Phil weighed 16 lbs. 9 1/2 oz. today. He will be 8 months old in six days. It's amazing how he can kick. He loves to lie on the big bed and kick while he watches the curtain blow. As soon as he sees it move he begins to talk—so sweetly—to it.... Yesterday morning Phil stood up, on his feet.... [H]is voice is bigger every day. He opens his mouth and roars, just for the entertainment of it. He doesn't cry; he shouts. It's like his earlier "talking" only much magnified.... He has a funny way of answering to his name. It reminds me [of] the way the kitty answers when I call him—a kind of little funny "Heh?" He has known his name since he was 3 weeks old.... His "eighth" birthday. Weighed 16-13 again.... His fourth tooth is through.... He spends a lot of time on his calfskin now and is learning ever so much about turning over and reaching.... I...take him on my lap at the piano while I labor over the Missouri Waltz. He watches and listens, ducking from one side to the other suddenly, and leaning forward to try to hit the keyboard with his own hands, and then all at once he leans back with his little hand against my breast and looks at me wonderingly with such a funny little grin—as if he wants to be sure it is a game for his amusement. As if he's now suddenly suspicious that I might be, after all, doing it for my own amusement.... He doesn't like it when he sees me sit or lie down and leave him to his own devices.... We took him to Greeley a few days ago, visiting, and he loved it. He had never got so much attention before and he thought it so lovely—laughed & talked to everyone. He liked to be right out with the gang.

It's hard to believe that the loving mother who wrote this detailed account was also the person who created such emotional damage in Phil.

In August 1930, Edgar was promoted to director of the western division of the NRA (Roosevelt's National Recovery Act), with headquarters in Reno. Dorothy and Phil moved to Berkeley and Edgar planned to commute from Berkeley to Reno.

In Berkeley, Phil grew to be a tiny, handsome child. His father remembered, "He loved life and sparkled with energy. He was not argumentative, but he was competitive. He had a temper, but it flashed and then cooled off.

"He loved to play hide-and-go-seek and had a navy in the nearby creek. He had the old men in the neighborhood competing with each other to make toys for him. Phil had a lot of pride. In the woods, one day, he fell over a root and hurt himself. He went behind a tree to cry so people couldn't see him."

Dorothy joined a Berkeley group that started one of the first preschools in the country, an experimental program sponsored by the University of California. Phil was a leader there. Edgar said, "He would even call the nursery school parents and talk to them on the phone like another adult. He amused the other children at nursery school by putting a slice of bread on his head at lunchtime."

The Institute of Child Welfare, the university preschool, sent a report on August 12, 1931, to the Dicks at 931 Shattuck Avenue:

Phil is a friendly and happy youngster. He is always busy. He seems to know just what he wants to do and without waiting for outside suggestions proceeds to do it. He is a lover of peace and often steps aside rather than have an argument. This is natural, normal behaviour and should cause no concern. When Phil feels his rights have been encroached upon, he is capable of protecting them. There have been occasions when he has held onto a treasured toy, protesting loudly when another youngster challenged his right to it. Phil's play is constructive and he shows fine powers of concentration. Sawing is one of his favorite occupations and he stays with it for long periods, shouting as each fragment is severed and drops to the ground. He talks remarkably well for his years, has intellectual curiosity and a keen interest in everything about him. He cooperates well with both children and adults and is a splendidly adjusted child.

When Phil and I were first married, I made an attempt to get together with Edgar. Phil had told me that he and his father had a falling out over politics in the mid-fifties and they hadn't communicated since. Hoping to mend the rift between them, I urged Phil to invite Edgar and his wife, Gertrude, to visit us. Edgar accepted—but at the last minute he phoned and said he was having trouble with his teeth and couldn't come. Phil said disgustedly, "That figures."

When I drove down to Menlo Park to interview Edgar, I found him outside, gardening. He told me about a wild squirrel he had tamed and what all the local birds had been doing. We went inside but it was hard to talk because of his fourteen-year-old cocker spaniel bitch's relentless barking. Gertrude said that Edgar wanted her to train the dog, but when she tried, Edgar would say under his breath to the dog, "Bark. Bark." Then he would tell Gertrude, "Give the dog some beefsteak," and she would get out a dog biscuit.

Edgar was built like Phil and stood like Phil. Gertrude showed me a photo of him in his prime when he was still playing football. He had been a big, athletic-looking man and very handsome. Now a cheerful octogenarian, he told me, "I live for my dog." He spoke in a kind of rural patois that must have been useful to him in his line of work as executive secretary of the California Cattlemen's Association. He had lobbied almost four hundred bills through the California legislature. He was especially proud of one that protected wild horses and burros. Gertrude said that Edgar had been a workaholic who came home only every ten days. That day, Laura came over to Edgar's house from Stanford and we all went out to lunch. However, Edgar would never go out with us on subsequent visits; he had seen a program on television about people choking in restaurants and felt it wasn't safe to eat and talk at the same time.
Several months later, Laura and I took Isa to meet her grandfather. Edgar was quite taken with her and made it immediately clear that Isa, not Laura, was now his favorite. Later, when Isa didn't come to visit him again, he called me up to say he wondered who was "keeping her away," and implied that it was me.

Edgar wrote a pamphlet, a piece of Americana, about his family and about his experiences in the Fifth Marines in World War I. He was the principal, the only resource for information about Phil's early years except for what Phil and Dorothy had told me many years ago.

Even after fifty years, Edgar expressed a bitter animosity toward Dorothy and blamed her for Phil's problems. He himself, he said, wanted Phil to be free,

"free as a bird," but Dorothy wanted to put Phil "in a box." Later, in the formal interview situation when he was being taped, he spoke about what a good mother Dorothy was.

As an adult, Phil remembered that his early relationship with his father was a good one. He had liked his dad before his dad "left." He remembered Edgar's stories about World War I. "My father was a hero in World War I," he said. Edgar showed little Phil his gas mask from World War I. It scared Phil. The face that Phil saw in the sky in Point Reyes in 1963 resembled this mask.

Phil got Edgar to take him to a radio station that broadcast a cowboy program. Phil wore his little cowboy suit and went with great anticipation. When they got there, there were just records, no cowboys. Edgar said, "I had to lie a little."

Edgar taught Phil to always tell the truth. "If I scolded Phil, he'd analyze it and come back and tell me. We'd talk it over. I'd admit it when I was wrong.

"When Phil was little, he was irritable. I would explain things to him. He needed a little lift. I was second oldest of fourteen, and I knew how to handle little children."

Father and son visited a friend of Edgar's who had a pet bull snake that slept in the basket on the porch. Edgar, who was afraid of rattlesnakes, had taught little Phil how to recognize them. Phil came in from playing outside and said to his father, "Jingle snake on porch." Edgar's friend laughed and said, no, it was her pet snake. But Edgar went out to see anyway and found that it was a thirteen-rattle rattler, the biggest ever killed in that area.

On another occasion, love of animals led Edgar and Phil to take matters into their own hands instead of calling the authorities. The people at a nearby ranch kept some rabbits in a cage in the sun with no food or water. Phil wanted to set these poor animals loose, so while the family was at church on Sunday, Edgar and Phil went to the ranch and let the animals out. But the animals returned and were put back in the cage. The next time, Edgar and Phil drove them twenty miles away and then let them out. "Phil was so pleased," he told me.

When Phil had to have his tonsils out, Edgar explained the operation to him in advance. He took him to the hospital on the bus. Phil said, "I'll see you later on today," confidently. "Dorothy took great care of Phil," Edgar said, "though she was too involved with Phil's glasses and his teeth and various medicines."

Did Dorothy and Edgar compete for the love of this charming and brilliant child? Did Phil, precocious in his ability to influence people, play them against each other? Edgar remembered one time when Phil wanted to go for a ride in Edgar's car. They were in the car waiting for Dorothy to come when Phil rolled up the windows and said, "Let's go, let's go, Daddy. Let's not wait for Momma."

Dorothy was the disciplinarian. Later, when the two of them lived alone and Phil had a tantrum, Dorothy would shut him in his room. Then he would tear his room and all his possessions apart. Dorothy taught him to take the consequences of his actions. In later years, Phil spoke approvingly to me of this aspect of his childhood.

In 1933, the Institute of Child Welfare, the University of California preschool that Phil attended, reported: "Philip has made excellent progress since his previous test. His highest scores are memory, language, and manual coordination. His reactions are quickly displayed, and just as quickly reversed. His independent initiative and executive ability are shown in rapidly varying techniques which are frequently replaced with strongly contrasting dependence. It might be well to guard against the development of this degree of versatility at his age."

Dorothy told Edgar she wanted a divorce. He said, still astonished fifty years later, "It came out of the clear blue sky. There was no discussion or anything." After Dorothy told Edgar she wanted a divorce, he asked her, "What about the boy?" Dorothy told him that she had consulted a psychiatrist, who said that the divorce wouldn't affect Phil.

When I was married to Phil, I had asked Dorothy about her divorce. She told me that Edgar was always suspicious of her whenever she went out, suspicious of "other men," except that there weren't any other men. She got tired of this. However, she said, she probably wouldn't have divorced him if she had realized how poor she and Phil would be afterward. Shortly after the divorce, Phil came to visit Edgar at his office, but he was restless and had to be taken home. In later years, Phil told Lynne, his stepsister, that he held the divorce against his mother.

It seemed odd to me that Phil had told me so much about his past when we were first married, but never had mentioned his grandfather, who had lived in Dorothy's Berkeley household for a while. Kleo told me, "Phil was afraid of his grandfather." Phil frequently expressed a strong hatred of old men. He told me on several occasions that there was "bad blood" in his family. I didn't know what to make of this odd statement. It seemed to me to be a very self-denigrating thing to say about your own family.

Years later, in a letter to Mark Hurst, his editor at Bantam Books, Phil wrote, "The other side of this DNA memory business, as you may already know, is that these DNA gene pool structures acquired from our ancestors determine our life script…. [M]y script, for instance, was 'written' most likely by my mother's father, and it programs me on a subliminal level and causes me to live the particular life…which has been plotted out for me, against my will and knowledge."

After Dorothy sent Edgar away, she and her mother, Meemaw, began living together in Berkeley. Meemaw would take care of Phil and do the housework and Dorothy would be the breadwinner. Then Meemaw's husband and Dorothy's father, Earl Kindred, the wanderer, showed up. Meemaw must have persuaded Dorothy to take him in as the former had always done in past years when he returned from his wanderings. Although as a teenager Dorothy had been furious when Meemaw let Earl came back home, this time, for unknown reasons, she let him stay. Did she think that Earl would be a father substitute for Phil and tell Phil this? ("The Father-Thing".)

Earl wasn't the only man who "wandered" in the early 1900s. Life could be bleak, and some people in rural areas suffered psychological isolation as well as economic hardship. The men who wandered in the early years of the twentieth century, prefiguring the hobos of the thirties, were often seeking a life as well as a living.

The Three Stigmata of Palmer Eldritch was written on the eve of Phil's departure from Point Reyes. Palmer Eldritch, a supernatural being coming from deep space back to Earth after a long absence, passes "something" to each person he comes into contact with—like a vampire. Then each one of them becomes a Palmer Eldritch (palmer is an old word for "wanderer"). The "something" continues to be passed from person to person, and, finally, there are many Palmer Eldritches.

In 1982, Phil commissioned Gregg Rickman to be his biographer. Phil died a month later. Gregg spent the next twelve years of his life researching the life of Philip K. Dick and wrote three books about him. He became troubled by some of Phil's actions, especially political ones, that didn't mesh with everything else he had found out about this man whom he admired so much. He did extensive research. He has detailed a circumstantial case about a childhood trauma when Phil was four years old in his book To the High Castle, Philip K. Dick: A Life 1928–1962 *(Valentine Press, 1989).*

Some Philip K. Dick scholars think that the loss of his twin sister at birth created Phil's psychological problems. Dorothy "went on" about this, Phil told me, and it wasn't good for him. There must have been some effect on Phil's psyche, perhaps more from his mother's talk than the actual event.

In 1935, when the Great Depression was in full blast, Dorothy moved with Phil to Washington, D.C. She had obtained a job as an editor in the Children's Bureau. There she wrote a government pamphlet on raising children. She put Phil in a Quaker boarding school at Sulphur Springs, Maryland. Phil told me, "I had trouble swallowing, didn't eat, and started to lose weight. This was due to grief and loneliness. My mother had to take me out of this school."

Phil attended day school, and the school reports from this period are uneventful. At times, Dorothy had housekeepers; at other times Phil was a lonely latchkey child, watching out the window of their apartment for his mother to come home.

Earl Grant Kindred died in San Francisco in April 1937. Later this year, eight-year-old Phil and his mother returned to Berkeley, and Dorothy became personnel director of the U.S. Forestry Department, a job she held until she retired. Meemaw lived with them again and took care of Phil.

The Berkeley that Dorothy came back to was like Athens during its Golden Age. Large, attractive homes on the hills overlooked the bay, across which the towers of San Francisco glittered in the clear air, Mount Tamalpais in the background. Light-colored stucco houses blended with frame and shingle houses on tree-lined streets that curved around the hills. In the pleasant climate, exotic trees, bushes, and flowers grew everywhere. Even the small bungalows down on the flat areas had their avocado and lemon trees.

Dorothy, always frugal, had managed to save a little money and wanted to buy property in Concord. Phil had a fit. He said he wouldn't ever live way out there. Vince Lusby said, "Dorothy lost a million-dollar opportunity, the way Concord land values went up in the next few years."

Berkeley was a special place. Professors and students from the great University of California dominated the cultural scene, creating an environment of fine art, music, and literature. Classical music stores stocked every record ever made. Bookstores, used and new, sat side by side on Telegraph Avenue, each with their own specialties. Avant-garde art galleries, movie houses, and coffee shops were scattered throughout the community.

At the political rallies being held at Sather Gate, intellectuals, students, and teachers from all nations and races mingled. The University of California at Berkeley was thought then to be the greatest university in the world. Every idea that made waves during the sixties and seventies was fermenting in Berkeley during the late thirties and early forties when Phil was growing up. There were many active members of the American Communist Party living in the community. The U.S. national presidential ballots of those years listed a Communist Party candidate for president as well as candidates for the Socialist and Socialist Labor parties.

Special programs were created for the children in the public schools and in the many parks. A club where the children could play chess, checkers, ping-pong, and pool was just down the street from Phil's house. When he and his friends hiked up the hill to Tilden Park, they went past the Berkeley Rose Garden, past the Greek Theater, and past the world's first cyclotron, where world-shaking breakthroughs in physics were occurring almost daily. Music was very important to Phil and to a number of his friends. One boy had a beautiful music room in his house, the closets and drawers bulging with sheet music by every conceivable composer. Another friend, down the street, was the son of a professor in the music department. Although Phil and his mother were poor, the culture he lived in was very rich.

For the spring semester of 1938, Phil decided to change his name, and Dorothy let him. He registered at the Hillside School as Jim Dick. Report cards from the Hillside School say about Phil, a.k.a. Jim: "Jim does fine work, his work shows good organization of thought and considerable maturity of expression.... Quite popular with his playmates. A fine sense of right...self-reliant...a reliable boy...efficient...business-like...courteous when given a position of leadership. He has a great degree of poise and self-possession for a boy of his age.... It has been a great pleasure to teach Jim. He is original and has added much to the group.... [H]e has a fine future ahead."

Thirteen
BOYHOOD IN BERKELEY

At thirteen, Phil had already taught himself to type and was contributing to Berkeley's daily newspaper. His mother saved every article that he had written. At fourteen he wrote his first novel, *Return to Lilliput.*
—from a conversation between Anne Dick and Philip K. Dick in the early 1960s

Phil and Dorothy lived in a small cottage in the backyard of a house at 1214 Walnut Street, a pleasant neighborhood a few blocks northwest of the University of California campus. Phil's friends entered from the rear of the lot that bordered on Live Oak Park. George Koehler told me, "The household was minimal, but adequate, cluttered, but the bed was made."

Dick Daniels was Phil's best Berkeley High School friend. When I interviewed him, he told me I should contact another one of Phil's best friends from junior high school days, George Koehler. I was able to locate George in Orange County through the California State Medical Board. George and his wife drove up from Los Angeles to Point Reyes in their motor home, and we spent an enjoyable afternoon picnicking and talking on my patio. George was a tall man who walked with a cane, the effect of the polio he'd had as a boy. He had studied psychiatry, medicine, and dentistry and ran an investment business. He had carefully thought about what he would say in the interview. His memories of Phil were organized and detailed.

Dorothy didn't come home from work until six o'clock; Phil was out of school at 3:30 and completely on his own. Even when home, Phil's mother, "didn't seem to direct him at all. She gave Phil the freedom to go his own way and do what he wanted. She was not bossy or mean. If Phil wanted to stay out somewhere to dinner he would call home; he was very considerate. Phil was an independent person but I noticed that he felt abused—about what, I couldn't make out."

Leon Rimov, a friend from junior high school, phoned me after Phil's death. Leon, an architect, businessman, and mountain climber, had an incredible memory for the events of forty years ago.

Leon perceived a somewhat different scene than George did: "Phil's mother was very young looking and ill a lot of the time. Phil was depressed because of his mother's illness. He was very close to Dorothy. She would never say "son"; Phil was the man of the house; he was like her little husband. There was a lot of friction between Phil and his mother. She was always telling him what to do and he would argue with her. He was in the way of her writing, too. Phil talked about going to see his dad; he talked of him with respect and enjoyed spending time with his dad."

Edgar had remarried and become the administrator and principal lobbyist for the California Cattlemen's Association, a prestigious job that paid well. A workaholic, he didn't find time to see his son often.

Phil had a lot of friends, but he didn't go around in a crowd. His relations were one on one. In junior high school, Phil already knew about *Rigoletto*, and was playing ping-pong and chess with George at the neighborhood boy's club. George said, "I wanted Phil to go swimming with me at the YMCA pool, but Phil told me that he had almost drowned when he was nine and since then had a terrible fear of water."

Phil attended nearby Garfield Junior High like other Berkeley college-prep kids and did very well. He was an avid reader, liked H. G. Wells, and was already collecting science fiction magazines. He received all A's and in Advanced English wrote "fascinating stories." The stories he wrote for class were not at all science fiction or fantasy stories. One was about how World War II would end. Another was about a summer trip on which he fished with his father at a river up north. George told me, "He enjoyed his father so much. They talked and cleaned fish but it was only for a day."

In school, Phil was interested in science and in intellectual pursuits. He and George invented and constructed modest scientific apparatuses out of wood for experiments. George remembered that in the shop course, Phil became frustrated trying to tin solder a small metal box. He told George, "If I die and go to hell, this is what I'll have to do for all eternity."

Leon remembered that Phil made lie detector boxes, "which fooled a lot of people. He enjoyed fooling people. Phil also made some weird kind of electric boxes with which he scared the teachers. Phil was always driving the teachers crazy about the Nazis; he was always figuring out how the Nazis would've done things; he drove a couple of teachers wild. Phil loved to play Nazi roles. He had a good sense of humor and had fun. He was always figuring out how things could be more efficient.

"Phil formed the Rocky Creek Club because he didn't like another group in junior high school. The Rocky Creek Club was supposed to 'take care' of this other group. Phil was always setting up good guys vs. bad guys situations. He was never satisfied with tranquil waters; he had to stir something up. Phil also formed a Bible club but he was not a religious fellow."

Phil had a crush on a girl named June Barrett. He composed a poem for her and tried to print it on a toy printing press with rubber type. He didn't talk about sex and girls with his friends, though. Once he and George saw a used condom in the street. Phil told George, "Don't touch it, you'll get a disease!"

Phil didn't have a bike; he bought records with his money instead. He loved all forms of classical music, and as well as collecting records, he played the piano quite well. George came over one day when Phil was playing a funeral march; then he played a funeral march by Chopin. "Who composed the first one?" George asked. "I liked that one the best." Phil said, "I did."

Phil was sick and pale and out of school from time to time. He also was hyperactive. He ate a lot of cookies and chocolate and was overweight. For lunch he would eat several candy bars and some ice cream. At one point, he told me when we were married, he had juvenile diabetes but it cleared up. He had asthma attacks throughout his childhood. More than one school friend remembered that Phil was always taking ephedrine at his mother's insistence— not very good for an adolescent brain.

George remembered: "Phil discussed a Rorschach test with me in seventh grade. Where did Phil learn about that when he was eleven? At that time, the average seventh grader didn't know anything about Rorschach tests! Phil, in fact, made up his own, and he and I played Rorschach test. Phil knew all about the Thematic Apperception Test, too. He knew the names of various phobias. He told me, 'I have some I can't fight.'"

For the school season, 1942–43, Phil went to a music-oriented prep school, California Preparatory Academy, in Ojai. He learned to operate the PBX at the school switchboard. It fascinated him. The boys all smoked, and he thought that was pretty neat, too.

A list he sent his mother asking for some records that she might send him at school gives some indication of his musical tastes:

Records I would like in order of preference:
Jupiter Symphony; Mozart. (Sym. 41) Victor. $4.00
Symphony #1; Brahms. $3.34 (Music Appreciation Records only). With album $3.97
Beethoven, "Emperor" Concerto, Piano Concerto #5. Victor played by Schnabel. Manual Secq. $3.50
Beethoven Violin Concerto in D maj. Victor. $5.00
Schumann, Piano concerto in A min. $4.50. Victor only
Firebird Suite by Stravinsky. $3.50. Victor
Bach, K.P.E. Concerto for Orchestra in D major. Victor. $2.50
Barber of Seville, Rossini. Victor. $8.50
Song of the Flea, Moussorgsky. $1.00
Till Eulenspiegels Lustige Streiche, Strauss. $2.00
Tschaikowsky, Symphone #3 (Polish). Victor. $5.50
Tschaikowsky, Symphony #2 (Little Russian). Victor, $4.50

Phil wrote many letters to Dorothy from Cal Prep, displaying varying moods: "I am perfectly miserable.... I'm so used to having all my things private and not to be touched.... I am getting sick and tired of knowing that the second I leave my room it will be messed up.... I just don't fit into the group here. I am afraid that I may decide to leave...."

Dorothy must have advised him to quit the school and come home, since he writes: "Gee whiz, I guess that I had just better not write unless everything I say is strictly cheerful. I AM NOT COMING HOME. I have no wish to, and I don't think that what I said in that letter could be interpreted to mean that I wished to come home.... I think that you and Meemaw are too ready to have me come home.... For goodness sake, don't tell me that I can come home, because it is just like when you would say, 'All right, you don't have to go to school today.'... When I get a letter like you sent me it REALLY makes me homesick.... You have hurt my feelings by suggesting that I am such a sissy that I can't stand a little work!"

And in another letter:

Now don't get the idea again that just because I am homesick I want to come home. I am just not that kind of a man, who would run away from something that was difficult to get used to....

If you write the Doctor say (instead of saying that I am not able to work, which I am) that I am behind in my studies anyway, and that working in the kitchen is making it almost impossible for me to keep up with my classes. Of course I CAN get my work done, by doing it when I should be at gym.... My asthma has been bothering me slightly.... I'm losing weight (my belt is too loose). I attribute it to the fact that 2 times a day we have potatoes, I do without, and so do not get much to eat....

I suppose that you can see by my letters that I am very changeable, but I can't help it. Sometimes I am sure I want to go home, sometimes I am doubtful, sometimes I am sure that I want to stay. I just don't know what to do, but I'm not doing anything for a while. I am without funds now, not even enough for a postage stamp. (I had to borrow for this.)

In another letter his mood changes:

I'll try to write as often as possible, and if I don't write very much, it is not because I am not thinking of you, but because I haven't time.... It is compulsory to go to church, besides going to chapel every day and vespers on Sunday. I'll be a lot different when I get home, I know that. I'm picking up good study habits, and am changing my character every day. To the better, I believe....

I think that I am doing pretty well here, leaving a soft and easy home to enter a boarding school and working for my education. I am very proud of myself, because I am homesick only every now and then.... Month end, 23 to 27, every one goes home. I will feel pretty lonely then, thinking of everyone with their families.... I don't mind working. Write Dr. Brush and find out how much more he wants to have me not do work, and then I'll work anyway, because I don't mind working.... However, if you could INCREASE MY ALLOWANCE, then I would not mind working at all....

Phil only went to this school for one year. He went back to Garfield Junior High School in the fall of 1943. During the last half of ninth grade, when he was fifteen, he had recurrent attacks of vertigo; the classroom would spin around him. After one of these attacks he couldn't get up out of bed for several days.

Earlier, in the summer of 1943, he had started to work part-time at University Radio, a job he would hold for the next eight years. University Radio did radio repairs and sold refrigerators, phonographs, washers, dryers, heaters, and television sets. Herb Hollis, the owner, was like a father to Phil. Later, Herb added an extensive record department and also opened Art Music, a very successful store on Telegraph Avenue near the university that sold only records. The people at University Radio and Art Music were like Phil's family and appear in book after book, even his last book, *The Transmigration of Timothy Archer*, written forty years later.

I went down the stairs into the basement of the Pellucidar bookstore in Berkeley where the science fiction was located to look for secondhand copies of Phil's published novels. I bought all his science fiction novels after his death. Even in 1982, they were already hard to find. The salesman, Jerry Kleier, turned out to be a knowledgeable Phil Dick fan. He loved the early novels but didn't care for the ones written in the seventies. I told him about my project and he told me that he knew the wife of Phil's old employer, Pat Hollis, who occasionally came into the bookstore and talked with him about Phil. He even knew her telephone number. I phoned "Perky Pat" Hollis and she met me at a charming little coffee shop in Oakland, just over the Oakland-Berkeley line. We sat and drank coffee while she told me about Phil and University Radio:

> Phil was a darling, very intelligent, very quiet, very kind, and a hard worker. He loved Beethoven. Beethoven was his hero. Phil and Beethoven had the same birthday, December 16. Phil really liked Herb. Phil had a wonderful sense of humor. He picked it up from Herb. Herb was a live wire, very positive, and always right. He was a good husband, a wonderful father.

It was Pat Hollis who had given me the name of Dick Daniels. She told me that he was the administrator of a large San Francisco Peninsula hospital and lived in Belmont, one of San Francisco's suburban cities. I looked through several phone books, called a number of Danielses, and finally located the right one. Several months later we met at Dick's hillside home.

We sat near his record player and his extensive record collection in the living room and drank coffee. I was using my new tape recorder for the first time. There was a little microphone on a wire attached to it. We talked for a long time, and Dick gave me wonderful information about Phil. I checked the tape recorder and none of it had come through. That treacherous little microphone had needed a battery. Some wonderful material had been lost. Dick had a battery, and we picked ourselves up and went on. I was happy to discover my Phil again in Daniels' memories. In fact, Daniels himself, who seemed to be a very nice man, reminded me a lot of Phil. I wondered, had Phil taken on some of Daniels' personality traits? Phil did this as he went though life. Dick Daniels had also worked at University Radio with Phil and gave me his thoughts about Herb Hollis and the other people there.

Dick said, "Most saw Herb as a decent, warm, charitable man who treated everyone well and had a wonderful sense of humor, yet Herb was very independent, had pet peeves, pet ideas, and didn't like authority. No one could tell him anything! He had a tremendous amount of energy and was a man of all trades: carpentry, plumbing, electricity, etc. He worked both Saturdays and Sundays."

Dick Daniels told me that one of the early contacts that Phil made at University Radio was Eldon Nicholls, the dwarf bookkeeper. Phil was very fond of Eldon. He became the model for Hoppy Harrington, the malignant repairman in *Dr. Bloodmoney*, although Eldon was afflicted by dwarfism, not phocomelia like Hoppy. Homer Thespian, one of the stream of "mad" radio repairmen working at University Radio, was part of the concept of Hoppy Harrington, too, and also perhaps the model for the schizophrenic boy in *The Transmigration of Timothy Archer*. Homer walked barefoot through the streets of Berkeley and went off to Napa occasionally to get shock treatments. He was extremely rude to Herb, who was very kind and tolerant toward him. Phil was in awe of Homer's impertinence. Then there was Jose Flores, a homosexual, a lovely young man who killed himself. Phil cried when he heard about Jose's death.

Phil started his sophomore year at Berkeley High School in January 1944. At this time, Dorothy and Phil lived in a small, modestly furnished two-story house, three or four blocks west of Grove Street, on Allston Way.

The house was somewhat messy, and Dick Daniels said it was "an eccentric household, even for Berkeley." Meemaw, who doted on Phil, lived with them at intervals between trips to Colorado or times when she lived with Dorothy's sister, Marion, in Richmond, an East Bay city north of Berkeley. Marion was hospitalized on several occasions with schizophrenia. Dorothy had always been close to Marion, and along with Marion's husband, Joe Hudner, was closely involved with her illness and treatment. Phil grew up in a household where a close relative was periodically committed to a mental hospital. It was an everyday experience.

Phil became best friends with Dick Daniels the first day the two attended Berkeley High School. Dick told me, "I walked into Fraulein Altona's class on the attic floor of Berkeley High School and Phil motioned emphatically for me to come over and sit down next to him. This began a relationship which was very close, a deep and important friendship, one of the most significant I've ever had in my life."

Daniels visited Phil's house: "Phil had an old Royal typewriter in his bedroom and was doing some experimental writing at that period, but he didn't show it around. He typed with the same kind of coordination that he used in piano playing. Phil was interested in literature and was reading science fiction extensively; he loved Heinlein. He had an enormous collection of science fiction magazines and books and haunted the secondhand stores looking for back copies of *Astounding* and *Amazing* magazines. I was always amazed that he could acquire such an immense pile of stuff and read it so quickly, cover to cover. There was no question he couldn't answer about the material that he had read."

Dick Daniels gave me a lead to Gerry Ackerman, but the latter was no longer in the Art History department at Stanford, as Daniels had thought. I finally located him at Pomona College. He generously sent me a long excerpt from his work-in-progress, a biography of his friend composer Dick Maxfield. He thanked me for getting him started on the part that included Phil. He was very encouraging and told me I had to buy a computer to work on, so I did. I don't think he liked the finished book, though; he never got back to me about it. I believe it must have upset him.

Gerry Ackerman had come from Santa Cruz. He described teenage Phil as "rounded in all his forms, a little thick around the middle. This may have been moderate heaviness or even just a normal, unathletic body. [He had] rather straight hair that fell down over his face and ears, the start of a moustache and a vigorous peach-fuzz on his cheeks, just an occasional pimple. He didn't care about his clothes, but simply wore the ordinary.... Good humored, full of enthusiasm for certain things, intellectual in that he was always posing questions, good ones. Always ready to take a walk or go on a trip into Oakland on the street car, or the bus, a good companion."

At school Phil had crushes from time to time on various girls. Dick Daniels noticed, "That winning openness made it possible for him to establish a relationship, although he would never go to a dance or any school activity; it would have been foreign for him. He also had a crush in a sophomore English class on a young new teacher, Mrs. Wolfson, a refreshing breeze of a teacher compared with others whose classes I had taken. Mrs. Wolfson was attractive, outgoing, and knew something about the world. Phil was greatly taken by her."

I interviewed Margaret Wolfson, Phil's high school English teacher, over the telephone. Phil had told me about her years ago. She was the ex-wife of William Wolfson, Phil's divorce attorney.

In her English class at Berkeley High, Margaret Wolfson found that the results of the assignments that she gave Phil were not what she had asked for, but the stories he handed in were so extraordinary that she suggested that he send one of them off to *Galaxy* magazine: "They were very professional, astonishing for a boy in high school."

Phil learned to speak fluently in German, read German, and later used some German in his novels. He studied physics and many years later told his stepsister, Lynne, "In high school I had to take a complicated physics test, but I had studied all the wrong things and didn't know the answers at all. I sat there in a total panic. All of a sudden I heard this clear, bell-like voice saying, 'It's really very simple.' Then the voice proceeded to give me all the answers!"

George Koehler developed polio and was in bed all summer. Phil came over to George's house to help him with his studies and to play games. He worried aloud to George, "I wonder if I have a mild case of polio."

Gerry Ackerman was at Phil's house frequently, too: "Since his mother lived, more or less, upstairs...Phil had the downstairs...to himself. He had his Magnavox, which he bought by working part-time at the record store, his stack of records, and his file of pulps. We had a freedom in this small front living room that I had never had any place else as a child."

Jerry's account of his own adolescence in his unpublished manuscript also told about Phil: "For a high school boy of that era, Phil had an extensive record collection and good equipment. Phil listened to Toscanini on Saturday and the New York Philharmonic on Sunday. Since the available recordings at that time (all shellac) were not so expensive (it was wartime), it was quite possible for an avid listener to have a critical opinion on all five available recordings of, for example, the Pastoral Symphony, and Phil did." Jerry remembered Phil's excitement when Bruno Walter's recording of Mahler's Fourth Symphony was released.

Once Jerry lent Phil his album of the Beethoven Sixth Symphony done by the Minneapolis Orchestra, conducted by Mitropoulos. "There was a passage in the storm sequence where Mitropoulos had encouraged both the sound engineer and the piccolo player to make an entry on a very loud high note. Phil told me the next day, 'Boy, I was enjoying that Beethoven you lent me, lying on the floor with my head inside the soundbox, when that piccolo came in and almost deafened me.' He must have had the set out from the wall and put his head in through the back behind the speaker."

At Christmas, Jerry gave Phil the Helen Traubel recording of the immolation scene from *Die Gotterdammerung*, which at $2.50 for a two-record album was an extravagant gift for a young boy. Jerry once lost a bet with Phil that a composer named Buxtehude really lived. "I remember we were crossing Shattuck Avenue at the time. He assured me he really had lived, and that Bach had walked fifty miles to hear him play. He demonstrated this to me in a book as soon as we got home."

Phil and Dick Daniels had long discussions about why Tchaikovsky wasn't as good as Beethoven. Phil played Beethoven on the piano and could memorize a composition very quickly. He loved early Beethoven, Haydn, Mozart, and Schumann. Phil used to delight in getting Daniels to talk about what was wrong with Tchaikovsky. Daniels remembered that he could be gulled into something like that. "I thought well of myself, was pretty pompous. Phil would make me listen to a piece of music I was unfamiliar with, convince me it was by Tchaikovsky and get me to say all kinds of stupid things about it. And then, reveal, 'Well, actually, this wasn't Tchaikovsky at all.' "All in front of other people. 'This was a work of Berlioz.' I had a tendency to be pretentious, and he would think of endless, inventive ways of nipping me in that tendency. A little sadism, a little putting himself up and me down, but mostly it was kidding. It was done with good humor and not really intended to be painful. He was constantly devising tricks and situations in which his friends could be embarrassed. That was simply part of his style and made life fun."

Dick Daniels convinced Phil to usher with him at the symphony. But Phil couldn't stand it and would never go again. Years later when we were living together, Phil told me that he had a terrible vertigo attack; something irreversible happened to his psyche when he was ushering at the symphony with Dick. He said that his being had sunk down into itself—from then on, it was as if he could only see out into the world with a periscope, as if he were in a submarine. He felt that he had never recovered his ability to perceive the world directly. (Just another little conversation with Phil.)

Phil told Dick Daniels that he had a morbid fear that he couldn't get to the toilet in time, so he didn't want to go to concerts. Daniels thought Phil made up strange reasons for not doing things he didn't want to do, that this was just a convenient ploy: "He used the excuse about the toilet and copped out of situations he didn't want to get into."

Daniels never saw Dorothy out of bed. She must have come home from work tired and gone up to her bedroom after fixing a simple dinner to read the books and magazines that she was addicted to. Daniels remembered that she was terribly thin and pale and had long black hair:

Phil's relationship to Dorothy was an odd one. He seemed kind of coldly distant, forthrightly answering her back, sometimes impertinently. She seemed to be amused by it. I would say it rolled off her back like water off a duck's. Phil was very sassy with her, more so with his parent than any other I knew. Phil came and went pretty much as he pleased. He kept regular hours, though; he was far from wild. He was quite well regulated from the standpoint of his habits, quite repressed, as most of us were at that time.

Phil was a very complex person, impossible to predict. He could be offended by any kind of directness. Something you might say in jest or whimsy, he would interpret as an assault of some kind and turn it into an unintended slight. He had a great capability for manufacturing drama around him. He was very precipitous in his behavior. He jumped to conclusions. You had to be able to watch Phil both as a friend and a manipulator; he was both at the same time. Reclusive though he was, he had a great capacity to attract people to himself. When he decided to put himself out, he could scrape up acquaintances virtually out of thin air. If he wanted to make friends with someone, he did it with great social ease, he moved right in. But he was usually standoffish.

"At Berkeley High, Phil never joined everyone on the slope," Leon Rimov told me, "where we all went to socialize and eat lunch and smoke. He kept to himself. The class at Berkeley High was very close and had lots of fun but Phil didn't take part. Phil never played ball in high school or did any sports."

Dick Daniels also had mentioned Pat Flannery to me. After calling the Berkeley High Alumni Association, (they invited me to join and come to their annual banquet), I finally found Pat Flannery in the Berkeley telephone book, the last person of my search. I made many calls to his wife, who didn't feel there was any way I would be able to see him in person; he was too busy. When I finally reached Pat on the phone he said that he was going to come out to Point Reyes to meet me, but it turned out that his wife was not in favor of this plan and we ended up talking on the phone. Even this phone appointment was hard to schedule. Finally, we did have a good phone conversation.

At Berkeley High, Pat was known as "Phil's shadow." He was a very quiet guy. He never spoke; he smiled. He was the same height as Phil with similar hair. He was in the same class, the same room. Pat met Phil in 1943:

> Phil was fourteen and very erudite, very intellectual. He expressed himself extremely well. He was also very opinionated and temperamental. He didn't care about his personal appearance. He liked simple things. He liked jigsaw puzzles; we spent hours putting them together. Phil and his mother were very close. Phil was thinking about changing his name to Philip Kindred, his mother's name. I observed a little bit of friction between Phil and his mother, but nothing out of the ordinary. Phil wasn't well in high school. He took ephedrine all the time for his asthma. He withdrew at these times. His mother was very involved with his illnesses.
>
> Phil had a subdued temper, which expressed itself in "So long! I'm leaving." He was a loner who didn't mind mixing when it was time to do so. I remember how Phil hated the Nazis and gave Walter Lanferman, who was from a German background, a really hard time.
>
> I taught Phil how to play chess. By the third game, Phil was winning every time. Phil liked new things and I was always finding new things for Phil to get in to. Phil and I both took an aptitude test in a magazine. Phil's test showed that he had scientific aptitude and my test showed that I had business aptitude. Phil told me, "Pat, you can come over and look through my microscope," and we made a bet as to who would be making more money ten years after college.

Phil showed Pat a story he had written based on the Faust legend but in a modern setting.

Pat continued, "Phil had a small circle of friends in which he was very influential. He was certainly very influential over me at that time. One time

Phil pushed me into a bramble bush. Another time he threw a dart and hit me in the hand and drew blood. I remember going with Phil to a movie, a frothy little movie called *Knickerbocker Holiday*. Phil got up in the middle, saying, 'I just can't take it. I'm leaving!' I left too, trailing along behind, although I happened to be enjoying the movie."

Gerry Ackerman was the only one among Phil's friends who had an idea that he, Jerry, was gay. Jerry used to occasionally, daringly, take "one of their hands in mine while walking. That, of course, only at night and usually on the always dark Allston Way. Once Phil told me that his mother had complained about the practice, so either she or someone else saw us walking hand in hand. He told me rather matter of factly about this, without scandal or admonition, as if it had no special import even in the interpretation his mother might have given the incident. This was not a regular occurrence with Phil, I believed it happened only this once. It didn't appeal to him and he submitted only out of friendship, perhaps a little curious and a little flattered as well."

Phil dropped out of high school in his senior year. His friend Pat Flannery thought "he was sick or something." Phil's picture doesn't appear in the Berkeley High Senior Yearbook.

Phil told me, "I dropped out of my last year of high school. I had a nervous breakdown and had to have a home teacher. I was walking down an aisle in a class and the floor tilted away under my feet."

Once a week, after this, Phil made the long bus trip to San Francisco's Langley Porter Clinic for psychotherapy. He told his friends at University Radio, where he continued to work part-time, that he went to Langley Porter because he was being studied as a gifted person, a continuation of studies that had been done since he was a young child. Did they tell him at Langley Porter to move away from his mother? This advice would have been consistent with the beliefs in vogue that most psychological maladies were of psychogenic origin and mainly the mother's fault. Phil told me that it was difficult for him to get away from Dorothy.

He rented a room in a boardinghouse that Gerry Ackerman had found, a house on Milvia Street in which some gay poets of that era lived: Jack Spicer; Robert Duncan; Philip Lamantia, who had a girlfriend; and Gerry Ackerman, Duncan's friend of the moment. Dorothy was upset about Phil moving to the Milvia Street house. She was worried that he was becoming a homosexual.

In the small world of San Francisco Bay Area intellectuals, my first husband, poet Richard Rubenstein, had also known Robert Duncan when Richard was auditing classes at Berkeley. In the late 1940s, when we were first married and had just moved to San Francisco, Philip Lamantia, who had become a well-known San Francisco poet at the age of seventeen, was an occasional visitor to our San Francisco apartment.

Gerry Ackerman remembered that one day, Phil and Jack Spicer were listening to the Kipnis recording of *Boris Gudunov*. Jerry waited for the music to end to knock on the door of Phil's room because he didn't want to interrupt them. When the music stopped and he finally knocked, they lamented, "You just wrecked our mood. Boris has just died."

Fourteen
A YOUNG MAN

By 1947, Berkeley was "as avant-garde a place as there was. Artists and writers were coming from New York to break into the life there. Every group had a black member and a homosexual member. People were involved with free love. Marriage was like musical chairs. Life was fun, stimulating, exciting."

—Vince Lusby

Berkeley was divided between the students and some of the faculty versus the old inhabitants. The former were deeply involved with left-wing politics and the McCarthy investigations. Both liberals and radicals were fearful of J. Edgar Hoover's FBI, which was secretly observing all the political activity and the radical bookstores. The Progressive Party office was just around the corner from University Radio where Phil worked. All Phil's friends were leftist. In the 1948 election, Phil voted for Henry Wallace.

Lois Mini and I corresponded after she moved to Bogota, Columbia. Lois had been married to one of Phil's best friends at University Radio, Norman Mini. I phoned her to see what she remembered about Phil's life. Lois suggested that I contact Vince Lusby. "He loves to gossip," she told me. She, herself, couldn't recall much, although she believed, "Phil was 'a naïf' [a person marked by a lack of worldly experience]."

Vince Lusby and his wife, Virginia, were easy to find. Vince and Virginia were still living in Richmond in the same house where Phil and I had visited them twenty years earlier. I hadn't realized how important Vince had been in Phil's early life. Vince, now in his sixties, had just had a triple bypass and a cataract operation. Virginia hardly seemed to have changed at all. Vince was very encouraging about my project and anxious for me to be the one to do a biography of Phil. He gave me the names of more of Phil's friends from the University Radio crowd: Bill Trieste, John Gildersleeve, and Betty Jo Rivers. I made the trek to Richmond several times to interview him and Virginia. After I met Pat Hollis in Oakland and told her I had seen Vince, the two of them got together and exchanged reminiscences.

Vince had met Phil in November 1947, when Phil was eighteen years old. He was still living at home and taking high school classes from a home teacher. Herb Hollis, the owner of University Radio, had brought Vince, a jazz expert, down from Sacramento to run Art Music, Herb's new record store on Telegraph Avenue. Art Music became enormously successful. Vince was soon running two radio jazz programs, one on KPFA and one on KRE. Vince and Phil became best friends, although Phil had some reservations because Vince had already been through several wives and a number of girlfriends. Vince soon became Phil's mentor.

Phil invited Vince to his home for Thanksgiving dinner. Vince noted, "Dorothy, Phil's mother, wasn't particularly sexy—I thought she was somewhat colorless. She served a fine dinner, though. Phil seemed to be boss of the situation—maybe it was just a pose. Kay Linde, who also worked at University Radio, was at this dinner, too. Phil thought Kay was the greatest thing on Earth. He was in love with her, but later I became her boyfriend."

Vince remembered that Phil was charming when his mood was right. He described Phil as a mild-mannered person, pleasant to be around, "and he could talk.... [H]e had a line of b.s. that wouldn't quit. He was a strange combination of wisdom and naïveté, but he wrote great graffiti in the bathroom—original, full of wit, some in verse."

Phil made a whole new group of friends at University Radio and Art Music. By then, he was a well-constructed, clean-shaven, active young man who got along well with his fellow workers. In a photograph of that period he is quite good-looking.

I phoned Bill Trieste, a premier Bay Area announcer, and was impressed with his rich baritone voice—the perfect voice for a radio announcer.

When he met Phil in 1948, Bill had just become an unpaid announcer on KPFA, the new educational radio station, one of the first in the nation. He worked at University Radio to earn a living, marking time while the transmitter for KPFA was being completed. Later, he became an announcer for the reputedly Communist radio station.

Norman Mini, a protégée of writer Henry Miller, was another employee at University Radio. Norman went to West Point in the thirties and was kicked out for his Russian sympathies and/or because he got drunk at the Yale–West Point football game. He then joined the Communist Party and was the first person in the United States to be convicted and sent to jail under the Criminal Syndicalism Act. Phil went to one Communist Party meeting with Norman and later felt as if he had been marked forever.

Another character who hung around University Radio was Inez Ghirardelli, a member of the famous and wealthy Ghirardelli family. Once she had been a debutante. Now she was emaciated-looking, wore men's trousers, suspenders, and shirts, and shaved her hair to a length of three-quarters of an inch. Even in Berkeley, she was considered extremely eccentric. Phil became a good friend of hers. Connie Barbour, a lesbian psychiatrist, was another member of the crowd. She became Kay Linde's girlfriend after Vince stopped going with Kay. Then there were Alan Rich, who later became a well-known music critic, Kleo Apostolides, and Chuck Bennett.

Phil, Vince, Norman, and Bill hung around together in the evenings, going to the famous bars of those days, the Steppenwolf and the Blind Lemon, to listen to Odetta and other folksingers.

Although Phil seemed to get along well with Dorothy at her home, he hid from her when she came looking for him at work, hoping to have lunch with him. People thought that Dorothy was his girlfriend. At that time she had long dark hair, and was thin and Garbo-esque.

"Phil did the bills at University Radio," Vince said. "He was an incredibly fast typist and had won contests. He sold radios and TVs. He swept the sidewalk. He sold records." Phil worked in the stockroom under the store, unpacking records. Phil and Vince used to joke that they wanted clothes the color of packing dust, so that when they had to run upstairs to wait on a customer, they didn't have to brush all the dust off their clothes.

Phil had some odd mannerisms and said he was being monitored by Langley Porter because, as a child he had an exceptionally high I.Q. Vince recalled, "He certainly was not a normal preppy type. He worried that he wasn't normal and surrounded himself with security mechanisms. He had to sit alone every day with his back to the wall on exactly the same stool in the balcony of the True Blue Cafeteria where he could see the door of the men's room." Phil told Vince he had a phobia that he wouldn't get to the men's room in time. He felt uncomfortable if his friends, at another table, looked at him while he was eating, because he had trouble swallowing.

It disturbed Vince that when he and Phil would lock up at night, Phil would try the doorknob, leave and come back a minute later, try the door again, shake it, and bang it; then they would get to the street, and Phil would have to go back again and try the doorknob, and shake and bang the door again. Phil's mood changed from month to month. Sometimes, he would be extremely reclusive. At other times, he would come out of his shell and be the life of the party. One night he danced with Lois Mini all evening, at one point falling over John Gildersleeve's feet.

Some days when he came to work, Vince remembered, Phil, with a dark look on his face, would march to the office in the rear where he kept the books, not looking to the right or left, not speaking to or acknowledging anyone. Vince noted that Phil could change his face, either voluntarily or involuntarily, so that he looked like a different person: "Something would trigger him, and his face would actually change."

That year, Phil passed the entrance exam at the university and enrolled, but he went for only part of a month. He got claustrophobia so badly that he couldn't stay in a classroom. He went to ROTC but didn't like it at all.

Phil acquired an interest in Gregorian and pre-Baroque music from Vince. Vince also introduced Phil to Gilbert and Sullivan, and Phil became a Gilbert and Sullivan fan. At University Radio, when things were dull, Vince, Phil, and the other clerks would go in a record booth and play records all day long. Vince couldn't get Phil interested in jazz, though. "Phil had to have frameworks, that's why he didn't like jazz." Phil hated *Kukla, Fran and Ollie*, but after Vince explained why they were so funny and charming, Phil changed his mind and decided that he loved them.

Phil had never been taught to drive. He practiced driving in Herb's University Radio truck with Vince's help. Phil took the driver's test seven times. He would always err in some way. He drove erratically.

Although he was still a virgin, not so unusual in those days when the sexual revolution was barely beginning, even in Berkeley, Phil told Vince that he believed that he was a homosexual. Vince said that back in 1947, the theory about homosexuality was much different. He said, "If you were a sensitive and creative man, chances were a hundred to one you were a homosexual who hadn't been 'brought out.' In time, I disabused Phil of this idea. He thought because he was a person who liked artistic things, loved music, and had creative impulses, he was gay. One of my arguments was, 'Go look at their records and books, Phil. They all have the same records and books.'" And Vince and Phil both felt Vince had saved Phil from being homosexual.

The next problem Vince addressed himself to was that Phil wasn't heterosexual either, because he'd never been with a woman: "University Radio was a sort of dating bureau. If the record clerks found someone they thought attractive, they'd give her a record to play in one of the booths. Then they'd find another record, similar to the one she'd asked for, and take it back to the booth and tell her, 'Play this; it's much like the first one.' She might end up listening to two or three albums, although she might end up not buying anything. That wasn't part of the scenario anyway."

One day, Phil met his first wife, Jeannette Marlin, when she came into the store to buy a record. Vince didn't find her to be "particularly artistic or musical. She couldn't pronounce the word 'Debussy,' but Phil evidently got some sort of vibrations. She asked for a record; Phil gave it to her and showed her a booth. He did the inevitable thing and took another record back and another, and subsequently—there was a large listening room in the basement next to the radio repair shop, and beyond, another room that was a storage area. You'll be familiar with both these rooms from reading *Dr. Bloodmoney*. Phil and his future wife cohabited in the basement of University Radio one night and he established his masculinity. They married shortly afterwards."

In those days, you very likely would marry the first man or woman you slept with. Phil was nineteen at the time, and Jeannette was twenty-six. Phil had to get his mother's signature in order to be allowed to marry. Dorothy didn't think that the marriage would work but she signed anyway, thinking that Phil would learn something from the experience.

Gerry Ackerman remembered visiting Phil and Jeannette in their new apartment. He came with composer Dick Maxfield. He wrote:

Phil and Jeannette lived in an old near-tenement apartment on the corner of Addison Way behind Walt's Drug Store.... [A]ll the rooms were joined together like railway cars, one behind the other. All was dark, messy, disorderly; the usual painting of the new apartment had not taken place, nor did there seem to be any furniture or charm.... Although they had been there some time, the place was full of unpacked boxes. Everyone else I knew rented a house, cottage, or part of a house with a garden or a tree or two. Apartment houses seemed alien to Berkeley life; no one that I knew lived in such a place.... I could only remember her as either an unfriendly or frightened presence, standing behind a stuffed chair with her hands resting on the back as if it were a shield.... Phil was seated in the rocking chair when we came in and...he greeted us and said good-bye to us without getting up. No coffee was served—almost unthinkable in the unwritten etiquette of Berkeley.

Six months later, Jeannette and Phil decided to divorce, and Vince appeared as a witness. Jeannette's complaint was that Phil kept playing three records that she couldn't stand, the three records that he had played for her in the booth the first time they met. Phil told Vince that he was glad it had all happened because he had been saved from homosexuality. Phil roomed with Vince for a while, until Vince married his fourth wife, Monica. Years later, Phil based a character in one of his literary novels named Nikki on Monica, and Vince and Monica's autistic child became Manfred in *Martian Time-Slip*. Phil found his own place on Bancroft, an apartment that he immediately painted. He moved in his large record collection, his Magnavox console, and stacks and stacks of science fiction magazines. Friends remember that he told them he was learning to write science fiction stories. The divorce with Jeannette must have been an amicable one because he had a photograph of her on the mantel. He said that he had liked Jeannette, because she had left him alone. At this time, Phil was caught up with German Romanticism and heavily into Wagner, and Germanic myths and legends. He played Wagner at full volume into the early hours of the morning until the neighbors banged on the walls.

In April 1949, Phil fell deeply in love with a popular co-ed, an English literature student who walked into University Radio one day looking for a classical record. Throughout Phil's later marriage to Kleo Apostolides, he kept telling her that Betty Jo Rivers was the "great lost love of my life." Kleo said, "Betty Jo would have been perfect for Phil—too bad she had to go off to Paris."

Betty Jo Rivers, a handsome, confident blonde, was an archaeologist for the University of California at Davis. When I was trying to reach her to interview her for this book, she was off on a dig for several months. Finally, her busy schedule allowed her to drive down from Davis to meet me at a little restaurant in Petaluma. We sat outside under an umbrella and gazed at the Petaluma River, and she told me about her relationship with Phil.

Phil decided that he was going to wait on Betty Jo before she even came into the store. He saw her through the plate glass window, Betty Jo said:

> ...with my new short haircut that looked to him like the helmet a Valkyrie would wear. He told me that he fell madly in love with me at that moment—he had a strong urge to jump right through the plate glass window. As soon as I walked in the store, he grabbed me by the arm before I even asked for a record. When I asked for something by Buxtehude, he immediately assumed that I knew music. Soon I was closed in a small listening room with stacks and stacks of records. He told me, "If you like this record, then you'll like this one and this one." Later when I put my coat on to get ready to leave, he asked if he could walk me home. As we walked, we talked and talked about music, Berkeley, "life." When we got to my place, a fair piece away on Hearst and Ninth, I hadn't had any supper and I asked him if he would like a sandwich. He turned absolutely green and said, "Eat with another person in the room?" and left. Later, he got so he could sit over a sandwich with me, but at that time he was afraid of crowds and messed up about public eating.

I sipped my Coke and chewed on my toasted-cheese sandwich, feeling a tiny bit... not jealous, exactly, but aware that this had been a big romance.

Betty Jo had been dating a fellow graduate student. She told me, "He got shoved out the door," and she and Phil became a couple. Phil wanted to give Betty Jo his most prized possession, his Magnavox console, but she refused: "Phil's attraction was all that talent boiling around, getting ready to explode. People of high creativity give off a kind of dynamic, something that is extremely attractive. But he didn't fit into any of my circles. It was difficult to take him anywhere—he was so extremely shy. We went to see my best girlfriend whose family was visiting. Phil was confused and felt inept. Later, he gave me copy of William James's *Varieties of Religious Experience*, inscribed 'To Betty Jo, in exchange for six social errors at once.'"

Phil used to comment on how easy it was for Betty Jo to be with people. He told her that as long as he worked in the store, he could deal with people, although he preferred being down in the basement unpacking records. "I met him in a period of intense ferment. He used to talk a great deal about why he was as neurotic as he was. He had a twin sister who was allergic to milk and died. He always felt it was like the German myth or legend about the person who has to look for his other half, that he was an incomplete person. He blamed the death of the baby on his mother. He talked about fear of crowds and fear of the presence of people around."

Although Phil wasn't particularly sympathetic to Betty Jo's preoccupation with academic studies, he was kind and patient with her because of the pressure of her approaching master's exam.

I used to study at his place. Getting ready for the master's was an ordeal. At that time, everything depended on the orals. Afterwards, a kind man gave a party for the tired, sleepless group that had just taken them. He handed everyone a martini in a water glass as they came in the door. I'd never had a martini. I drink little, and I have no tolerance for alcohol. "Here, this will relax you," he said. "And," I thought, "this is a party and I'm grown up, have my master's, and now this is what I'm supposed to do." Well, as I went into a daze and knew I was passing out, I looked around and noticed it wasn't just me. There were people falling on the rug. I had the sense to get to the phone and call Phil and say "Get me home." I have a hazy memory of him appearing at the door. He told me later he had to look through all those prone bodies before he found mine. He threw me over his shoulder in a fireman's carry and deposited me in a cab, muttering in my ear about "irresponsibility and drinking." The next day, I woke up with a classic hangover, and Phil made me some coffee and scolded me solidly. I later noted that there was a Betty Jo in one of his novels who was a drunken linguist.

When, years later, Phil told me this story about Betty Jo, it became a pitiful story about an abused lover whose girlfriend went to a party, became drunk, went in the bedroom with another man, and then had the lover come to pick her up.

Betty Jo received a fellowship to go to France. "My mind was all set on this scholarship and on going abroad. Phil asked me make a choice between him and going to France. I didn't have any doubt about what I wanted to do. I asked him, 'Do you want me to send you pictures of this? Of that?'"

"I don't want you to go," he said.

After Betty Jo left, Phil fell under Connie Barbour's influence. She had made a pass at Betty Jo but had told Phil that Betty Jo had flirted with her. At this period of his life, Phil went to parties and gave parties for his friends, making fancy rum drinks and serving bacon and eggs in his apartment.

I phoned Kleo Apostolides Dick Mini, who now lived in St. Helena, and we made a date to go out to lunch. When I parked in front of her small cottage, loud strains of Italian opera wafted out to greet me. Kleo was in her kitchen, the many bottles of wine she had just made sitting on open shelves. She was professionally interested in writing and encouraged me with my project.

She had married Phil's old friend Norman Mini a few years after she and Phil had divorced, and they'd had two children, now grown. A widow now, Kleo enjoyed encouraging young people to read. She knew everything that was going on wine-wise in the Napa Valley, California's most prolific wine-producing region. She gave me some information about Phil's life in the early fifties, but she didn't share her feelings or any personal matters with me. She felt it would have been improper to do so. I thought she was most gracious to receive me and felt somewhat abashed in her presence.

Kleo Apostolides was eighteen years old, a striking-looking brunette with dark eyebrows accenting her face, when she met Philip Dick. Phil was recovering from his love affair with Betty Jo, but soon he and Kleo were living together. "I met Phil at Art Music in 1949," Kleo said. Everyone hung out at Art Music then: Alan Rich, Chuck Bennett, and good friends Connie Barbour, Eldon Nicholls, and Norman Mini.

Kleo and Phil went out in the evenings to the True Blue restaurant in Berkeley and sometimes took the train to San Francisco to go to the coffee houses in North Beach. One evening they went with Margaret Wolfson, Phil's former high school teacher, and her husband, William Wolfson, a young attorney.

"We married in, I think, May or June of 1950. Phil was straight and it was Phil's idea to get married," Kleo told me.

Vince Lusby said, "Kleo and Phil's romance was an all-right relationship based mostly on their common interest in Italian and German opera. They both believed in free love."

William Wolfson, Margaret Wolfson's husband, and later Phil's attorney, saw Kleo as mousy, and thought, "Phil played the role of Pygmalion to her Galatea."

Alan Rich found me. He had read my letter about Phil in Horizon *magazine; I hadn't even known they'd printed it. He remembered coming out to Point Reyes to visit us in the early sixties. Kleo had thought that Alan was still a music critic for the* New York Times, *but in 1983, he was living in Los Angeles, where he had a music service. I phoned him several times, each time enjoying the splendid classical music on his answering machine.*

He told me, "Kleo was a music nut, a vocal nut. Phil and Kleo married because of their common musical interests, principally Italian opera. I saw no strong emotional base between them."

John Gildersleeve thought, "Kleo and Phil were friendlier than most married couples. They were really good friends. Phil was definitely the dominant figure. I wondered if Phil thought I was coming around to see Kleo, instead of him. He acted rather odd when I came around. I had quite a reputation as a ladies' man in those days."

Phil and Kleo started looking for another place to live. "At one point," Kleo told me, "Phil and I moved to Sausalito for one day to an apartment on the bay. Phil looked out the window and became extremely disturbed by being so close to the water. We moved back to Berkeley the same day."

Phil had told me that he and Kleo bought a very old small house at 1126 Francisco Street for $2,000. He said it was financed by Dr. Apostolides, Kleo's father. But Kleo said, "This is not true. My father never gave us any money for the Francisco Street house.... When Phil and I first got together, he had already put the down payment on the house; it was *his* house, and that is why all I asked for and got in the divorce was the '55 Chevy; we paid it off together, and no one ever helped us in paying it off."

Lynne Hudner remembered the house well: "It was a somber, musty-smelling house in the bad part of town with two bedrooms upstairs, a kitchen, and a front room too small to be called a living room. Phil and Kleo had nothing, only a few chairs that didn't match. But there were lots of books and records in bookcases made of apple crates and pictures on the walls. Phil, sitting in his dark, huge, filthy old easy chair, was an omnivorous reader and read Styron, Sigrid de Lima, Malamud, James Joyce, Beckett, and the other literary writers...writing in the late forties and early fifties.... Kleo had no interest in domestic arts or clothes. Both Phil and Kleo wore dirty jeans all the time. There were a whole mess of cats, one named Magnifa."

Vince told me, "Phil and Kleo argued about everything—how to make coffee—they fought all the time." Phil describes the house in his 1980 story for *Playboy* magazine, "Frozen Journey," and in his last novel, published thirty years after his Berkeley days, *The Transmigration of Timothy Archer*. Kleo remembered that Phil became apprehensive about things going wrong with the house.

Phil told me a story about his life there: "One day, a fly buzzed and buzzed, circling around in the living room. I watched it for a while and then I began to hear a tiny voice talking." He didn't tell me what it said, and I was so amazed at his experience I didn't ask.

Phil used to sit on his porch railing and watch the kids play at the school across the street until he realized that some older women who lived next door watched him every time he sat there. He became afraid that they would think he was some kind of a sex fiend, so he didn't watch the children anymore.

In 1951, Herb Hollis fired the whole bunch that worked at University Radio, including Phil. Vince Lusby said, "It was Norman Mini that got Phil fired. There was some sort of intrigue going on at University Radio. On top of this, Norman told an obscene joke to a customer. Herb, a prude, fired him and later fired Phil for talking to Norman when he came in the store. At that point Phil listed his vocation as a writer, because the unemployment benefits were better. If the Unemployment Bureau couldn't find you a job in your line, they had to pay you benefits. At that time you could list yourself as anything. Although Phil had written some things earlier, he really became a writer at this time."

Phil stayed home full-time to work on his writing. Agoraphobia seemed to be a determining factor for his writing career. An early story, "The King of the Elves," describes the beginnings of this lifestyle.

"Phil's output, even at the beginning, was so voluminous," Kleo said, "that when I went out to get the mail one day there were seventeen returned manuscripts lying on the porch. Phil was writing literary fantasies and science fiction, all mixed. I read the manuscripts and criticized."

Phil was a protégé of Anthony Boucher, the editor of *The Magazine of Fantasy & Science Fiction*. Phil went a few times to his private class, but he was so uncomfortable in a group situation that he had to send in his manuscripts in to be criticized. Phil sold "Roog," his first story, to *The Magazine of Fantasy & Science Fiction*. He papered the walls of the small center room of his house with rejection notices. Later, he sold some of the stories that had been rejected to the same magazines that had spurned them.

Alan Rich remembered, "Phil's first writing consisted of impressionistic portraits, thinly disguised, of people he knew. I was a character named Max who always read the *New York Times*. I was uncomfortable with this portrait."

Kleo paid a large share of the couple's household expenses, working full-time, while Phil was beginning to write and publish: "We had a simple lifestyle— Phil was making a little money from his writing and I was working—we had little to spend."

Phil had told me that one of his treats was boiling canned milk to make Depression pudding. He made this dessert for me once in Point Reyes, and it was surprisingly tasty. Kleo told me, "I don't even know what Depression pudding is.... We ate meals of ten-cent chicken-giblet gravy on potatoes once a week. But," she said with mock indignation, "we did not have ground horse meat; we got whole steaks from the pet-food store and broiled them."

Phil frequently described his early poverty as being characterized by eating hamburger bought from the Lucky Dog Pet Store. When I lived with him, he liked to talk about how poor he'd been and how ingenious at getting by on almost no money. He told how he'd gone from store to store buying loss leaders, and how he and Kleo had eaten for only $10 a month. One of their entrees was a popular noodle dish prepared with gravy that only cost a dime.

Jack Sanders, who later became an editor of *New York Magazine*, gave Phil and Kleo their first car. For years Phil talked about this car, a Raymond Loewy Studebaker Starlite coupe. He put it in at least one of his novels. After the Starlite coupe wore out, the couple bought a black 1938 Cadillac that got four miles to the gallon from a place like Looney Luke's (Phil's prototype car lot in several novels) on San Pablo Avenue. The Cadillac wouldn't go uphill. It turned out to have a couple of dead cylinders. They traded it back to Jalopy Jungle after a short time, although they had loved that car, and bought a Renault.

Vince remembered when Phil and Kleo decided to take a trip to the Mendocino coast "to have a wilderness experience." They packed provisions and camping equipment in their Renault. They arrived, made camp, ate dinner, and curled up in their sleeping bags. But they couldn't sleep—they heard noises. They didn't sleep all night long. The next morning they packed their things in the car and came back to Berkeley.

One day, there was a knock on the door of the Francisco Street house. Kleo said, "It was two FBI agents wearing suits and dark grey fedoras, looking exactly like one would imagine FBI agents would look. Their names were Jones and Smith, they said, and they wanted us to identify the people in a photograph of a crowd scene at Sather Gate—a Socialist Workers' Party meeting. I looked over Phil's shoulder at the picture and giggled, pointed my finger, and said, 'Look. There I am.'" Kleo went to all the radical rallies but was too independent to join any particular group or party.

The real name of one of the agents was George Scruggs. He became a good friend of the Dicks and helped Phil learn to drive; Phil and Kleo had a cordial relationship with the FBI or at least with one FBI agent. He asked them if they would go to the University of Mexico—the FBI would pay them to spy on the students there. They said no to that idea. Later George retired to run a hardware store.

A year after Kleo and Phil married, Phil's mother remarried her late sister Marion's widower, Joe Hudner. Phil was extremely disapproving of this match. Kleo said, "Dorothy made a strange marriage to her brother-in-law nine months after his wife died. Phil was angry about this match and suspicious about Marion's death. He blamed Dorothy. Dorothy had been deeply involved in Marion's many hospitalizations, and, in desperation, she and Joe had put her in a private experimental nursing home, where Marion had been allowed to remain in a catatonic posture too long and died. Phil was just starting his writing and felt rejected, because Dorothy had a new, ready-made family."

Lynne Hudner said, "Phil, my cousin, became my stepbrother; Dorothy, my aunt, became my mother."

Joe Hudner, an artist, an intellectual, a blue-collar worker, and an extremely versatile man, was only five foot five, though he didn't seem small. A warm, compassionate man, he was a second-generation Irishman. His father was a blacksmith, and Joe had practiced blacksmithing since he was a young man. He had been a professional sculptor in the WPA program in the thirties and danced naked at bohemian parties. He learned carpentry and built buildings, furniture, clocks, and cabinets. He had sung in opera and acted in plays. He was psychic, deeply involved with his own brand of metaphysics, with a foot in another world. Raised a Roman Catholic, he had a prejudice against organized religion. He was a person with strong opinions and lots of energy, a Socialist, although not a party member. The marriage between Joe and Dorothy turned out to be a good marriage. Joe was protective of Dorothy. Shortly after they married, Dorothy retired on disability pay. Their warm, compatible relationship lasted until Joe's death in 1971.

Kleo, heavily influenced by Phil's negative views, had a different tale. "Dorothy was an early feminist, contemptuous of Joe, Edgar, Phil, everyone. Dorothy found no male worth the dirt he walked on. She was a hypochondriac who lived in her illnesses and her pills."

After Kleo and Phil had been married a couple of years, "Phil became uncomfortable about leaving the house. He couldn't even walk to the movies. He was uncomfortable in crowds from two people on up." Kleo's father, Dr.

Apostolides, prescribed Semoxydrine, a trade name for amphetamine, for Phil's agoraphobia. Phil also suffered from tachycardia and took a drug, Serpasil, for this condition.

He wanted to get back into the record business and took a job at Tupper and Reed, a record store on Shattuck Avenue, but his agoraphobia was so bad that he couldn't function there. He went back briefly to manage Art Music in order to help his old friend, Pat Hollis, after Herb died, but he was too uncomfortable there, too.

Kleo said, "He was depressed that he was cut off from so much because of his agoraphobia. Though Phil loved music, he could no longer go to concerts. Only recorded music was available to him. He was interested in the writing of Samuel Beckett, but when I bought tickets for *Waiting for Godot*, Phil couldn't go see it.

"Phil…projected various personalities at different times. Phil really lived in the pages of his books…on paper. Phil's was a life of hiding."

Lynne remembered, "Phil had a brooding quality about him when he lived in that Francisco Street house. Those moods of Phil's were awful, those black, black moods. He would sink into a horrible lethargy, completely enclosed, you couldn't reach him. Dad became angry at Phil at times, because of the tumultuous relationship between Phil and Dorothy. Dorothy wouldn't say anything, but she would get sick, and Dad blamed Phil. Dad always took Dorothy's side."

Neil said, "Phil would take a little bit of reality and anticipate negatively what people's reactions would be, then act as if these were their [actual] reactions. He would act out his pictures without testing…."

Phil often walked over to his mother's house to visit her, because she and her new husband, Joe, lived only a few blocks away. Dorothy read and criticized Phil's early manuscripts.

Kleo said that Phil's novel *Nicholas and the Higs*, was about a friend: "The main character was unsuccessful, and never knew why. He wore powder blue suits, left home, never knew why. He left his wife, never knew why. Jim Briskin, the radio announcer in the novel *The Broken Bubble of Thisbe Holt*, [sic] who announced for the program on which Looney Luke advertised his cars, was based on Don Sherwood, a famous Bay Area disc jockey. *The Broken Bubble of Thisbe Holt* had a character named 'Mary' in it. Mary really existed; she was a tough, good-looking lady with long dark hair who worked at the drugstore across from University Radio. She taught Phil about sex. Phil was in love with her for a short time."

Later, in Point Reyes, Phil told a story of being offered the script-writing job for *Captain Video* at $500 a week, big money in those days, but he would have had to fly to New York, and he felt he was too nervous, he couldn't do this. Also, he realized that in order to produce a weekly show, he would soon use up all his material. Kleo told me that this story wasn't true.

Ray Nelson, Phil's good friend after Phil left Point Reyes, wrote me about a party he went to at "Kleo's" house years before he met Phil:

I was living with my parents in the Berkeley hills, and had come down to the South Campus neighborhood to hang out with some other science fiction fans at the Garden Library bookstore…the center of Bay Area fantasy and science fiction fandom…. So many fans gathered, together with a sprinkling of KPFA radio volunteers, that someone said, "Let's have a party!"…"Let's go to Kleo's…she has a house!"… Note that nobody said, "Let's go to Phil's" or "Let's go to Kleo and Phil's, or the Dicks."… I can't remember anyone that day mentioning Phil even in passing.

…[W]e all caravanned over to 1126 Francisco Street…. Carrying our jugs of… "Dago Red"…we trooped up the front walk, across a small porch, and into the rather dim and musty-smelling interior. I glimpsed some pictures of nudes on the wall, and an old upright piano, then we continued on into the relatively well-lighted kitchen…. Berkeley student-types never liked to get too far from the refrigerator…. The cigarette smoke got thick. The discussions got deep…. At some point I became aware that someone was playing the phonograph rather loud, forcing the conversationalists to raise their voices in order to be heard…. Someone yelled into the next room, "Can you keep it down in there?"… The music continued to boom…classical music. Wagner…. [S]omeone said to me, "Can you talk to him?" with an angry gesture toward the next room. I had the reputation for being very diplomatic. "Okay."… I went into the other room. The shades were drawn…and no lights were lit…. I made out the figure of a man sitting hunched over in a shabby armchair. He was clean shaven, thin and hunted-looking, and wore jeans, sneakers, and an army surplus shirt. He looked like a typical student, with straight, messy hair, a broad forehead. I judged him to be somewhere in his middle twenties.

"Hi," I said grinning. He…did not even turn his head to look at me. Somewhat disconcerted, I added, "Uh, pardon me, but…." He said nothing. My own words died in mid-sentence. There was such an intensity in his eyes, in his posture, that the notion wandered into my head that he was insane. Did I dare demand that this strange statue of a man...turn down the volume of his hi-fi? You never know when someone like that might get violent.... I began over. "Uh, could you tell me the way to the bathroom?" He did not speak, did not look at me, did not betray the slightest awareness of my presence. Wagner's "Ride of the Valkyries" continued to rattle the windows.... I wondered suddenly if he might be dead, but then I noticed a movement, so slight as to be almost invisible. He was nodding his head, ever-so-little, in time to the music.

Vince went with Phil to a party given by Allan Temko for writer Herb Gold. Phil had just sold his first science fiction novel, *Solar Lottery*. Vince told me, "Temko had recently come back from being educated in Paris. He and the various writers at the party were discussing what they had sold. Phil said he had sold a novel, and Temko said 'What sort of stuff do you write?' Phil said, 'science fiction,' at which point everybody exploded into ridicule. Temko, wearing pink denim pants and a green striped shirt, started dancing around singing songs about people who write science fiction. I left with Phil—it was a horrible experience for him. Even if you weren't Phil Dick, it would've been a horrible experience."

John Gildersleeve, the editor of the University Press for many years, had had an office around the corner from University Radio. Retired now, he and his wife, Grace, lived in the small town of Fort Bragg on the rugged Mendocino coast. I phoned him to arrange an interview. The two of us tried to get together on one of John's infrequent visits to the Bay Area, but we could never coordinate. In the summer of 1983, I drove up the coast to the Gildersleeves' home with my friend Angelina Hnatt. Great, foggy, forested hills appeared in the headlights of our car as we neared Fort Bragg. John and his wife had invited us to stay in their Maybeck-style redwood home on the edge of a great ravine, a half-mile from the ocean's edge. The house was filled with artworks and surrounded by rhododendrons and azaleas. It was lined with books. Bookshelves covered the bedroom walls in the guest room, where we spent the night. In the morning the first thing I saw as I opened my eyes were the complete writings of Trotsky.

When we sat down to talk, to his chagrin, John couldn't remember much from those long-ago days. He told me, "Phil gave me some of his first stories to read. I felt all of them went to pieces in part. I thought Phil was spoiled because he didn't have good editing in the beginning. Phil made up the stories as he went along. His typing was incredibly fast."

John was always discovering some little hole in Phil's stories, something unexplained: "I discovered a flaw in *Solar Lottery*. The hero had a bomb implanted in his side. If he got within a certain distance of something or other, this bomb would go off. In the first part of the book, he gets within this distance. I asked Phil, in front of Kleo, 'Did you make a change, take care of that contradiction?' Phil wouldn't answer, and when Kleo asked what we were talking about, he said to her, 'Oh, it's just a little joke between John and me.'"

Phil was fascinated with a story John told him: "When I was a little child, my grandmother told me to remember sitting on her lap, because when she was a little child, she had sat on the lap of one of Washington's soldiers. Phil went into ecstasy over this story, the idea that only a few generations separated us from the founding of the nation."

Eventually, John and Phil fell out. John kept finding logical flaws in Phil's writing. Phil dismissed John as "just a proofreader."

Phil remained friendly with Vince Lusby, who now was married to Monica and had an autistic child. Phil was interested in this child. At that time, autism in small children was thought to be a form of schizophrenia caused by the mother. It was believed that the mother didn't talk enough to her baby. Vince was writing a novel about this child and took little heart-shaped green pills, Dexamyl, a form of amphetamine, to help him write. In that era, many writers used amphetamines.

Phil published eighty-five science fiction stories and seven science fiction novels between 1951 and 1958, as well as seven literary novels. The literary novels weren't published until after his death. Most of the major themes that appear in Phil's later writing appear in the novels and stories of the fifties. Among them: a killer robot with six personalities; and another robot, "The Imposter," who is a bomb but thinks he's human, as does the reader, until he/it explodes. In *The World Jones Made*, seven humanoid creatures live in an artificial world, unable to survive in the real world. They look longingly out of their bubble at San Francisco, but when they try to leave, they collapse. Jones, a fortune-teller, can see a year into the future. There are drugs in this story, and a policeman is the protagonist. "The Golden Man" can see a half-hour ahead and can always find a woman to keep him out of society's traps. Shadrach Jones in "The King of the Elves" has been lured into becoming the king of the elves, instead of working at his prosaic job running a filling station. He's wanted and needed in the kingdom of the elves and is a king there. The leader of the trolls, whom he has killed, looks like one of his friends. In "Progeny," Phil uses the name of Janet Doyle, a woman with whom he had an affair. "The Turning Wheel" deals with Elron Hu. (Phil's mother was a Dianetics auditor and wanted to "clear" Phil.)

In "Colony," everything in that world is out to "get" the colonists, from pseudo-microscopes to pseudo-spaceships. In "Expendable," the bugs are out to get everybody (except for the spiders). Eventually, the spiders will win, but it's too late for our hero. (Phil loved spiders and was always telling me that spiders were mankind's friends. He would have liked to have a tarantula for a pet.) In "Paycheck," Jennings I foresees and engineers, by use of a time scoop, the successful escape and job rehabilitation of Jennings II, whose memory has been destroyed.

Lots of worlds in ruins (in "Breakfast at Twilight," the worst weapon is a woman) or worlds soon going to be in ruins. Foster in "Foster, You're Dead" was named after Edgar Dick's youngest brother, who died as small child. In "Service Call," a swivel will control men's thoughts in order to prevent atomic war. "The Impossible Planet" tells the story of an old lady who wants to return to the planet of man's birth; she does return, but can this bombed-out, grey ruin be the fabled green Earth? "Elwood Builds an Ark" in his backyard. "Prominent Author" writes the Bible. "The Father-Thing" was a forerunner of Jack Finney's *Invasion of the Body Snatchers*.

In July 1955, Phil and Kleo took a car trip to Colorado, Kansas, Wyoming, and Montana. The Hudners were in Mexico that year, and when they came back they stayed at Phil and Kleo's house while looking for a place. Kleo said, "Dorothy insisted on moving out on the day that we returned. She said she didn't want her twins, Lynne and Neil, in the same house as a young married couple." It wasn't long before Kleo fell out with Dorothy and Joe.

In spring, Betty Jo Rivers returned to Berkeley. She found that the Phil of 1956 was different from the Phil she had dated in 1949:

He had been published and made a name for himself; he could at least walk down the street comfortably; his sense of humor seemed more developed. Phil and Kleo immediately asked me to come over, which made me feel happy. I was struggling when I arrived in Berkeley, with two children and a third on the way, and not much money. It was two months before my husband [black artist Heywood Rivers] could join us. Both Phil and Kleo asked if the children and I wanted to come and stay with them. I thought this was a far cry from the person who couldn't have people around him.

My impression was that Phil and Kleo were happy and that Kleo was protective of him. The only strain I saw was that it was obvious that Kleo wanted children and Phil made it plain that he didn't. She took wonderful care of him, tried to keep the whole place a studio for him. When we did find a place, they gave us kitchen equipment—I still have a Phil and Kleo Memorial Frying Pan....

Marge and Jerry Hirsch, whom I had known in Paris, lived across the street from Kleo and Phil in a tiny fifty-dollar-a-month cottage. Jerry was a psychology professor.... Marge was pregnant. Phil wrote the story "Human Is" with the Hirsches in mind. It bothered Phil a lot that the pulps would axe his work any way they wanted. He would send them three hundred pages, and they would print one hundred fifty. He had no control over the editing. The story "Foster, You're Dead" had already become an international classic at this time. I felt the little boy, Foster, who wanted to live in a bomb shelter, mirrored Phil's worst neurosis.

Phil told me about the time he was listening to KPFA discuss the lead story in a Russian magazine [that was] equivalent to *Life* magazine in this country. It was "Foster, You're Dead." Phil thought he was having a hallucination. "Foster, You're Dead" was reprinted in many countries, but Phil received no money for it because of the copyright laws or rather because of the lack of copyright laws. It was a story that could have been construed as pro-red, talking about American terror tactics.

I was apprehensive driving to a lower-income, black neighborhood in Oakland to interview Maury Guy, now Iskandar, but I ended up pleasantly surprised. Maury and his wife lived in a pleasant old frame house at the end of a dead-end street, a charming place filled with plants, books, and interesting fabrics. Both Maury and his wife worked in a drug-intervention program. Maury talked so much about Phil and about Joe and Dorothy that he filled up three tapes on both sides.

In 1956, Maury Guy, a tall, black intellectual and poet, moved into the Hudner's rental cottage, which was located behind their Hearst Street bungalow. He became close to Joe and Dorothy and he and Phil became close friends. Phil confided things to Maury that he didn't tell anyone else.

Maury told me:

[Joe and Dorothy] had a tragic cast to their lives.... Both of them were somewhat melancholy—writers—artists who had been forced to give up their careers. I remember Joe, inhaling an inch of his cigarette with the first draw...doing semi-humorous political cartoons. Dorothy had a terrible kidney problem. Joe was a marine machinist, had a horrible job working in oily bilges, but he didn't have the inner strength to get his talent off the ground. Both of them had magnetic charm. Phil was terrified of his mother. He painted her as the "dark witch of the universe." I could never make out how Phil could see Dorothy this way. Phil blamed all his problems on his mother. He would come over and bawl his mother out because he couldn't leave the house.

Phil never turned on his charm to work me. I didn't get all that shuck and jive. I remember the day I met Phil on the gravel path at the back of Dorothy and Joe's house. Phil was wearing jeans, scuffed oxfords, a lumber jacket, and a grumpy expression on his face. He had just been quarreling with Dorothy. Dorothy and Joe were great parents, supportive, marvelous people, but both Phil and Dorothy were prisoners of the holy agony—they loved each other, but their relationship was filled with pain.

Phil told Maury that he felt that he had been crippled psychologically and it was because of his mother and his father. He told Maury that, when he was eighteen, he had started to lose his mind the last year of high school. The forces of evil were overwhelming him and he suffered such anxiety that he had to quit school, and after this he felt he was handicapped. He told Maury that it wouldn't do any good for him to get psychiatric help and that he had a sense of shame when he had to go to Langley Porter Clinic. He had planned to go on to college to study math, philosophy, or piano but was unable to.

"He felt anger, bitterness, pain, all unresolved. He had no psychiatric care, no religious discipline. Everything boiled up in the direction of his mother. He was trying to work it out with his mother and it didn't work. Phil was afraid his mother was going to 'get' him. Why, I don't know."

Phil told Maury that he wanted to write about the nature of man and the nature of reality, and if he couldn't get his serious literary writing published, he would "'do it in science fiction.'"

In 1958, Dorothy and Joe bought a cabin in Inverness. Phil and Kleo drove out occasionally to spend the night or a weekend there. The couple liked the West Marin area so much that they decided to move there. Phil wanted to grow things, get close to the soil. In the past his family had been farmers and he, himself, had grown all kinds of small crops in Berkeley. Also, there was less pressure from people out in the country. At the end of summer, Phil and Kleo sold their Berkeley place and bought a small house in the town of Point Reyes Station.

Just before they moved, Meemaw, Phil's grandmother, died in the hospital in Berkeley only half an hour after Phil and Kleo had visited her. Dorothy was furious that they hadn't stayed, that they weren't there when Meemaw died, but the two of them had no idea that Meemaw was going to die at that particular time. Kleo had loved Meemaw and she and Phil had visited her frequently in the hospital.

Maury Guy visited Phil and Kleo at their new home in the country. He thought they seemed idyllically happy and that, finally, Phil had found a point of equipoise. The new house was on the corner of Manana and Lorraine streets. Soon, Phil and Kleo met their neighbors: Avis Hall, across the street on one side, and Jerry and June Kresy, on the other. Some mornings, Phil stopped by Avis's house to have coffee with her and then walked with her to the post office to get his mail.

Kleo and Phil were sitting at the table in their kitchen early one evening two months later, early October 1958, when there was a knock at the front door.

"I wonder who it is?" said Kleo. "Tell them to go away," said Phil. "I don't want to see anybody."

"Oh no, we want to meet people in this area," she told him.

AFTERWORD 2009

AFTER PHIL LEFT, I began to question the very concept of identity. He didn't seem to have a fixed identity, or did he have several? If he were the person I had thought he was, he couldn't possibly have acted the way he did. (Do we ever know anyone, including our own selves?) Is it possible that our identities shift and change continually—sometimes so slightly and slowly that it is unnoticeable—but occasionally, in someone like Phil, rapidly and dramatically? Could identity be a myth our parents had about us when we were small, a myth that we became? Phil was a psychic shape-shifter. He was also a great actor. He would have been a great spy. He changed his personality with every woman he related to. He changed it every time he changed his life situation. He changed it every time he was interviewed. He was a powerful influencer, with his great verbal ability, his modest-sounding words, and his ability to read people. He played with all our lives as well as his own, turned us into fictional beings, and melded us into universes of his own creation.

A lot of young men idolize the Phil they meet in his writing. I think men need to preserve a little wildness, something that gets more or less stamped out by our culture and by domesticity. If it weren't for women, men would live very different lives. Phil stayed wild, although on the surface he seemed very civilized. He knew some important things about relating to other people and influencing them: First, be nonthreatening; second, become everything they want you to be and more. Underneath his modest manner, he was a forceful, powerful person (who felt very weak and who was very sorry for himself). My commitment to our relationship empowered him, too, something he didn't understand. (Women are usually small atomic-energy machines for their special man, who may not even perceive this.) Still, it was very stressful for him to fill the role of husband and father in a middle-class family. The financial aspects of his writing life evidently put a great deal of stress on him, too, something I realized when I did the editing for this 2009 edition of *Search* (almost a half-century later). But with all his talent, Phil didn't know how to get women to stay around. Underneath his immense charm, he didn't have any model for hanging in there.

A frequent view of a male writer or artist is that it is difficult for him to function in a bourgeois marriage—the house, the children, the grocery shopping, the car, the Bluebirds troop, going to church, going to the beach, birthday parties, the children's colds—but Phil seemed to love all this and used it happily in his writing.

Many people have never experienced an intense romantic love; they don't even believe in it. Perhaps a close childhood relationship with a parent is a prerequisite. For some persons, the door into the Room of Love dissolves behind them. Loyalty and commitment don't seem to be as strong values in the United States as they once were. Commitment can be a good thing for two partners and their children; things don't always go well at the moment, but if you hang in there, they work out in the long run. My romantic commitment to Phil—most of what I knew about relationships came out of novels—wasn't easy, but it made me transcend my earlier self.

In Point Reyes Station, Phil wrote mostly novels. He wrote a few stories, but nothing like the quantity he had written in Berkeley. Two significant Point Reyes short stories became parts of *Ubik* and *Do Androids Dream of Electric Sheep?* Phil was just finishing *Time Out of Joint* when he met me, but it was mostly written in his Berkeley period. *The Game-Players of Titan*, one of the early books written in Point Reyes, also came largely from notes and ideas that had originated when he lived in Berkeley. The novels written or developed in Point Reyes were *Confessions of a Crap Artist*, *The Man Whose Teeth Were All Exactly Alike*, *The Man in the High Castle*, *We Can Build You*, *Martian Time-Slip*, *Dr. Bloodmoney*, *The Simulacra*, *Now Wait for Last Year*, *The Three Stigmata of Palmer Eldritch*, and, as we were separating, *Clans of the Alphane Moon*, *The Crack in Space*, *The Zap Gun*, and *The Penultimate Truth*.

THREE 1982 DREAMS

1. IN FRONT OF the Palace Market, a young, handsome Phil is holding his racing bike in one hand and with his other holding the hand of a slender blonde girl dressed in a dirndl skirt and sandals. I, my present self, tries to talk to him, to tell him who I am. He gazes intently at me, puzzled, trying to understand. The young blonde woman is motionless, fixed in the dream space like a figure in a tableau.

2. Phil and I are in a hotel room. He is very ill. I call room service for a doctor. A stout German psychiatrist arrives and, taking the situation in at a glance, phones for an ambulance. The ambulance attendants arrive and take Phil away on a gurney. The hotel room suddenly has an inch of water on the floor. ("I am made of water" is the first sentence of *Confessions of a Crap Artist*.) Later, the German doctor brings back a small Phil, big-headed, bald, and curled up like an embryo in a small, square wooden box. The hotel room expands into a great cathedral, and suddenly a throng of real people, Phil's fictional people, and creatures are all around: My daughters Hatte, Jayne, Tandy, and Laura; Lord Running Clam; Kirsten; Juliana Frink; Mr. Tagomi; Joan Simpson; Tim Powers; Pete Freid; Leo Runcible; Maren Faine...

I am expected to make the funeral oration. I step forward. "Phil, you were mad at me because I loved you and knew you were okay and expected great things of you. You see, I was right—as usual." In the box, the small Phil, who isn't dead after all, turns his head and starts dictating into a tape recorder. Then, suddenly, he flips over and dies for good. His voice starts coming out of my mouth, and he gives his own funeral oration to the assembled throng: "I'm sorry I can't stay for the whole wake, but I'm unavoidably called away. Bless all of you—enjoy your lives, enjoy all the little things. Don't mourn for me—my life is complete—I'm at peace." The funeral service is over; the little box is now

Phil's coffin. Just as the lid is being closed, I drop a blobby gold ornament into it, a small metal figure of a man striding forward carrying a walking stick, a little child on his shoulder.

3. I am riding in a convertible with Phil. He is driving and full of good spirits. I notice large red blotches on his face. He impudently leans over and kisses me on the cheek. "Where were you all my life?" I say to him indignantly, as if he were an hour late for dinner. "What's the use of your kissing me and being so charming now?"

"You did okay without me," he says.

"Why do you have those horrible spots all over your face?" I ask him.

"You should see what I really look like," he says, and as he turns his face toward me, I see that the whole left side of his head is empty space.

My last words to him as the dream fades away: "I tried to be your Boswell, too."

A LEGACY

I STILL DON'T really understand what Phil's problem was—drugs? Mental illness? Drugs making a mild mental illness worse? Childhood trauma? Not being socialized as a child?

Posthumously, he sent many interesting and entertaining people to visit me. The BBC came twice: a pleasant man with a tape recorder early on, later, a group filled with deception and carrying a video camera. PKD scholars and serious fans came to visit me from all over the United States and from most of the countries of Europe—Spain, England, France, Germany, Switzerland, Denmark, and Italy—and one from Iran.

Larry Sutin, the official PKD biographer, stayed with me in Point Reyes Station on two occasions. I drove him around the area, talked extensively with him, and loaned him a file drawer of materials and tapes as well as the manuscript of *Search*. He acknowledged part of this material. (If he had acknowledged it all, it would have looked as if his whole book had come from mine.)

Emmanuel Carrère, the French novelist and movie producer, stayed with me while doing research for his imaginative biography of Phil's thoughts, *I'm Alive and You Are Dead*. My daughter Hatte cooked him fresh salmon sautéed in butter and lemon slices. He drank two bottles of good California wine with it, one red, one white. I gave him my manuscript. I don't think he used any other sources. He ran with the "dream autobiography" idea.

It seemed logical to first send my book to Phil's agent, Russ Galen. He wrote me in May 15, 1985: "…[I]t seems to me (and again I'm seeing this through an emotional fog so can't say anything for sure) that you've done a wonderful job of capturing what it was like to live with Phil in those days—the domestic, day-by-day side of things. And you've certainly brought him vividly to life as a character, as a personality…. [R]eading…[your manuscript] brings Phil back for me." But Galen felt he was too close to the subject matter to handle my book. He wished me luck.

Top science fiction agent Virginia Kidd liked *Search* and tried to place it. After her initial reading, she said, "So that's what really happened? We'd heard so many things." I was surprised that people would be talking about my relationship with Phil back in Pennsylvania. Virginia was sure my book was going to go over in a big way, and that I would be giving talks and signing books all over the country. She sent it to all the top houses, but that was in the mid-eighties before there was so much interest in Philip K. Dick. There were some literary politics involved, too, and my credibility was put into question. Discouraged and disgusted, I gave up. Then in 1992, Professor Sam Umland, who taught a course on PKD at the University of Nebraska, worked with me on a revision and arranged for the publication of *Search* by Mellen Press. It is still publishing a hundred-year library edition priced at $119.

Virginia Kidd gave a manuscript of *Search* to Tom Disch, a close friend of hers, and he and I began an occasional correspondence that some years later after the death of his partner turned into a friendly e-mail interchange lasting until his death by suicide on July 4, 2008. He was very angry at Phil because Phil had turned him in to the FBI, but he thought Philip K. Dick was the best writer there was. Along with himself, Phil was one of the only two writers Tom admired.

I met my best friend, Miguel Díaz Fernádez of Segovia, Spain, via the Mellen edition of this book when he wrote me January 25, 2000, regarding his Ph.D. dissertation on PKD. We have been e-mailing and phoning for ten years.

In 2001, Darryl Mason, a talented Australian writer, came from England and stayed with me off and on for much of the summer to work on his biography of Phil for a contract with Albion Press. Too bad he never finished it. Phil is too much for some people.

An Argentine documentary crew came here in 2006 to do a documentary about Philip K. Dick and stayed with me the weekend they filmed in this area. In the evenings, we drank Argentine wine and had dinner in front of an open fire. I still correspond with two of them: the sound man, Sebastien Lipsicz, who was recently working with Francis Ford Coppola, and the director of the PKD documentary project, Dario Schwartzstein, who next went off to Basel, Switzerland, to video interview Dr. Albert Hoffman, the inventor of LSD, now 101 years old.

Tony Grisoni, who wrote the script for *Fear and Loathing in Las Vegas* and other avant-garde independent films, came from London and stayed with me two days in the summer of 2006 while doing research for a biopic about PKD.

There are three biopics in the works and a German biography has already come out.

Now Phil is world-famous and the world has become "Dickian" or maybe "Phildickian." Twelve of his books have been or are being published in the Library of America—he's been literarily canonized. His books are outselling many other American great authors: Melville, Hawthorne, Henry James, Thomas Jefferson. Meanwhile, almost no one here in Point Reyes Station has ever heard of Philip K. Dick.

If you go to the *New York Times* book page and scroll down the slot that says "Authors," you will find Philip K. Dick's name in the most distinguished literary company of today's world. Click on him, and several pages of articles come up.

Michael Dirda of the *Washington Post* referred to Phil in an article for that publication as one of the most influential writers of the twentieth century. *Time* magazine puts Phil's *Ubik* in their list of the one hundred most significant novels written since 1923.

Then there are the movies: *Total Recall* with our governor, Arnold (a new version is coming out, too); *Blade Runner*, now a classic, with Harrison Ford; *Minority Report*, by Steven Spielberg with Tom Cruise; *Paycheck*, by Ang Lee with Ben Affleck. Some lesser-known films are *Screamers*, *Imposter*, *A Scanner Darkly*, *Next*, and the French film *Barjo*.

Phil's old house is still here in Point Reyes Station and looks almost the same as when he and Kleo moved there in the fall of 1958. The white picket fence has been replaced by a natural wood fence with no pickets, but I couldn't climb over it anyway now.

Only a few people who knew Phil still live here. I see Sue Baty once in a while, and we play Boggle. Judge Baty, who married Philip and Nancy, is still around. Occasionally, I see Inez Storer at the Bovine Bakery. Missy Patterson works at the *Point Reyes Light* (the *Baywood Press* in Phil's novels).

Phil was a unique super-being who made my life wonderful for a while and then terrible for a while. Recently, when I revised the early chapters of *Search for Philip K. Dick*, I enjoyed those happy times again, a period when Phil wrote many of the books that made him world-famous.

INDEX

Ace Books 48, 175
Ackerman, Gerry 234–235, 239–240, 245
agoraphobia 11, 190, 254–255
Allen, Bob 43, 84
Amazing Science Fiction 37, 168, 234
amphetamines (*see also* "Beans") 104, 116, 123, 131–132, 136, 144, 156–157, 183, 254, 257
Apostolides, Kleo, *see* Dick, Kleo
Apostolides, Dr. 250, 253–254
Archer, Edna Matilda see Kindred, Edna Archer
Art Music 31, 232, 242, 249, 254
asthma 229, 231, 238
Astounding Science Fiction 37, 234
autism 257, 246
Bach, Johann Sebastian 40, 46, 179, 230, 236
Bailey, Mike 155–156, 162
Barbour, Connie 243, 248–249
Baty, Judge David 132, 269
Baty, Sue 93, 132, 269
Baywood Press 16, 41, 61, 84, 96, 269
"beans" (see also amphetamines) 144–145, 150–151
Bhagavadgita 66
Beckett, Samuel 38, 250, 254
Beethoven, Ludwig von 46, 64, 230, 232, 236
Bennett, Chuck 243, 249
Berkeley 23, 27, 31, 35, 39, 43, 46–47, 51, 57, 59, 61, 65, 68, 71–74, 76–77, 85, 97, 99, 102, 104–105, 112, 131, 205, 207, 219, 222–225, 227–8, 232–4, 241, 243–244, 246–247, 249–250, 252, 255, 258, 260–261, 264
Berkeley High School 31, 50, 57, 74, 79, 84, 94–95, 115, 130, 227, 233–239
Berner, David 159–162
Binswanger, Ludwig 79
Blake, William 17
Blaylock, Jim 164, 171, 185, 204, 206
Book of the Golden Flower, The 60, 66
Borges, Jorge Luis 17
Borman, Martin 65
Boucher, Anthony 251

Bradbury, Ray 171
Bradley, Marion Zimmer 112, 123–124
Breen, Walter 112
Buber, Martin 125
Busby, F. M. 155
Busby, Nita 164, 177
Busby, Tessa *see* Dick, Tessa
CIA 16, 121, 142–143, 147, 150, 168
California Preparatory Academy 229–231
Captain Video 58, 255
Carla 145
Carr, Carol 117, 137–138, 163
Carr, Terry 137–138
cats 27, 39, 48, 78, 96, 99, 105, 114, 121, 130, 140, 145, 178, 183–184, 188, 194–196, 216, 250

Characters
    Abendsen 70
    Archer, Angel 205
    Arnie 80
    Arctor, Bob 83, 141
    Austurias, Mr. 84
    Barefoot, Johnny 116
    Bloodmoney, Dr. 43, 65, 79, 84–85, 233, 245, 264, 271
    Bluthgeld, Dr. *See* Bloodmoney, Dr.
    Bohlen, Dr. Jack 59, 79–80
    Bohlen, Sylvia 80
    Bundy, Bob 63
    Childan, Robert 70
    Dangerfield, Walt 85
    Denkmal, Dr. 94
    Irmgard 136
    Esterhazy, Blanche 81
    Fat, Horselover 196
    Febbs, Surly G. 95
    Fergesson, Jim 85
    Flores, John 43
    Frauenzimmer, Maury 63
    Frauenzimmer, Pris 61, 63
    Freid, Pete 95, 265
    Frink, Frank 70
    Frink, Juliana 70, 265
    Gloria (Knudson) 196, 197
    Hambro, Claudia 28, 46
    Hardy, Dean and Ella 85
    Harrington, Hoppy 85, 233
    Hnatt, Emily 53, 93, 103

Hnatt, Richard 53
Horstowski, Dr. 64
Hume, Charley 31, 53, 55
Hume, Fay 55–57, 179
Isidore, Jack 50, 55, 179
Kasoura, Betty 70
Keller, Bonny 65, 84
Keller, George 84
Kongrosian, Richard 92
Lotta 131
McConchie, Stuart 85
Mayerson, Barney 103–104
Rybys 183
Powderdry, Lars 95
Pris 136
Proxers 105
Rosen, Leo 57, 63
Rosen, Louis 63, 64
Sarapis, Louis 116
Sharp, Kathy Egmont 116
Stockstill, Dr. 84
Straud, Orion 84
Sweetscent, Kathy 95–96
Sweetscent, Dr. Eric 95–96
Tagomi 70, 265
Terance, Dr. 43
Topchev, Lilo 95
Tree, Mr. *See* Bloodmoney,
Vepp, Dr. Jack E. 43

Christensen, Bill 64, 77, 87–91, 101
Christian Science 39
"Cindy" 15, 141, 143–145, 148, 150, 152–153, 156, 161, 168
Civil War 38, 68
claustrophobia 244
"Clint" 145–150, 152
Coleridge, Samuel Taylor 52
comics and comic books 38, 95
Communism 40, 225, 242–243
Daniels, Dick 227,232–238
Davidson, Avram 111
Davidson, Grania 111–114, 117–124, 142–143, 151
Davis, Grania *see* Davidson, Grania
Desert Fathers 66
Diamond, Anne 114–115, 126
Diamond, Bernard 115
Dianetics 258

Dick, Bessie Mack 214
Dick, Christopher Kenneth 172, 178, 181, 183, 185, 187, 205
Dick, Dorothy Kindred 47–48, 59, 65, 77, 79, 88, 101–102, 105, 131, 136, 142, 151, 155, 170, 172, 198, 212–225, 227–229, 233, 237, 239, 242–243, 245, 253–254, 258–261
Dick, Edgar 15, 202, 213–216, 218–223, 228, 253, 258
Dick, Isolde Hackett (Isa) 129, 134, 148, 171, 220
Dick, Jane Charlotte 47, 209, 213–214
Dick, Kleo 15, 25–29, 32–35, 46, 113, 123, 129, 173, 187, 198, 206, 222, 243, 246, 248–261, 269
Dick, Laura Archer 59–62, 69, 76–77, 96, 121, 133, 139, 141, 152, 172–174, 184, 188–189, 193–194, 196–198, 200–208, 218, 220, 265
Dick, Tessa 15, 163–164, 168–172, 175–179, 181, 183, 185, 187–188, 190, 203, 205, 207
Dickens, Charles 17, 49
Disneyland 16, 62, 170, 174
divorce 16–17, 35, 40, 83, 104–105, 114–118, 126, 132, 158, 170, 177, 206, 222, 235, 246, 250
dogs, 27, 45, 73, 77, 94, 96, 118, 132–133, 136, 145, 148, 220
"Don" 143, 145–147
Doyle, Janet 76, 258
Dr. A 31–35, 86–93, 106, 114–115, 138, 150
Dr. J 92–94, 99, 102, 115, 122, 125
Dr. S 90–92
Drake, Sir Francis 42
drugs 26, 87, 93–95, 101, 104, 123–124, 131, 136, 141–144, 147, 149, 157, 165, 183–184, 186, 188, 257, 267
Duncan, Robert 239–240
Durkheim, Emile 39
Eichmann, Adolf 65
Ellison, Harlan 199–200
Encyclopedia Britannica 37, 52, 63, 105
ESP 197
FBI 16, 121, 147, 150, 152, 164, 168, 241, 252–253, 268
Feinstein, Janet *see* Doyle, Janet
Finney, Jack 258
Flannery, Pat 238–239
flying saucers 28, 46, 76, 156
Freud, Sigmund 38, 130
Friedan, Betty 74
Fullerton, CA 152, 155, 160, 163–164, 169, 171, 175, 177
"Fuzzy" 138–139, 170
Galen, Russ 182, 267
games 28–29, 81, 235
Garfield Junior High School 228–229, 231
Gegenearth 40
German 39, 68, 94, 175, 201, 214–215, 235, 238, 246–247, 249, 268–269
Ghirardelli, Inez 243
Gilbert, David 199

Gilbert, W. S., and Sullivan, Arthur 47, 244
Gildersleeve, John 71, 241, 244, 250, 255
Gold, Herb 256
Gomez, Joe 45
Grand Prix du Festival 189
Graveson, Alys 81, 132, 136, 138
Gryphon 26
Guy, Maury (Iskandar) 63, 70, 85, 87, 131, 259–261
Hackett, Maren 97, 123, 130–132, 134, 206
Hackett, Nancy 15, 95, 97, 123–125, 129–139, 141–142, 145, 148, 170, 172–173, 187, 189, 197, 206, 269
Halevy, Al 117, 123
Hall, Avis 23, 35, 261
Handel, George Frideric 46
Handelsman, Anne 30, 35–36, 57–58
Handelsman, Maury 30, 35–36, 57–58, 63, 80
Harcourt Brace 58–59
Haydn, Franz Joseph 132, 236
Hesse, Herman 27
Hirsch, Jerry 259
Hirsch, Marge 259
Hnatt, Angelina 256
Hnatt, Mike 31, 53
Hoglind, Sue 164, 166
Hollis, Herb 25, 232–233, 242, 251, 254
Hollis, Pat 232, 238, 242, 254
homosexuality 102, 239, 244–246
horses 45, 133, 155–157, 169, 185, 189, 216, 220, 252
Hovel 64, 100–101, 115
Hudner, Dorothy *see* Dick, Dorothy Kindred
Hudner, Joe 47–48, 59, 77, 88, 131, 136, 142, 149, 151, 218, 233, 253–254, 258–260
Hudner, Lynne 73, 101, 105, 117, 127, 135, 138, 142, 172, 198, 216–217, 222, 235, 250, 253–254, 258
Hudner, Marion 216, 233, 253
Hudner, Neil 47, 149, 151, 172, 217, 254, 258
Hugo Award 12, 96, 148
Hynes, Lorraine 61, 68, 100
hypertension 172, 183, 205
I Ching 66, 77, 87, 111, 148
Inferno 26, 30
Iskandar *see* Guy, Maury (Iskandar)
James, William 247
Jamis 156–161
Jeter, K. W. 164, 168, 185, 187, 203
jewelry 12–13, 61, 68–69, 85, 88, 122, 125, 133, 173, 198, 204, 271
"Jim" 145
Johnson, Samuel 38

Jones, James 26
Joyce, James 27, 159, 250, 269
Jung, Carl 65–66, 163
KGB 16, 186, 197
KPFA 40, 84, 242, 255, 259
Kafka, Franz 17, 27, 38
Kaiser Hospital 59–60
Kennedy, John F. 62, 96
Kindred, Earl Grant 215–216, 223–224
Kindred, Edna Archer 213–216, 223–224, 230, 233, 261
Kindred, Dorothy Grant *see* Dick, Dorothy Kindred
King, Martin L. 62
Koehler, George 227, 235
Kresy, Jerry 28, 51, 69, 73, 80, 138, 261
Kresy, June 34, 51, 87, 93, 261
Landor, Walter 43, 95
Lanferman, Walter 95, 238
Langley Porter Clinic 90–93, 124, 239, 243, 260
Lee, Gwen 164
Leibnitz, Gottfried 39
Levy, Linda 15, 164–168
Lincoln 16, 38, 62–64
literary novels 26, 38, 49, 57, 59, 63, 65, 125, 179, 205, 246, 250–251, 257, 260, 269
Lovecraft, H. P. 37–38, 76
LSD 103, 124, 137, 268
Lusby, Monica 246, 257
Lusby, Vince 76, 85, 116, 224, 241–246, 249–252, 256–257
Lusby, Virginia 76, 85, 116, 241–242
Mad Magazine 38
Magazine of Fantasy and Science Fiction 26, 37, 111, 251
Magnavox record player 37, 46, 64, 114, 116, 235, 246–247
Mailer, Norman 56, 79
Mandrake the Magician 38
Manson, Charles 146
Marais and Miranda 46
Marin General Hospital and Marin Medical Clinic 129, 136, 150
Marlin, Jeannette 15, 245–246
marriage 16, 30–31, 36, 41, 46, 73–74, 85–87, 91–92, 97, 100, 102, 105, 122, 130, 132, 135, 138, 172, 175, 193, 199, 241, 245, 253, 264
Martians 75, 80, 103
"Mary Lou" 145, 148, 168
Maxfield, Dick 234, 245
McLuhan, Marshall 159
McMahon, Joanne 164–166
McNelly, Professor Willis 152, 155, 160–161, 163–166, 171, 177
Meemaw *see* Kindred, Edna Archer
Mexico 35, 40, 77, 89, 111, 120, 258

Miller, Henry 28, 243
Milne, E. E. 38
Mini, Kleo *see* Dick, Kleo
Mini, Lois 43, 51, 72, 76–77, 241, 244
Mini, Norman 43, 76, 173, 206, 241, 243, 249, 251
Moore, Ward 68
Mozart, Wolfgang Amadeus 95, 117, 230, 236
mushrooms 41, 60, 71–72, 83, 103, 137
music 29, 31, 46–47, 52, 54, 61, 84, 98, 132–133, 144–145, 159, 224–225, 229–230, 232, 236, 240, 242–246, 249–250, 254–256
National Science Fiction Convention 121
Nelson, Kirsten 15, 112–113, 117–121, 124, 130, 133, 136–137, 142, 170, 194, 197, 265
Nelson, Ray 93, 112–113, 117, 120–121, 123–124, 136, 142, 152, 207, 255, 273
Neurotica 26
nervous breakdown 105, 137, 139, 190, 239
Newcomb, Jack 117, 123–124, 130
New-Path 141
Nicholls, Eldon 233, 249
Nixon, Richard M. 62
Noseworthy, Frank 158
obituary 209
Oedipus Complex 30
Oko, Adolph 42
Oko, Gladys 42
Orr, Robert 71
paranoia 137, 188
Partch, Harry 98
Plattes, Dr. 43
Point Reyes Station 12, 16, 23–27, 33, 36–37, 41–42, 56–57, 62, 72, 77, 80, 83, 91–92, 97, 100, 104–105, 113–116, 118, 124–127, 133–138, 141–142, 152, 172–175, 181, 186, 188, 193–194, 197–198, 204, 206–7, 209, 211, 221, 223, 227, 238, 249, 252, 255, 260, 264, 267, 269, 271
proletarian writer 49, 59, 95
Psychiatry 15, 26, 31–32, 35, 63, 79, 89–90, 92, 106, 115, 127, 130, 135, 149, 178–179, 181, 186, 217, 222, 227, 243, 260, 265
Psychology 32, 38, 53, 79–80, 92, 102, 115–116, 130, 137–138, 156, 174, 181, 188, 196–197, 202, 217, 223–224, 239, 259–260
psychokinesis 85, 92
psychomotor seizure 169
Pope John XXIII 40
Powers, Tim 163–170, 174, 177–179, 183–186, 190, 204–208, 265
Pauling, Linus 66
Pike, Christopher 206
Pike, Bishop James A. 132, 134–137, 205
quaternity 66
Rich, Alan 77, 243, 249, 251
Rickman, Gregg 17, 206, 223

Rimov, Leon 228, 237
Rivers, Betty Jo 15, 241, 246–249, 258
Robeson, Paul 47
robots 16, 62, 79, 257
Ross Psychiatric Hospital 89–90
Royal Electric typewriter 37, 105, 234
Rubenstein, Hatte 23–25, 32, 38, 44, 60, 75–77, 81, 84, 86, 89–91, 94–95, 100, 105, 109, 114, 135, 142, 173, 175, 179, 189, 265, 267
Rubenstein, Jayne 23–25, 32, 38, 41, 69, 75, 84, 92, 105, 142–143, 149, 173–174, 188, 194, 209, 265
Rubenstein, Richard 23–28, 30–32, 35–36, 38, 42, 45, 67–68, 86, 126, 240
Rubenstein, Tandy 23, 25, 32, 62, 68, 72, 75, 77, 84, 97–98, 132–134, 142, 172–174, 265
ruins 258
Russell, Henryetta 122, 133
Sandburg, Carl 38
Sanders, Jack 71, 252
Santa Venetia, CA 131, 134–153, 273
Sausalito 35, 43, 142, 250
Sauter, Doris 171, 181–187, 190, 203–205, 208–209
schizophrenia 16, 63, 70, 91, 93, 233, 259
Schopenhauer, Arthur 39
Schubert, Franz 40, 47
Science Fiction Studies 177
sculpture 27, 48, 50, 53, 61, 96, 98, 113–114, 149
"Sean" 145, 147, 151
sheep 21, 24, 27–28, 51, 54, 70, 76–77, 114, 140
"Sheila" 15, 141, 143–151, 193
Sherwood, Don 254
Simpson, Joan 15, 183, 186–191, 193, 196–197, 265
Smith, Ginger 168
Spicer, Jack 239–240
spinet piano 16, 61, 138
St. Columba's Church (Inverness, CA) 97–99, 132, 173, 204, 206, 209
Stein, Joel 164–165, 168–169
Stevens, Chris 42
Stevens, James 37
Stevens, Joan 42, 78
Stevens, Pete 63, 78, 85, 95, 138
Storer, Inez 69, 73, 112, 126, 269
Stratton, George 84
Stratton, Jan 84
stroke 80, 208
Subud 63, 70, 87
suicide 96, 113, 119, 122, 134–136, 155, 159–160, 178–179, 185, 196–197, 268
Surrealism 49
Synanon 125, 155, 159
synchronicity 66

tachycardia 39, 204, 254
Tao Te Ching 67
Tchaikovsky,Pyotr Ilyich 47, 236
telepathy 152, 197
teratomas 79, 85
theology 17, 53, 95, 97, 99, 103, 132, 174, 182, 203
Tibetan Book of the Dead 66
Teller, Edward 40, 84
Temko, Allan 40, 256
Thespian, Homer 233
Thompson, Bill 43
"Tom Swifties" 67
Torrence, Ray 187
Tumpey 39, 96
Treasury of Jewish Folklore 38
twins 29, 47, 79, 85, 96, 172, 173, 194, 209, 213–214, 216–217, 224, 247, 258
University of British Columbia, Vancouver 155
University of California, Berkeley 27, 40, 74, 76, 80, 219, 224–225, 227, 232–233
University of California, Davis 246
University of California, Fullerton *see* Fullerton, CA and McNelly, Willis
University of California, Santa Cruz 135
University Radio 31, 76, 85, 116, 231–233, 239, 241–247, 251, 255–256
Vancouver, B. C. 152, 155–156, 160, 162, 167, 169, 172
Vancouver Science Fiction Convention 152, 155
vaulting 157, 173, 185, 188–189, 198
V-Con *see* Vancouver Science Fiction Convention
vertigo 84, 231, 236
Wagner, Richard 32, 39, 246, 255–256
Wallace, Henry 241
Walsh, Michael 156–159
Walsh, Susan 156–159
Washington, D. C. 31, 80, 163, 215, 224
Watts, Alan 40
Wells, H. G. 228
West, Nathanael 37
Westercon 168
Western Hospital 208
Williams, Paul 15, 207, 209
Wilson, Mary 15, 164, 168
Wolfson, Margaret 57, 115, 235, 249
Wolfson, William 63, 115, 120, 126, 150–151, 235, 249

Works
    A Maze of Death 116
    A Scanner Darkly 83, 141, 143–145, 165, 189, 269
    A Time for George Stavros 59
    Blade Runner 136, 205–206, 269

Clans of the Alphane Moon 104, 264
Confessions of a Crap Artist 12, 23, 28, 31, 33, 35, 40, 46, 50–51, 53–56, 58, 179, 186, 216, 264–265, 271
Cosmic Puppets, The 26, 38
Crack in Space, The 98, 104, 264
Counter-Clock World 111, 129, 131, 135
Dark-Haired Girl, The 168
Deus Irae 125
Divine Invasion, The 103, 183
Do Androids Dream of Electric Sheep? 136, 205, 208, 264
Dr. Bloodmoney 43, 65, 79, 84–85, 233, 245, 264, 271
Exegesis 17,174, 183, 185, 187
Eye in the Sky 26, 49
Flow My Tears, the Policeman Said 137, 144, 151
"Foster, You're Dead" 258–259
Galactic Pot-Healer 67, 142
Game Players of Titan, The 71–72, 264
Ganymede Takeover 93
"Human Is" 38, 259
Humpty Dumpty in Oakland 59
"King of the Elves" 251, 257
Man in the High Castle, The 12–13, 68–72, 85, 96, 111, 115, 123, 172, 187, 264, 271
Man Who Japed, The 26
Man Whose Teeth Were All Exactly Alike, The 12, 42–43, 57, 104, 264
Martian Time-Slip 12, 57, 73, 79–80, 85, 136, 187, 246, 264, 271
Now Wait for Last Year 12, 95, 102, 264
Owl in Daylight, The 164
Penultimate Truth, The 104, 264
"Roog" 200, 251
Simulacra, The 57, 92, 264
Solar Lottery 26, 256–257
Three Stigmata of Palmer Eldritch, The 12–13, 53, 93, 98, 100, 103–104, 158, 223, 264, 271
Time Out of Joint 12, 26, 39, 48, 264
Transmigration of Timothy Archer, The 134, 205–206, 232–233, 250
Ubik 135, 174, 186, 200, 264, 269
Unteleported Man, The 104
VALIS 104, 174, 178, 181–184, 196, 202
Valisystem A 174, 184
We Can Build You 16, 57, 61, 63, 264
"What the Dead Men Say" 104, 116
World Jones Made, The 26, 257–258
Zap Gun, The 43, 95, 264

Wright, Jack 98
Wright, Patty 98
X-Kalay 155, 159–166, 169

About the Author

Anne, Philip K. Dick's third wife, lived with him in Point Reyes Station during a period in his writing life when he wrote the novels that made him world-famous: *Confessions of a Crap Artist*, *Martian Time-Slip*, *Dr. Bloodmoney*, and *The Three Stigmata of Palmer Eldritch*. He accurately chronicled the beginnings of Anne's jewelry business in his most famous novel, *The Man in the High Castle*.

Anne was born in West Englewood, New Jersey, in 1927. After moving to St. Louis, she attended the Principia secondary school and graduated from Washington University in 1947. After the death of her first husband, poet Richard Rubenstein, she studied metal sculpture with Harry Crotty at College of Marin and later based her jewelry designs on the welded sculpture techniques she had learned there. Her bronze and silver jewelry has been sold in museum stores and galleries throughout the United States and abroad. Retired from the jewelry business after forty-seven years, she continues to write novels and poetry. She still lives in the same house where she lived with Philip K. Dick and raised her four daughters.

"Dear Anne, I just finished reading your biography of Phil, and I must say I am impressed. Besides being a remarkably accurate and lifelike picture of the man, it is also a rattling good tale, like a real-life detective story...."

—Ray Nelson

"Anne's detailed account of her years with Philip K. Dick is a must-read for anyone discovering the autobiographical elements in his writing. No other biography gives the reader as strong a sense of how he crafted his fiction, where he got his characters, and what made him tick. Parts of Anne's memoir are instantly recognizable to PKD's readers as they describe the inspiration for many of his most bizarre fictional scenes."

—David Gill, San Francisco State University; The Total Dick-Head blog

"The secret of Phil Dick's greatness, as with so many other great men, is his... third wife, Anne. You can see her influence in the development of his novels, their increasing awareness of the human/family/sexual element. Most SF writers simply didn't pay attention to such things, which are the entire concern of mainstream fiction. Dick was almost alone among the SF writers of his day in trying to write mainstream novels himself. And what is their constant theme? His battles with, and bafflement by, and love of Anne, the Other who never left his thoughts...."

—Thomas M. Disch, author of *Camp Concentration*

"[*Search for Philip K. Dick*] shows that if we choose to, we can see through the flaws, and find the shining divinity that is there. Even in his worst times in Santa Venetia, he was still trying to help people."

—Laurene Jensen

"I found the manuscript utterly engrossing on two levels: first, as a sympathetic yet clear-eyed study in the round of an extraordinary personality, and second, as a source of innumerable clues about PKD's work. I consider it prime source material for anyone interesting in PKD the man or the writings of PKD. I not only understand him better now, but have fresh insights into several of the novels and short stories...."

—Meritt Abrash, Rensselaer Polytechnic Institute

"...an amazingly thorough job, even though...dealing at times with people who could have been hostile. And then [Anne Dick] wrote the whole complicated story in clear, fast-moving, and entertaining prose."

—Floyd M. Shumway, Yale University

"In all the critical literature-review-type books, yours comes as a breath of fresh air."

—Perry Kinman "Razzelweave," PKD zine, Japan